"*The Bonfire Moment* sheds light on these hidden challenges startup teams often grapple with, reminding you that your team's dynamics can make or break you. Rich in insight and grounded in organizational psychology, this is a must-read for every leader."

—*Bill Coughran, partner at Sequoia Capital*

"One of the things I am most proud of about Fitbit was the team we built. Building the team was not easy. *The Bonfire Moment* takes you from the time you are forming your starting team to how you grow it to lead a multibillion-dollar company. It acknowledges that there are a lot of trade-offs as you create and shape your team along your startup's journey. It provides rubrics on how to think about those trade-offs and on the signposts you will see along the way. It is a great read for one just starting out and for those who are well underway."

—*Eric Friedman, cofounder of Fitbit*

"If the people working toward a company's mission are at odds, the chances it will ever be fulfilled—much less sustained long-term—are low. *The Bonfire Moment* lays out the ways dysfunction can derail meaningful work and provides well-tested tools for making sure that, through transparency, good leadership, and humility, your startup's culture is truly mission oriented."

—*Eric Ries, bestselling author of* The Lean Startup *and founder of LTSE*

"Getting the people side of startups is so hard, and there is not a lot written that is practical and gives founders and future founders a way to peer around the corner, which is why *The Bonfire Moment* is an important read for anyone wanting to create something from nothing."

—*Garry Tan, president and CEO of Y Combinator*

"If you've ever wondered, Why is it so hard to get things done around here? Martin and Josh offer not only a structured teardown of why but also a practical guide on what to do about it. For anyone aspiring to leadership—startup or otherwise—*The Bonfire Moment* will leave you with examples, frameworks, and language you can't unsee."

—*Gorick Ng,* Wall Street Journal *bestselling author of* The Unspoken Rules

"Drawing on the rich lessons learnt from Google's Startup Accelerator Project, *The Bonfire Moment* sheds light on the people problems that founders sweep under the rug and provides a practical tool kit for startup teams to confront uncomfortable truths and feelings and emerge stronger as a team. In short, a vital playbook for founders."

—*Huggy Rao, Atholl McBean Professor of Organizational Behavior and Human Resources at the Graduate School of Business, Stanford University, and author of* Scaling Up Excellence *and* The Friction Project

"*The Bonfire Moment* is a proven recipe for rebooting team relationships, building better culture, and making your workplace the place everyone wants to work."

—*Jake Knapp,* New York Times *bestselling author of* Sprint *and* Make Time

"Anyone who's built a startup knows it comes with its highs and lows. Martin and Josh get it; *The Bonfire Moment* is like having a trusted mentor guiding you through those turbulent periods. Many startups have changed course after attending their one-day workshop. Try running a Bonfire Moment for your team—it could be what gets you unstuck!"

—*Jason Scott, cofounder of ANIM and Black Angel Group and host of* Unicorn Hunter

"I have worked with Martin on effective organizational structures to best support Google's research teams. This is a complex area, since there are many different research teams, projects, and desired directions, and designing effective structures that support collaboration without feeling overly stifling is critical to achieving long-term breakthroughs. Martin provided many wise words of advice over the years, and I'm excited that, through this book, Martin and Josh will provide this sort of wisdom to a broader audience."

—*Jeff Dean, chief scientist, Google*

"*The Bonfire Moment* is the missing manual for startups that want to scale with integrity, self-awareness, and a solid team foundation. No more sweeping people issues under the rug, fanning the flames for future discord and flameouts. Eminently practical, with detailed facilitation guides throughout its well-researched, road-tested program, this book will become a founder's go-to guide for building world-class teams."

—*Jenny Blake, award-winning author of* Free Time *and* Pivot

"Clear, thoughtful, and abundantly practical, *The Bonfire Moment* is the missing manual for the hardest part of leading: working with other people. Its guidance on creating the moments that fire up teams is welcome and long needed."

—*Jerry Colonna, author of* Reunion *and CEO of Reboot*

"*The Bonfire Moment* will help you confront the paradoxes faced by leaders, capturing many of the lessons I gained during my years of leading product teams. At a time when many leadership guides are riddled with platitudes, this book stands apart, grounded in data and real-world experience."

—*Jonathan Rosenberg, New York Times bestselling author of* How Google Works *and* Trillion Dollar Coach

"While ideas, products, and business models are crucial, *The Bonfire Moment* presents a strong case that the collaborative spirit and the strength of the team are what determine the success of any early-stage business. Gonzalez and Yellin draw on robust research and their extensive experience in guiding a diverse range of entrepreneurs and business leaders toward success. This book is an essential guide for any leader who values an inclusive approach to building a high-performing team."

—*Julia Austin, senior lecturer and faculty cochair of the Arthur Rock Center for Entrepreneurship, Harvard Business School*

"There is nothing soft about 'soft skills.' They are hard to learn, and they are the biggest contributor to your success. Gonzalez and Yellin are the compassionate yet clear-minded mentors you'll need in the toughest moments of your leadership journey."

—*Kim Scott, New York Times* bestselling *author of* Radical Candor *and* Radical Respect

"Martin and Josh share the hard, unvarnished reality of building enduring companies: creating the right team culture is hard work but establishes undeniable upside for both the business and the people. *The Bonfire Moment* is an indispensable guide for anyone trying to beat the odds in growing a new venture, whether in a small startup or a big organization."

—*Laszlo Bock, cofounder of Humu and Gretel.ai, former Google SVP of People Operations, and* New York Times *bestselling author of* Work Rules!

"*The Bonfire Moment* is a must-read for anyone (emphasis on *anyone*) looking to build a successful startup. Weaving real-life examples with tactical tips for preserving your mental health while building a company, Martin and Josh artfully unpack the actions and mindsets that differentiate the best startup founders. The stories and lessons in *The Bonfire Moment* are proof that successful founders can come from all backgrounds and that bringing together an inclusive, resilient founding team is essential to creating a long-lasting company."

—*Liz Fosslien,* Wall Street Journal *bestselling coauthor and illustrator of* No Hard Feelings *and* Big Feelings

"In this concise guide, Gonzalez and Yellin, pioneers at Google for Startups Accelerator, share their crucial insights. You'll learn how to anticipate and avoid common people problems, as they provide you with actionable gems. An indispensable resource for founders navigating the challenges of entrepreneurship."

—*Noam Wasserman, dean of Yeshiva University's Sy Syms School of Business and bestselling author of* The Founder's Dilemmas *and* Life Is a Startup

"*The Bonfire Moment* makes a compelling case that startups can increase their chances of success by getting the people elements right and offers a practical guide to help you do that. This is an important book for anyone building breakthrough technology that will shape our future."

—*Peter Cho, managing director, partner, and global people chair of BCG X*

"Gonzalez and Yellin hit the nail on the head—growing a startup is about growing an organization. Scaling human groups effectively is, in many ways, far more complicated than coming up with the business model or getting funded. The authors do a terrific job of weaving together insights from research as well as their own experience at Google's Accelerator in a book that will be a handy manual for every (aspiring) startup founder hoping to successfully scale up."

—*Phanish Puranam, Roland Berger Chaired Professor of Strategy and Organisation Design at INSEAD*

"*The Bonfire Moment* is a remarkably well-researched, engaging, road-tested, and, above all, practical guide that teaches you how to identify and avoid the people problems that sink startups. I am especially smitten with the step-by-step instructions that Gonzalez and Yellin provide to help leaders and teams develop their own homegrown strategies for avoiding such traps—which are based on their workshops with more than ten thousand people in hundreds of companies."

—*Robert I. Sutton,* New York Times *bestselling author of eight books, including* Scaling Up Excellence *(with Huggy Rao),* The Friction Project *(with Huggy Rao),* The No Asshole Rule, *and* Good Boss, Bad Boss, *and professor of management science and engineering at Stanford University*

"Martin and Josh go beyond the Silicon Valley campfire kumbaya to shine real light on how to navigate the people and culture traps that determine a company's success or failure. Soft skills are some of the hardest things, and they've developed a framework that works."

—*Scott Hartley, cofounder of Everywhere Ventures and bestselling author of* The Fuzzy and the Techie

"This book should be required reading for all entrepreneurs and for managers who are under startup-like pressures. *The Bonfire Moment* has created a science where previously there was only art. It's loaded with fascinating stories and practical principles you'll wish you'd known five years ago."

—*Steve Chen, cofounder and former CTO of YouTube*

"In a world obsessed with technical prowess, financial strategies, and grand visions, Martin and Josh reveal a fatal trap that too many startups fall victim to—ignoring the critical people issues that lurk beneath the surface. With vivid examples of promising startups that appeared destined for unicorn status, only to crumble due to unaddressed interpersonal challenges, this book serves as a stark wake-up call for entrepreneurs. Blending their decades-long experience working with startups with cutting-edge academic research to guide readers toward success, *The Bonfire Moment* is a beacon for new ventures—trailblazing the path around common traps and, ultimately, redefining what it means to build a company that lasts."

—*Valentina A. Assenova, Edward B. and Shirley R. Shils Endowed Term Assistant Professor of Management at the Wharton School, University of Pennsylvania*

"As chief of staff at Google Brain, Josh built the right team structures, processes, and leadership forums to enable collaboration and impact at one of the world's most complex and successful AI innovation environments. These same skills are front and center in his workshop for startups. *The Bonfire Moment* will be a valuable partner to innovators all over the world."

—*Zoubin Ghahramani, vice president of research, Google DeepMind, and professor of information engineering at the University of Cambridge*

THE
BONFIRE
MOMENT

THE BONFIRE MOMENT

Bring Your Team
Together to Solve the
Hardest Problems
Startups Face

Martin Gonzalez & Joshua Yellin

HARPER
BUSINESS
An Imprint of HarperCollins*Publishers*

HarperCollins books may be purchased for educational, business, or sales promotional use. For information, please email the Special Markets Department at SPsales@harpercollins.com.

FIRST EDITION

Artwork by Meagan Greer and Justin Ng

Library of Congress Cataloging-in-Publication Data
Names: Gonzalez, Martin, author. | Yellin, Joshua, author.
Title: The bonfire moment: bring your team together to solve the hardest problems startups face / Martin Gonzalez and Joshua Yellin.
Description: First edition. | New York, NY: HarperBusiness, [2023] | Includes bibliographical references and index.
Identifiers: LCCN 2023043055 (print) | LCCN 2023043056 (ebook) | ISBN 9780063297012 (hardcover) | ISBN 9780063297029 (ebook)
Subjects: LCSH: Teams in the workplace—Management. | New business enterprises—Management. | Organizational behavior.
Classification: LCC HD66 .G656 2023 (print) | LCC HD66 (ebook) | DDC 658.4/022—dc23/eng/20230921
LC record available at https://lccn.loc.gov/2023043055
LC ebook record available at https://lccn.loc.gov/2023043056

24 25 26 27 28 LBC 5 4 3 2 1

To the innovators around the world whose bold endeavors flare with the intensity of a bonfire: may this book be a helpful partner in your endeavors.

Contents

Contents

A Note to the Reader

Teams Are Harder than Tech

"Engineering is easy; people are hard." We'll never forget this line from Bill Coughran, a partner at Sequoia Capital who cut his teeth as a researcher at the legendary Bell Labs and went on to run some of Google's most successful products, like Search and Maps. Coughran recognized that most people at tech startups believe that their success will ultimately be determined by three factors: technology, market fit, and raising enough capital. Deliver on all three, the thinking goes, and any startup can scale at rocket speed.

This widely held assumption ignores one key challenge that doesn't get nearly as much attention. According to researchers from Harvard Business School and McKinsey & Co., 65 percent of startups fail because of people issues,[1] not flawed technology, a misguided product, or a lack of cash. A vast majority fail because they can't figure out how to get the right team on board and working well together.

Take a close look at the story of a successful team, and you'll always find two intertwining plotlines. First there's the public story, often retold on the stages of startup conferences, on podcasts, and at launch events. Spurred by the brag culture of the startup world, founders craft a narrative that's bold yet simple: "We raised x million dollars, hired y people, and entered z new markets in our first two years." This story is easy to follow and exciting.

But there's another story that takes place, often behind closed doors, away from the scrutiny of the public, the media, or investors. It's much messier, often featuring private mental battles and painful team conflict. It's those moments when people lost faith in the idea, disagreed on how to pivot, or got into gridlock over the best way to spend their limited cash. It's also how they persevered and recovered when the stress erupted into ugly, damaging arguments. Accomplishing x, y, and z against this backdrop is all the more impressive—and yet we're trained to hide the complicated reality of human collaboration.

What gets a team to the finish line, it turns out, isn't so much their countless late nights working passionately on a product. It's how they respond when doubt creeps in and progress stutters, when pressure builds and that little voice in their heads tells them they're probably doing more (and receiving less) than their teammates, when they need to let go of that loyal friend who offered so much help in the early days, or when they worry that they're underqualified for the job and fear being exposed as impostors.

This book is about this second plotline: the people issues that sink even the most promising endeavors.

A Problem as Old as Technology

Examine the history of technology and you'll find many iconic pioneers who struggled to become effective leaders, hang on to talented people, and turn their ambitious visions into reality.

Take William Shockley, one of three inventors of the transistor, a foundational innovation that led to the creation of today's computers, smartphones, and every digital device you can think of. Winner of the 1956 Nobel Prize in Physics, Shockley was by all accounts brilliant—but his brilliance stopped short of his understanding people. He earned a reputation as extremely difficult to work with. He was always certain he was the smartest person in any room, and he never let anyone forget it. He was the textbook case of "a genius with a thousand helpers."

When his employer, the Bell Labs research center in New York, refused to promote Shockley to senior management, he quit to launch Shockley Semiconductor Laboratory. He hired several PhDs from MIT and moved to California in the earliest days of what became Silicon Valley. Right from the start, Shockley Semiconductor had a paranoid, authoritarian, and tyrannical culture. Legend has it that when a staffer suffered a small cut on their finger, Shockley insisted someone on the team was responsible for the wound and called in the police to subject the entire lab to a lie detector test.[2]

By 1957, Shockley's best people were fed up, and eight of them— soon to become famous as "the Traitorous Eight"—quit as a group to launch a new company, Fairchild Semiconductor, which continued to develop and commercialize the transistor and integrated circuits. Shockley could have shared in the success of those "traitors" as their work became standard tech in almost every computing device. More important, he could have built a legacy that stretched well beyond his early technical achievements. Tragically, his excellence in building technology was no match for his ineptitude at building teams.

Of course, oppressive bosses are not the only type of bad managers. There's also a long history of beloved leaders who excel at creating a welcoming and inspiring team experience but then stumble because they can't hold people to high standards or hard deadlines.

Consider the company that built the prototypes of what eventually became the first smartphone, almost two decades before Steve Jobs changed, well, *everything*, by launching the iPhone. This company was General Magic, founded in 1990 by Marc Porat, Bill Atkinson, and Andy Hertzfeld. "I had wanted to create 'engineering heaven' for engineers, and so I raised money to do that. They were free to imagine and play and invent and write," Porat recounts.[3] He was charismatic and spellbinding when presenting his vision of the future. General Magic abolished dress codes, which may seem quaint now but was revolutionary at the time. Bunnies roamed freely around the building to inspire creativity, and meetings were conducted with employees sprawled out on the floor. The best and brightest engineers and designers flocked to join this wild alternative workplace.

These talented, eager techies roamed as freely as their rabbits:

they had no managers, no schedules . . . no neckties! And innovation flourished. Ideas for the USB, software modems, small touchscreens, networked games, streaming TV, and the e-commerce model were all born in this creative den. Side projects were not seen as distractions; they were supported as potential paths to breakthroughs. Before long, the media had anointed General Magic as the next big thing in computing. When the company went public in 1995, the stock price rapidly doubled.

When the pressure mounted to launch a working device, trouble came to paradise. The company had not built the muscle to hold people to deadlines or manage operational risk. Having no taste for discipline, Porat and his cofounders pushed their self-managed environment beyond its capacity. As Darin Adler, one of the free-range engineers later asked to manage the team as director of software development, recalls: "The deadline is everything—meet this date or miss your opportunity to change the world. I don't think we had anyone saying that."[4] There was little he could do to undo the beloved culture of near absolute freedom.

You've almost certainly never heard of General Magic, because they went out of business in 2002 after several years of losses, layoffs, and missed projections. Their visionary phone was finally launched, but while it excited investors and media, the consumer public didn't get it. The company sold a meager three thousand units at launch, largely to the extended networks of the "Magicians" (i.e., their employees). Consumers who did purchase the phone complained that its network didn't work well, its revolutionary touchscreen and software were glitchy, and its battery died quickly.

Of course, cultural problems weren't the only reason General Magic failed. The internet was in its infancy, the public yet to be educated, and however "magical" the company's technologies, they would need several cycles of iteration to resolve the glitches. Nevertheless, the company's cultural problems predestined it to failure. Even the visionary himself, Marc Porat, eventually agreed: "In retrospect, it would have been welcome in our culture if there was a really tough leadership that could have taken control of what we were designing, with exactly what features, how much time it would take, and how to minimize risk. In other words, all the things which are fundamental in good technology management. That was missing."[5]

In the long arc of technological innovation, failures like Shockley Semiconductor's and General Magic's aren't true failures; their alumni go on to great careers and future discoveries. For example, General Magic alumni include technology heavyweights such as Megan Smith (US CTO during the Obama administration), Tony Fadell (creator of the iPod and iPhone and founder of Nest, which Google later acquired), Kevin Lynch (former CTO of Adobe and creator of the Apple Watch), and Pierre Omidyar (founder of eBay).[6] Still, we'll never know what miracles General Magic might have brought to market, and on what timeline, if only it had better harnessed the genius in that deep pool of talent.

Trying to Understand the "Madness of People"

Teams that pursue ambitious goals will inevitably suffer contention and internal criticism. They need to get good at managing and recovering from personality conflicts while keeping standards high. History shows that it's easy for very smart people to get this balance wrong. The very same people problems that tech teams faced in the 1960s, '70s, and '80s still exist today. While progress in technology has surged like lightning, progress in human dynamics has moved much slower.

Recently, we've heard jaw-dropping trainwreck stories about the founders of unicorns like WeWork, Uber, and Tinder. People issues have plagued companies of all sizes, and only some of them have worked through the grueling conflict and recovered. We can only wonder how much more successful some of these companies might have been.

It's tempting to think these were tactical miscalculations, anomalous mistakes by companies that were mostly doing well. Yet if you look at any company that blows up because of people issues, you can rewind the tape six, twelve, or twenty-four months to where the challenges started. And you'll see that these were avoidable problems—if only they had been addressed early enough. You can almost always point to an inciting incident: the sidestepping of a robust conversation around equity splits, the sloppy hiring of an industry veteran, or a half-hearted attempt to paper over a conflict with forced harmony. These interpersonal issues often start small, deceptively insignificant to waste time on. After all, there are more concrete, important challenges to wrestle with. But over time, the people problems grow until all those concrete challenges crumble beneath them.

Should one idea resonate above all others from these pages, let it be this: *Ignoring people issues in favor of technical, financial, and strategic issues is a fatal trap. Those deceptively minor, hard-to-quantify team challenges will undermine your success if not confronted with resolve.*

Sir Isaac Newton once said, "I can calculate the motions of heavenly bodies, but not the madness of people." Our hope is that this book will help you better understand the madness of people and gain powerful tools to prevent that madness from derailing your goals.

How We Created the Bonfire Moment

This book was inspired by the work we've done in building Google's Accelerator program for startups since 2015. The Google for Startups Accelerator invites some of the most promising growth-stage startups[7] from around the world to Google's campuses and takes them through a boot camp–style experience. Its mission is to support thriving, diverse, and inclusive startup communities of every stripe, in global startup hubs that include Africa, North America, Latin America, Asia, and Europe. Google for Startups also runs special programs for underrepresented groups such as Black and women founders. And they partner with ecosystem builders like incubators, startup spaces, and venture capitalists (VCs) in cities around the world.

Initially, these Accelerator programs focused on the so-called hard stuff: innovating technology, developing new products, growth hacking, and refining user experiences. Josh, whose team pioneered the Google for Startups Accelerator, had an early sense that their curriculum also needed to address organization and leadership challenges. Josh himself had built several teams and had experienced firsthand that mastering the hard stuff was not enough.

Around the same time, Martin, who was based in Google's Singapore office in 2015, was building out a no-frills leadership workshop based on how Google trains its own leaders, and on state-of-the-art research about startups. Martin's team was advising Google's senior leaders on their people and culture challenges, and this was his 20 percent project.[8]

A pilot program was approved with a small budget, and we set out to help founders solve their people problems with an intense, in-person workshop. Our first pilot location was Jakarta, Indonesia. To our surprise, the startups didn't just find the workshop incredibly valuable, they found it *more* valuable than other compelling Accelerator workshops on machine learning, growth hacking, and user experience.

To make sure these initial responses weren't an anomaly, we tried the same workshop in Bangalore, followed by Singapore, São Paulo, Tokyo, Tel Aviv, Bogotá, Warsaw, Muscat, San Francisco, London, and Toronto. Founders everywhere continued to give us rave reviews, and our workshop became the consistently highest-rated experience of the Accelerator. Consequently, program managers across the globe were asking us to train facilitators so they could continue to run the workshop. Josh was convinced that we had stumbled upon a huge unaddressed need.

Over the past nine years, we've reached startup teams in more than seventy countries. At the end of every workshop, participants have frequently asked for materials to run their own bootleg version for their teams. Or they ask where they can buy the book that captures all of our ideas and tools. They've always been disappointed to hear there isn't one. Until now, only a select group of startups admitted to Google's Accelerator could access this exclusive workshop.

Finally, we've distilled the insights and strategies of our sought-after single-day program into this book. We've captured the people problems that have been surprisingly consistent across countries, cultures, and industries. We've engineered into our methodology a process for extracting insights about yourself and your team and learning to have important and, at times, uncomfortable conversations. We've drawn lessons from the hundreds of startups we've worked with closely. Each element of our methodology and tool kit has been road tested hundreds of times, and we've kept only the parts that startup teams told us were useful.

We've come to call this workshop the Bonfire Moment.

Imagine, for a moment, what it's like to be standing near a raging bonfire. Fire can be a wild and destructive force. Yet here you and your friends are, basking in the light and heat of a carefully controlled inferno. You can inspect the flame up close without being consumed by it. In this space, everyone's senses are heightened. The sleepy become alert. Problems and grievances can be examined in a new light.

That's the kind of experience we inspire with our workshop. Working collaboratively on a near-impossible goal under severe time constraints can sometimes feel like being *in* the fire. Our workshop allows teammates to step back from the flaming pit and consider their collaboration—and especially its flashpoints—in safer, cooler air. The Bonfire Moment is a structured place and time to regroup, get back in touch with their mission, bandage relational wounds, and prepare for the next push. We know that startups are starving for this type of help, and getting it can mean the difference between success and flameout.

How This Book Is Different

Business books that offer help to entrepreneurs tend to fall into one of three categories.

One is the victory lap, in which an entrepreneur tells their story of hustle, struggle, and success. These books are often inspiring and fun to read and make an important contribution to the world. But they are prone to survivor bias—the assumption that we can extract a success formula from the victorious without also looking at why others have failed. When you read such books, you can easily fall under the spell of a simple story told with the benefit of hindsight. The true startup journey is never that clear. This book will share stories of triumph alongside detailed accounts of setbacks, and lean on a large corpus of data and anecdotes to uncover what effective founders do that the ineffective don't. We think there's a lot to learn from both.

Then there's the academic book, which holds the highest bar of evidence to back up every bit of guidance. We love these books because they challenge our intuitions and parse out good advice from bad. But they can be dense and not always straightforward in their practical applications. So we've done the work for you and sifted through decades of research, both from academia and from our own tour around the world. We'll help you question some of your assumptions with the use of data, provide proof points for others you've held subconsciously, and offer concrete, practical actions you can take.

Finally, there's the framework book, usually written by a smart consultant. They offer a neat, simple framework to explain any example, good or bad. Some of these books are wildly popular precisely because they provide an easy way to understand the world. But challenges in startups are multifactorial, so a neat framework is usually oversimplified. We agree with H. L. Mencken: "For every complex problem, there is a simple solution that is elegant, easy to understand, and wrong." Yet we understand the value of simplifying complexity: it provides a starting point to address big challenges, allows you to take action, and ensures the concepts are memorable and therefore more likely to be used. In this book, we candidly narrate the trials of building a startup, not shying away from its messiness. Simultaneously, we provide mental models and conceptual scaffolds that highlight issues deserving your focus. Our approach is to offer simplicity only where it aids understanding. But we strive to heed Einstein's advice: to make everything "as simple as possible, but no simpler."

We've combined the best parts of these book archetypes to give you something even more helpful. This book is based on the patterns we've seen in our work with startups in every corner of the world, from seed-stage companies to three-thousand-person, post-IPO companies. We've collected lots of data along the way, using people analytics techniques that offer rigor and precision where there hasn't always been. You can think of this book as a large-scale body of quantitative and qualitative observations—ten thousand people working at hundreds of companies in seventy countries. We offer only the solutions that we've seen help teams get unstuck, along with inspiring stories of teams that got it right (and some that got it wrong).

Who Should Read This Book

Not everything in this book will apply to you 100 percent of the time. The insights, stories, and tool kits were honed by our encounters with startups, but you'll get tremendous value from them even if you've never worked at a startup and have no plans to do so in the future.

Startups are unique in that their goals tend to exist outside the realm of possibility. "10x, not 10 percent" and "moonshot thinking" are mantras in this world. Founders are hugely ambitious, aiming to make the impossible happen. But startups are also typically under tight resource constraints, and many shut down when they run out of money. They have a very short runway to either take off or crash, which contributes greatly to the intense environments we talk about in this book.

Despite these unique characteristics, startup teams have much in common with other kinds of teams, from those at corporate giants to those at nonprofit organizations operating on a shoestring budget. Whenever big ambitions and driven people come together, they can create intense team dynamics that often have the same exciting results as startups—but on the flip side, many of the same problems.

The startup stories in this book might feel right on the nose for some readers, or perhaps like an extreme version of what others are experiencing today, but we're confident they'll sound familiar. We also believe the insights they've produced will bring the power and light of a bonfire to your biggest challenges, no matter where you work.

How to Use This Book

Part I explores why teams are harder than tech. We examine why startups that seemingly have everything going for them still fail—underscoring the economic benefits of getting the people stuff right. The chapters in part I delve into the four traps we've observed start-ups predictably fall into. We bring to bear the data we've collected from our work across every major startup hub in the world and from academic research that convinced us of the value of the Bonfire Moment. Along the way, we share some practical ideas for you to put into action.

Part II equips your team with strategies and tools to avoid or escape these traps. These chapters are based on the four time blocks we've developed for our full-day workshop, and they include step-by-step instructions, templates, and guidelines to run your own DIY version. Every workshop requires a leader, so consider appointing a team member or a trusted mentor to effectively guide the group through the process. Regardless of how you customize the process, the most important thing is that you jump in. This book will give you everything you need to create your own Bonfire Moment.

We wrap up part II with ideas for extending the impact of the Bonfire Moment into a regular, ongoing practice for your team. Following through on the dialogue that's triggered in the workshop is essential; failing to do so will allow old patterns of behavior to reemerge. We'll show how startups have adapted our tools into permanent rituals, and how they've experienced profound changes as a result.

Our Promise to You

We can't promise that this book will make any team wildly successful. Only a huckster would try to sell you a foolproof formula for success; there are far too many variables at play, including sheer luck. But what we *can* promise is a road-tested means to anticipate and address the biggest people problems that disrupt even the most promising teams. Our proven methodology will de-risk your efforts.

Use this book like you would a good mentor; come back every so often to keep the ideas and practices fresh. You can return to various sections whenever you recognize that your team is falling back into these traps.

The process of developing a strong and healthy team never truly ends. Let's go!

Part 1 /

WHY TEAMS ARE HARDER THAN TECH ...

Chapter 1

Startups Have a People Problem

We're kicking off a workshop at 9:00 a.m. in a large Google meeting space. About forty people from various growth-stage startup teams are sitting at tables around the room. We may be in Silicon Valley or New York or Toronto, or it could be São Paulo, Tel Aviv, Bangalore, or Singapore. Regardless of where we are, the vibe is almost always the same: some members of the group are excited to be here, some have a wait-and-see attitude, and some really, really wish they were somewhere else.

We understand the third group's frustration and skepticism. They are all participants in a Google for Startups Accelerator, a highly selective program offering growth-stage startups tailored technical, product, and leadership training. Today they've been told to give up a full day to attend this workshop about, of all things, people issues. "Why would serious entrepreneurs and technologists waste a whole day on touchy-feely stuff?" they think. We see them grit their teeth and silently resolve to endure this so they can get back to what they consider their real work.

There are no pleasantries or breaking-the-ice exercises. Instead, we start the session by jumping right into a "sixty-second case study" about two startup founders, asking everyone to play a quick game of prediction: Which one is more likely to succeed?

The first is Alex, the CTO of a small startup that's working on an on-demand app. He has great ideas but often feels frustrated that the junior engineers can't keep up. Alex hired them all from the same distinguished university, and they all seemed like quality software engineers on paper. But after months of daily stand-ups, weekly flare-ups, and long nights doing quality control, Alex gives up on them. He decides to lay off five junior engineers (using the excuse that he has to downsize) and replaces them with two more experienced and much better-paid engineers.

This fix seems to work. They ship a better product that year, boosting their daily active users beyond their investors' expectations, which allows the startup to raise more funds. But soon after, Alex's brightest engineer quits. Asked why, the engineer replies, "To be honest, I don't have much to learn from you. I'm not growing in this job. I'm moving to another company where my new boss promised to mentor me." Alex is gutted—and worried that his six-month product road map is now at risk.

As the room processes this unfortunate conclusion to Alex's story, we shift over to Dani, the CEO of a startup in the agriculture tech space.

With the charisma she honed as a community organizer in high school and college, Dani now leads her twenty-member staff with the ease of a naturally gifted leader. She gives an inspirational speech every Monday morning. She makes a habit of walking the floor to check in with people and pump them up, encouraging their highest aspirations. Dani cares about loyalty, so she really takes care of her early employees.

Jacob, her first hire, is a go-getter with a collaborative style that reminds Dani of her own younger self. She sees great potential in him and wants to help him grow his career. "I'll make him a team leader," she thinks. She knows he doesn't have experience leading a team, but she believes he'll figure it out, just like he always does. She gives him a pep talk about her vision for his new role, and sends him off without further support. She then turns her attention to other pressing matters.

Soon after, members of Jacob's team begin to knock on Dani's door, complaining that they aren't getting enough direction from him. She hesitates to give Jacob tough feedback—she's had only praise for him in the past, and this shift feels uncomfortable. Surely he'll find his rhythm. But months later, Jacob's team is badly underperforming on their OKRs,[1] and one of his stars has threatened to leave if things don't improve. Feeling terrible about it, Dani sees no choice but to let Jacob go.

Now we ask the room a simple question: "Who do you think is the better leader, Alex or Dani?"

A few people raise their hand to make the case for Alex. He was under time and resource constraints yet did the best he could. And he delivered! If he hadn't pulled through, the startup wouldn't have survived long enough to work on its people challenges. Then a few others make the case for Dani. She was clearly a more inspiring leader who was invested in her people. She took a chance promoting someone promising, but those bets don't always pay off.

Others in the room protest that neither is a good leader. When it's time to vote, we insist they pick one; "none of the above" is not an option.

"Who thinks Alex is the better leader?"

Invariably, fewer than half of the participants raise their hands, some of them with slightly rebellious energy—as if they assume we're squarely on team Dani because, well, we're the "people people."

"Who thinks Dani is the better leader?" Again, fewer than half of the participants raise their hands. We gently chide the abstainers.

Then we change the questions: "Who here is more like Alex? Who here is more like Dani?" To everyone's amusement, the people who thought Alex was a better leader think they are more like him. And the same for Dani's supporters.

Fascinating. Chuckles fill the room. One explanation: people like their own leadership style and will defend someone similar. Or perhaps a better explanation: people see their own errors in those made by either Alex or Dani and are therefore more forgiving of those types of mistakes.

We throw two new questions at the room: "Who would hire Alex? Who would hire Dani?" The debate energy often shifts at this point. A show of hands reveals that most people would hire Alex. Not all, but most.

And then a final question: "Whom would you rather work for, Alex or Dani?" Most people choose Dani. They'd hire Alex but would prefer to work for Dani!

"Did you see that? Did you see the wild inconsistency of this group? Most of you would hire the person you'd hate to work for!"

As this paradox sinks in, there's nervous laughter. Then pensive silence. We don't speak again until you can hear a pin drop. Everyone in the room is now laser-focused on us. We've just established the first key message of the day: the people stuff is hard. And getting it right can be the difference between a startup that fails and a startup that succeeds.

No one in the room is cynical, indifferent, or resentful about being in the room anymore. It's dawned on them that this touchy-feely people stuff is actually quite important. They're all in.

It's now about 9:30 a.m., and we're on track to run a workshop that can transform their businesses and maybe even their lives.

Rocket Science Is Easier

You most likely launched or joined a startup because you care deeply about an important, difficult challenge you want to help solve with cool technology. You probably spend most of your workday wrestling with hard, complex, vexing problems. And when you joined the startup world, you probably didn't imagine that your colleagues would be among those hard, complex, vexing problems.

Perhaps you've heard the cliché "This isn't rocket science!" used to compare the "soft" problems of people with the "hard" problems of innovation. The irony is that humans have gotten incredibly good at rocket science. Since way back in the 1970s, NASA has been able to send a rocket 400,000 kilometers to the moon and land it within 0.2 kilometers of the touchdown target.

Contrast that with our struggles to understand and predict human behavior. Social scientists are thrilled when they can explain human behavior with 50 percent precision using their most advanced experimental techniques; they call this a strong correlation. The other half is essentially unaccounted for. Somewhere out there an actual rocket scientist is laughing . . . or crying!

The tools we use to understand people are constantly improving, yet building and maintaining a great team culture remains hard, complex, and vexing. As we mentioned in the introduction, a Harvard and McKinsey study found that 65 percent of funded startups fail primarily because of people problems.[2] In 2020, this study was replicated by researchers from Harvard, Stanford, and the University of Chicago. They surveyed close to seven hundred venture capital firms across the world and found a similar picture. The top reason for startup failure, by far, was people-related.[3]

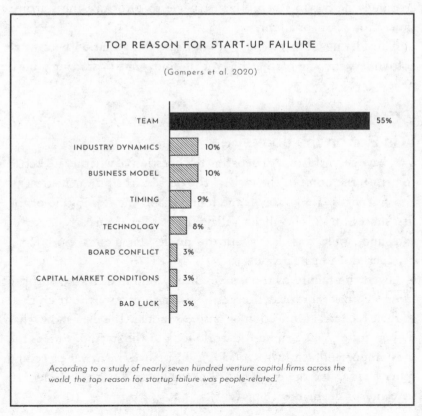

TOP REASON FOR START-UP FAILURE

(Gompers et al. 2020)

TEAM	55%
INDUSTRY DYNAMICS	10%
BUSINESS MODEL	10%
TIMING	9%
TECHNOLOGY	8%
BOARD CONFLICT	3%
CAPITAL MARKET CONDITIONS	3%
BAD LUCK	3%

According to a study of nearly seven hundred venture capital firms across the world, the top reason for startup failure was people-related.

The biggest people challenge is usually conflict within the founding team. Cofounders get frustrated because their teammates aren't pulling their weight, aren't committed enough, don't have the skills they were supposed to have, or have different priorities for the product, fundraising, or exit plans. A business founder may assume the technical founder knows everything there is to know about building a world-class product. The technical founder may feel frustrated that the business founder consistently overpromises to customers and investors and underappreciates the complexity of the work or the technical risks of moving too quickly.

The list goes on. As they scale, the startup's leaders find it incredibly tough to recruit good people, and they take too long to let go of unproductive, toxic teammates. They also become less effective at making decisions, because consensus is their first instinct but is increasingly harder to reach. They struggle to prioritize the startup's time, effort, cash, or all three.

Considering all these issues, it's not surprising that 55 percent of cofounders end the partnership within four years of starting a business.[4]

VCs Bet on the Jockey

VCs have a long history of debating the question of whether it's better to bet on the horse or the jockey. The horse is the product, strategy, and financials. The jockey is the founder and the team. One of the first successful VCs in Silicon Valley, Thomas Davis, an early backer of Intel and Apple, was clear about this point: "People make products; products don't make people."[5]

Given the failure factors we've already outlined, it's no surprise most VCs pay more attention to the strength of a startup team than to their technical innovation or business model. The data shows that 47 percent of VCs around the world look to the startup team as the most important factor when deciding on an investment, far exceeding other factors like the product (13 percent), the business model (10 percent), or the market (8 percent).[6]

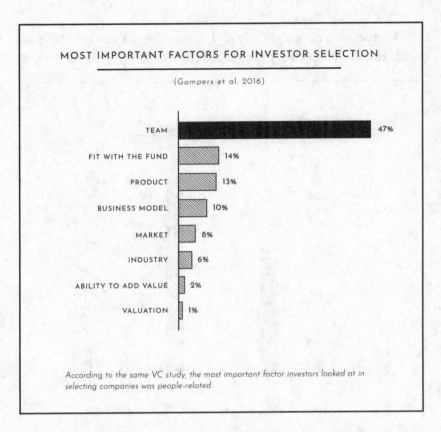

MOST IMPORTANT FACTORS FOR INVESTOR SELECTION

(Gompers et al. 2016)

TEAM — 47%

FIT WITH THE FUND — 14%

PRODUCT — 13%

BUSINESS MODEL — 10%

MARKET — 8%

INDUSTRY — 6%

ABILITY TO ADD VALUE — 2%

VALUATION — 1%

According to the same VC study, the most important factor investors looked at in selecting companies was people-related.

And the evidence doesn't stop there. There is now rigorous research demonstrating that strong teams ultimately make a huge difference in achieving big goals.

Stanford professor Charles O'Reilly and his colleagues[7] asked the question: How does a tech company's culture affect its financial performance? They found that within the tech sector, getting your team culture right helps explain 50 percent of a company's market valuation and 51 percent of analyst buy/sell recommendations.

A strong culture is always important—even more so during tough years. A study on company performance that spanned four decades found that companies with a strong culture dramatically outperform their peers during financial crises and recessions. Just take a look at the thirty-month period of the dot–com crash from 2000 to 2002 and the eight-month period of the global financial crisis in 2008 and

2009 depicted in the graph below.[8] The benefits of a strong culture are subtle in calm waters but pronounced in a storm.

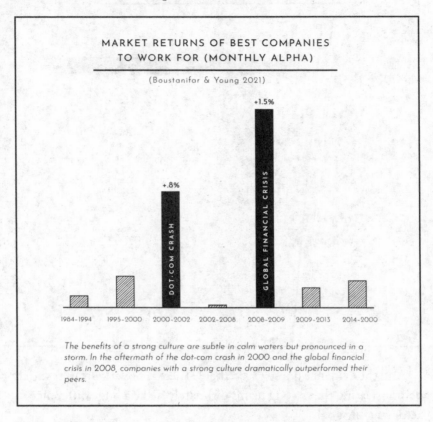

MARKET RETURNS OF BEST COMPANIES
TO WORK FOR (MONTHLY ALPHA)

(Boustanifar & Young 2021)

The benefits of a strong culture are subtle in calm waters but pronounced in a storm. In the aftermath of the dot-com crash in 2000 and the global financial crisis in 2008, companies with a strong culture dramatically outperformed their peers.

We've sat with CEOs of billion-dollar enterprises working hard to rush into new markets and reach scale. Time after time, they tell us they have a bigger market than they can address. They have great product ideas and sources of capital. The biggest constraint on their growth, by far, is hiring enough good people and then getting them to work effectively as a team.

Two Ways to Ruin a Team

Let's return to Alex and Dani, who are actual startup founders we know, with only their names and a few details disguised. We listened to their painful experiences. We took account of the pressures they faced, the personalities at play, and the egos at risk. Unfortunately, their stories echo those of hundreds of other entrepreneurs. Alex and Dani both failed at the most difficult task of leadership: walking the tightrope between delivering results and building a strong team culture. Between performance and people.

Under pressure to reach the impossible expectations of his start-up's product road map, Alex's response was to push his team to maximize their output. He was a trained engineer but had no training in leading a team before being thrown into the deep end. Despite Alex's unexpressed but ultimately good intentions, he felt there was no time to consider what the team needed from him; instead, he focused on what he needed from them. It's no wonder that his best engineer concluded, "If no one here is looking out for me, I might as well look out for myself."

In contrast, Dani wore her good intentions on her sleeve as a charismatic, people-oriented leader. She took a very public risk on Jacob when she promoted him. She had high hopes, but those hopes weren't backed up by a thoughtful plan to support Jacob and help him lead his new team. Her gut-level decisions about people were often trailed by sloppy follow-through. She also had an aversion to conflict, preferring to focus on rah-rah team spirit.

Dani made several mistakes, but her biggest came at the end of the cycle of back-channeled complaints. Sure, Dani listened to the negative feedback from Jacob's team and gave them the guidance they weren't getting from their boss to address their short-term needs. She also gave Jacob a pep talk. What she didn't do was take the much harder step of sharing specific feedback with Jacob and coaching him on how to guide his team. Before long, the situation was completely out of hand, and her business was at risk, just like Alex's.

Learning Soft Skills to Solve Hard Problems

Fortunately, there's a third approach that avoids the mistakes of both Alex and Dani. You don't have to risk your team to meet deadlines

(Alex) or coddle your team at the risk of your OKRs (Dani). Instead, you can lead like Aldi.

Aldi Haryopratomo is a startup founder who obsesses over solving hard, meaningful problems while also building the kind of team culture that delivers consistently outstanding results. After a stint at the Boston Consulting Group, followed by Harvard Business School, Aldi founded one of Indonesia's earliest tech startups. His company, Mapan, sought to create banking services for millions of Indonesian families ignored by the big banks.

Mapan brought new financial products and opportunities to the community that met them where they were—from a business-in-a-box model that helped women in rural parts of Indonesia sell prepaid cell phone credits to a rotating savings and lending product that gave families access to more affordable goods and services. Aldi was asked by Gojek, one of Southeast Asia's most successful tech companies, to lead its fintech group, Gopay, as its founding CEO, which was assembled through the acquisition of three fintech startups, Aldi's Mapan (lending company), Midtrans (payment gateway), and Kartuku (offline payments provider).[9] Aldi led Gopay in its first few years, preparing it to go public in 2022 before leaving to cook up his next startup while serving on the boards of Indonesian healthtech and agritech companies.

We met him in 2015 at Google's Accelerator program in Singapore, where we gathered some of the most promising growth-stage startups from Malaysia, Vietnam, Thailand, Singapore, Indonesia, and the Philippines. What followed were many deep, enlightening conversations about the inner workings and struggles of his startup.

When you ask Aldi about his approach to culture, he'll excitedly start by introducing himself as a "social hacker" and a student of human behavior. To summarize his core belief: *Everyone has aspirations for a better future, and when placed in a social structure that furthers their goals, most people will consistently make good decisions.* Aldi studied how megachurch and cult leaders build loyal followings, then applied what he learned to redirect those strategies toward good (and, we underscore, nonmanipulative) goals.

For instance, while at Mapan, he created community groups for his customers so that they could support each other in achieving their financial goals. The all-women groups meet for weekly rituals in which they sing together about their mission, to help them stay committed to their dreams of providing for their families. They recite a statement of commitment to each other, to their families, and to making progress toward their goals, and the colors and symbols of the community are prominent.[10] To his team that supports these communities, he communicates using clear, repetitive messages and compelling stories about the people they serve. He sets the bar high for the team.

"I'm fully convinced that a good culture has an incredible economic upside," Aldi told us with passion in his voice.

As proof, he recounted a surprising call of gratitude from a woman in a community group the day after a major typhoon hit her part of Indonesia. The day of the storm, she had been scheduled to receive a delivery from Mapan. She figured it was hopeless, of course, given the weather— and yet somehow, through some magic, Aldi's delivery person did turn up that day, soaked to the skin, on a motorcycle in the pouring rain. He smiled and presented her with a completely dry package.

How did he manage this? Well, the delivery person knew that these families saved money for weeks for valuable household items that made their daily lives a little easier, such as rice cookers and electric fans. He knew they were counting on him. So he did something small yet profound in its impact. He braved the storm and used the jacket off his back to keep the package dry.

Organizational psychologists have a term for these types of self-initiated, extraordinary actions: discretionary effort. It's the difference between what someone *has to do* as part of their job description and what they *want to do*."[11] It's a passion to go the extra mile, and what level of effort someone exerts in situations where the choice is up to them. Discretionary effort is the reason why great innovation happens and why teams persist when goals seem impossible. It enables teams to excel in good years and do even better during financial crises, recessions, pandemics, and typhoons.

Charlie Kim, founder and co-CEO of Next Jump, has a snappier

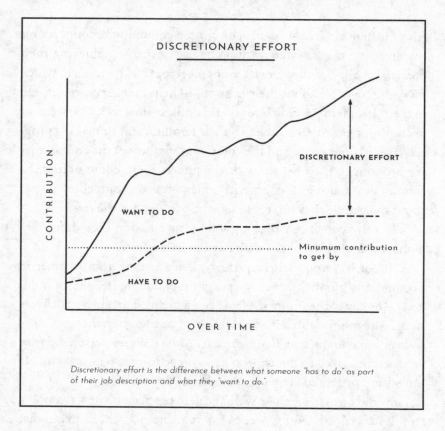

DISCRETIONARY EFFORT

CONTRIBUTION

WANT TO DO

DISCRETIONARY EFFORT

Minumum contribution
to get by

HAVE TO DO

OVER TIME

Discretionary effort is the difference between what someone "has to do" as part of their job description and what they "want to do."

way of talking about the same idea. His company calls it a culture of GAS ("Give a shit"), and they've built a team of people who do. Aldi's startup was full of people who cared a lot about the mission, which became a huge factor in their success. Unlike Alex or Dani, Aldi successfully found a balance between having high expectations of his team and inspiring them to meet these goals, leading to markedly different results.

Aldi is one of several truly outstanding founders whose insights you'll find in this book. Their stories are all unique, yet there are consistent patterns in how they lead their teams to deliver on their impossible goals.

Four Predictable Traps That Derail Startups

Before we get to the tools and tactics to build a team like Aldi's in part II of this book, the rest of part I will dive deeper into the four biggest traps that hinder startups. These traps are subtle and deceptive; while they may initially appear enticing and even beneficial, they carry significant drawbacks that tend to surface abruptly and unexpectedly. They chip away at the commitment and effectiveness of a team before most people even become aware of them. Our work with founders starts with helping them recognize the warning signs, which are often invisible until you're trained to notice them. Then founders can put structures and practices in place to de-risk their teams.

Here's an overview of these traps to set you up for the next few chapters. Then in part II, we'll show you how to overcome the four traps with the Bonfire Moment.

The trap of speed. Operating at high speed comes with a fairly predictable downside: deprioritizing long-range thinking and downplaying or ignoring a team's potentially toxic dynamic. This sets the team on a destructive trajectory. The role of a leader is to find the right balance between getting stuff done and investing in people; between *what you do* and *how you do it*. To build world-class, quality products *and* a dream team that works well together. But in any time-starved team, these conflicting priorities play tug-of-war, and the task list usually wins over people. We'll share fascinating research on how early choices defining a team's culture can help predict its likelihood of failure or success.

The trap of the inner circle. Most startups (including new units within big companies) tend to begin with a tight inner circle of the founder's former collaborators, close friends, and sometimes even family members. The data shows that converting extremely close personal relationships to stable business partnerships is a difficult feat.[12] The inner circle resists healthy conflict, disagreement, and unpleasant conversations—but our data shows that these are all essential to quality work.

The trap of the maverick mindset. Many entrepreneurs are drawn to startups as an opportunity to challenge norms and disrupt mature industries. But when they direct that same energy toward upending seemingly traditional management practices, founders often find that some of those practices have survived for good reasons. Founders embracing a maverick mindset may try to force egalitarianism by splitting equity equally while leaving expectations unspoken; create fuzzy power-sharing arrangements; resist introducing hierarchy for fear that it will create bureaucracy; build a culture that over-relies on heroics; or work furiously to stamp out all conflict, even the kinds that are unavoidable or healthy. Such moves can all be very damaging.

The trap of confidence. When you're pursuing impossible growth targets, taking on bigger and bigger responsibilities, adding to your team rapidly, doubling revenue every six months, and facing one obstacle after another, it's natural to start doubting your abilities. Common unspoken questions include *Am I the right person to lead this team? How do I hide the fact that I've never done this before? Am I having a patch of bad luck, or am I just incompetent?* Our data suggests that the most effective founders are not nearly as self-confident as the least effective ones, who don't ask for help often enough.

We've introduced you to a lot of thorny people problems in this chapter, but we can reassure you that hundreds of startups have applied our process to understand them, bring them out into the open, and solve them. In the next chapters, we'll guide you through the traps with more inspiring stories from leaders who have escaped them.

Chapter 2

The Trap of Speed

There are two games startups must play: the short game and the long game. Both are important, but the long game is often forgotten in the daily battle to survive.

The short game: develop an idea, build a prototype, launch a beta, find product-market fit, pitch for funding. The short game is about constantly monitoring your two key resources—cash and time—and asking, *How do I build this startup with the least amount of cash, in the shortest amount of time?* It's no surprise that two of the most important metrics in the early days are burn rate (*How much cash are we spending in excess of revenue?*) and runway (*How many months can we survive on our cash reserves at the current burn rate?*). In the short game, speed is paramount.

Then there's the long game: keep technical debt[1] low, select for investors who offer smart money,[2] find valuable mentors, build a team that will go far with you, and persevere through setbacks. The long game decisions you make on day one will look different from the ones you make on day five hundred, but don't be mistaken: they begin on day one, when you choose your cofounders. On day five hundred, it might be employee number thirty, or your first investor, or whether you will give people fancy job titles. Long game founders see how far and how big they can get, and work to eliminate any points of failure in the product and in the team. In the long game, foresight is paramount.

Both games are important, but they are fundamentally at odds with each other.

The short game values being scrappy. The long game values doing things well.

The short game looks for fresh, fragile ideas. The long game knows that ideas are a dime a dozen and execution ultimately matters most.

The short game asks, *Are we viable?* The long game asks, *How big could we get?*

The short game requires a great product. The long game requires a great team.

In the short game, the leader is the chief bricklayer. In the long game, the leader is the chief architect.

Given how both games vie for your time, the single toughest challenge for your startup is how to win the short game without risking the long game. If you can't answer this question, you may have already fallen into what we call the trap of speed.

Don't misunderstand; the short game is extremely important. Many startups desperately need to move fast to beat their competitors when launching a great idea. They may need to rush to get real-time feedback. So there's a case to be made for putting your heads down, working crazy hours, and letting the empty pizza boxes and soda cans pile up. Under extreme pressure, fueled by adrenaline, everyone performs triage on their daily task list, with anything important but not on fire sliding into the background. You do have to prove that your product works and that early adopters will pay for it, as conditions for securing funding.

The problem is that the first or second or even third round of funding is not the finish line, as many first-time entrepreneurs mistakenly assume. Each round is merely the start of another push toward the next mountain to climb. So the frantic time crunch continues, becoming a permanent part of the team's rhythm, rather than a short-term solution to a short-term problem. No one ever feels like they have a moment to breathe, and problems within the team tend to stay on the back burner—until they become too big to ignore. At that point, an obsession with lightning speed at the expense of setting a solid foundation for the team jeopardizes your chances of winning the long game.

That's the trap of speed. Your hyperfocus on the short game can ultimately be just as damaging as running out of cash or falling behind a competitor.

A $50 Million Snap Decision

Let's consider a classic mistake we see teams make too often: rushing to take on a cofounder to fill an urgent gap in the founding team.

Imagine you're right at the start of your journey, and you need an experienced sales executive. Through a mutual friend, you meet a mid-career senior sales manager at a big, prestigious company who's eager to jump into their first startup. They offer to invest some cash and join you full-time, to reel in your first few big customers. In exchange, this person asks for a 25 percent equity stake and the title of cofounder.[3] At this point, you have nothing but a pitch deck, a prototype app, and some informal user research.

Let's pause and take a moment to ask, *What is the true value of accepting this cofounder on these terms?* At first, it seems like a great deal. You immediately get money in the bank and an expert who will handle all of your sales activities—which you would hate to do yourself—freeing you up to focus on what you really love, building the product. If that's enough to persuade you, you might be overly focused on the short game.

Here's how a long game evaluation might look. Let's say your startup takes off, and in a few years it has a unicorn valuation of $1 billion. After several rounds of funding, your cofounder's share is diluted to 5 percent, which amounts to $50 million. We find that most cofounders are recruited on the basis of just a few conversations, a LinkedIn check, and maybe one reference call to a common contact. Most people would have done a lot more research to buy a $30,000 car!

So let's lay out a balance sheet on this head of sales. On the assets side, you have all the big customers they've brought in, and their cash contribution. On the liabilities side, you have anything they've done that has destroyed value. What if this cofounder turned out to be like Alex or Dani from chapter 1? You'd have to account for the toxic culture they created, the good talent that quit as a result, and the many times a big potential customer told you that they don't want to deal with your head of sales. At a unicorn valuation, you've lost the long game despite crushing the short game. Now how do you feel about that $50 million expense?

This was exactly the crisis that a couple of young founders in London confided in us. They had partnered with a seasoned industry executive who came with a very rigid way of doing things, including a bureaucratic style of allocating blame and managing consequences. Their only recourse was to clean up their mess by forcing out their head of sales—but not before the trap of speed had already done a lot of damage.

Hyperbolic Discounting

Behavioral scientists call this kind of judgment error—focusing on the short game at the risk of the long game—*hyperbolic discounting*.[4] Humans consistently underestimate the value of things that will benefit us far into the future.

This tendency has been tested by a wide range of experiments that sound like, well, fun party tricks. Subjects of these studies are asked questions such as: "Would you rather receive $100 today or $120 next week?" and "Would you rather receive $100 a year from now or $120 a year and a week from now?" Most respondents would rather receive $100 today than wait a week for $120. But if they have to wait at least a year anyway, they don't mind waiting an extra week to bump it from $100 to $120. This confounds believers in rational economic thinking, because those two scenarios are identical, with the only difference being that the one-week delay will happen either now or a year from now.

We prefer Jerry Seinfeld's take on this. He captured the irrationality of hyperbolic discounting in a stand-up routine called *Night Guy versus Morning Guy.* Night Guy can stay up as late as he wants, with no consequences. But what about feeling terrible in the morning after less than five hours of sleep? "That's Morning Guy's problem," Seinfeld says. "Night Guy always screws Morning Guy.... There's nothing that Morning Guy can do to get back at Night Guy. The only thing Morning Guy could do is to try to oversleep enough times so that Day Guy loses his job, and Night Guy has no more money to go out."[5]

Our bias for the present is hardwired from our origins as hunter-gatherers. If your ancestors found a scrawny, bony antelope, they would expend energy immediately to hunt it down, kill it, and eat it. They wouldn't let the bony antelope pass to save their strength to possibly chase a heftier one later. What if a heftier antelope didn't show up for another two weeks? You can't be picky when you don't know where your next meal is coming from.

Translated to the modern world, this instinct explains why it's easier to sell medicine to treat a disease than insurance to protect against future risks. Or why people fail to take fairly easy steps to protect their data, despite saying they value personal data privacy.[6]

Hyperbolic discounting looks like the chart below. Activities that benefit us at present are valued accurately. Activities whose benefit we perceive to come in the future are erroneously given a discount factor. One might argue that the discount factor is correctly applied, because there's a risk that any anticipated rewards will not materialize in the future. However, studies have shown that although the likelihood of these future rewards is uncertain, we tend to underestimate their probability anyway.[7]

It's important to draw a distinction between procrastination and discounting. Procrastination is a motivational problem: *I see the value of going to the gym instead of binging Netflix, but I can't bring myself to go.* Hyperbolic discounting is a computational failure: *I believe our short-term challenges are more important than strengthening our team culture or waiting to find the right person for a critical job.* In our experience, procrastination is an easier problem to solve. Addressing hyperbolic discounting requires a mental reframing that usually happens

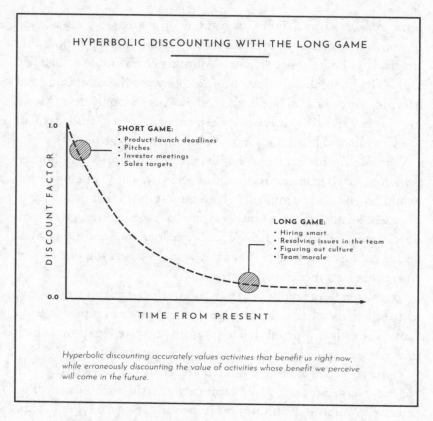

HYPERBOLIC DISCOUNTING WITH THE LONG GAME

SHORT GAME:
• Product launch deadlines
• Pitches
• Investor meetings
• Sales targets

LONG GAME:
• Hiring smart
• Resolving issues in the team
• Figuring out culture
• Team morale

1.0

0.0

DISCOUNT FACTOR

TIME FROM PRESENT

Hyperbolic discounting accurately values activities that benefit us right now, while erroneously discounting the value of activities whose benefit we perceive will come in the future.

only after the miscalculation leads to crisis. It's no wonder that many startups come to us for help shortly after their best engineer leaves unexpectedly, or they've had to do layoffs.

A startup team that focuses on the short game is unconsciously acting like a clan of hunter-gatherers from thousands of years ago. They are as terrified of running out of cash as our ancestors were of running out of food. They'll worry about the future some other time, when things are less crazy and the dangers less urgent. Convincing them to change their ways won't be easy.

Avoiding the Trap of Speed

Not every startup falls into the trap of speed. Some of the most enduring ones keep one eye on the long game as they hustle through their daily crises. They make time to find the right people to bring onto the team. They address toxic behavior early and decisively. They create an environment that turns A players into an A team.

During Google's first few years, founders Larry Page and Sergey Brin usually spent one full day each week working toward the long game, which included recruiting and interviewing the people who would take the company into the future.[8] They invested significant time and attention in developing a unique workplace culture that would become legendary.

Larry, whom we consider one of the most brilliant organizational strategists of our time, liked to tell the story of his grandfather, a Detroit factory worker. This man died a little bit each day on the assembly line, suffering from a lack of autonomy, with no freedom to use his creativity to make things better, and from a need to cater constantly to power-tripping managers. His employer cared only about workers' hands, not their heads or hearts. Larry wanted his startup to attract brilliant people and make them feel alive. From the very start, he built an organization that trusted people to do the right thing. He understood that if he created the right environment, innovation would thrive.

He also believed that the best people weren't looking for new jobs; they were deeply engaged in challenging projects at their current companies. Long before bright engineers would claw their way into an interview with Google, Larry and Sergey knew they couldn't rely only on job postings. Rather than requesting résumés from prospective employees, the early team at Google shared their own résumés. This allowed potential colleagues to understand the caliber of engineers they'd be working with.

Another founder who instinctively tried to avoid the trap of speed is Liran Belenzon, who cofounded BenchSci right after getting his MBA, along with David Chen, Elvis Wianda, and Tom Leung. BenchSci applies machine learning across the entire history of biomedical research to help scientists expedite preclinical research. By providing AI-powered guidance on formulating hypotheses and planning experiments, they enhance the success rates of the discovery of new life-saving drugs. As of 2023, their pioneering platform was being used by more than fifty thousand scientists, including at sixteen of the top twenty pharmaceutical companies and more than forty-five hundred research centers worldwide.

Google's Gradient Ventures fund invested in BenchSci in 2018, a key milestone on their way to raising a total of $200 million and growing to about four hundred employees across North America and the United Kingdom by 2023. As part of Google's investment portfolio, the BenchSci team tapped us for guidance on culture and people issues. But when we sat down with Liran, we found that we could probably learn more from him than he could from us. He's not your typical CEO, and we think he will be one of the most consequential CEOs of his generation.

Liran deals with hard science, but he also understands the importance of getting the culture right. As an engineering manager at BenchSci told us, "Your title and your role aren't limitations on the amount of influence you can have in shaping the various tracks of development in the company." The culture BenchSci has built is the antithesis of the notoriously hierarchical and credential-dependent world of Big Pharma and elite academic science.[9] Liran deploys many initiatives to nurture the BenchSci culture, including spending a lot of time dissecting how renowned organizations like NASA, the Navy SEALs, Nike, Apple, Google, LinkedIn, and Netflix built their cultures to shape BenchSci's approach.

We're especially impressed with a program he calls "Paid to Part Ways." Having grown past the hundred-employee milestone in 2021, BenchSci was getting too big for Liran to screen each new hire personally. He knew that the standard recruitment process was an imprecise game of prediction. Most of the time, you're relying on the weak signals of a résumé, several interviews, and maybe a written technical test or a business plan presentation. BenchSci's employee churn was significantly lower than the tech industry average (25 percent voluntary churn in North America in 2021). Yet they saw many more people leaving as the company got bigger, especially within the first eight to twelve months. They learned that in most of those cases, employees or their managers had realized that it wasn't a good fit within just a few weeks.

Liran suspected that people stayed on for two pragmatic reasons: to avoid the hassle of another job hunt and a hit to their income, and to avoid looking like a job-hopper on LinkedIn. But in the meantime, while waiting to leave, they were subpar, unenthusiastic teammates who were dragging down the performance of others.

So why not, he thought, pay them a full month's salary if they quit within the first three months? That way the company would cut its losses through a voluntary early departure. And employees would walk away grateful to have some money to tide them over during the job hunt. Also, with only three months on the job, ex-employees could just drop it from a résumé or LinkedIn profile. But the biggest benefit of all? Employees who decide to stay are forced to make a conscious choice to opt in, making them even more committed to BenchSci's mission.

As of early 2022, Liran told us, only one person has requested the "Paid to Part Ways" benefit. And the company is stronger than ever, included on Canada's Great Place to Work list for the third year in a row.[10]

Asked why most tech founders don't focus on people issues, given the clear payoff, he replied, "People think that investing in your people requires hard work and only has a long-term return. They are wrong on both counts. Sure, it's work, but it isn't a lot of work. And the benefit is felt immediately. Potential employees decide to join or not join. Your team decides to stay or not stay. They're energized or hating their jobs."

The Economics of Early Decisions

Long game founders like Larry Page and Liran Belenzon are exceptions. Many founders have told us things like, "I manage products, not people," or "Team culture is a luxury that can wait." If you're still inclined to believe statements like that, consider the conclusion of one of the most seminal studies ever done on tech startups: your early decisions about people and culture play an instrumental role in your startup's future success.

The Stanford Project on Emerging Companies set out to answer two primary questions: How do founders of tech startups approach organizational and people challenges in the early days of building their companies? And do these activities contribute meaningfully to their endurance and performance?[11] Study authors Michael Hannan and James Baron, professors of management and organization behavior, respectively, at the Stanford Graduate School of Business, began a decade of data collection in 1994 on more than two hundred tech startups in Silicon Valley. Their timing was perfect for this longitudinal study, catching the dot-com bubble, the crash of 2001, and the tech rebirth that followed. Their work is worth exploring in depth.

Their first important finding was that three dimensions define a company's *organizational blueprint*, as they called it.

1. **Selection criteria (i.e., what they look for when hiring):** Companies tend to prioritize one of three things. Some prioritize *skills*, such as expertise in a specific programming language. Others prioritize *exceptional potential* over current skills, perhaps in part because they can't yet afford technical experts, but also because they dream of building deeply innovative tech, rather than reproducing what has worked before. Still other companies assume that skills and potential are common, so they prioritize *cultural fit*, sometimes filtering job candidates through peer interviews or informal meetups with the full team.

2. **Source of commitment (i.e., why people work there):** The authors found three basic reasons why people join and stay at a startup, summarized as *money*, *work*, and *community*. Good compensation has the weakest and most tenuous appeal, because talented people who focus on money tend to be job-hoppers, always open to the next offer. Startups that stress

interesting and challenging work draw candidates who care more about the mission and the chance to work on cutting-edge technology. We knew an engineer who summed up the appeal of working at SpaceX—the startup that's trying to put a human colony on Mars—as "Long hours, low pay, hate your boss, make history!" Finally, some startups emphasize a *sense of community* as the main source of attachment and commitment.

3. **Management approach (i.e., how they coordinate and control the work):** Management approaches exist on a spectrum, from very hands-off to very tightly controlled. The researchers observed that *informal control through peers or a well-defined culture* was one of the more common approaches. Bridgewater Associates has an extreme version of this, with peers providing real-time feedback in meetings through an iPad to sharpen each other's judgment. Some startups offer near absolute autonomy to high-caliber recruits, and rely on *professional standards* to keep the quality of the work high. Others operate more traditionally through *formalized processes* or manage the work themselves through *direct monitoring*.

Table 1: Dimensions of Organizational Blueprints

What we look for when hiring	› Skills › Exceptional talent/potential › Fit with the team
Why people work here	› Good compensation › Interesting and challenging work › Sense of community
How we coordinate and control the work	› Peer and/or cultural control › Reliance on professional standards › Formalized processes › Direct monitoring

In studying those two hundred startups, the researchers found that five blueprints—that is, five combinations of the three dimensions—were most common.[12]

1. The *Star* model seeks to recruit only outstanding people and gives them the resources and autonomy they need to do their jobs.
2. The *Engineering* model operates with a scrappy, intense, skunkworks mentality. The goal is to build something amazing with minimal management constraints. (This was the most popular blueprint in this study, not surprisingly.)
3. The *Commitment* model hires people who are a strong cultural fit, and wants them to feel a strong family spirit, so they will persevere through the tough days and will want to stay for many years.
4. The *Bureaucracy* model focuses on documentation and organization. Every job description is clear, and every project is rigorously managed.
5. The *Autocracy* model aims for an old-fashioned, purely transactional workplace: labor is exchanged for compensation, but neither side gets emotionally invested.

Table 2 summarizes what each of these models prioritizes across the three dimensions and what percentage of the companies studied followed each model.

Now let's turn to the big question: How does the choice of organizational model affect the trajectory of a startup? You'll begin to see here how the people decisions you make in the early stages of your startup will matter in the long game. The researchers focused on three metrics: the likelihood and speed of going public, the likelihood of failure,[13] and, for companies that went public, the growth or decline in market capitalization. All three metrics varied widely by organizational blueprint, even after statistically controlling for exogenous factors such as relative levels of VC financing, IPO volume per industry,

Table 2: Typology of Organizational Blueprints Based on
Three Dimensions

Blueprint (% of companies studied)	Dimensions		
	What we look for when hiring	Why people work here	How we coordinate and control the work
Star (9.0%)	Potential	Work	Professional standards
Engineering (30.7%)	Skills	Work	Peer/cultural control
Commitment (13.9%)	Fit	Community	Peer/cultural control
Bureaucracy (6.6%)	Skills	Work	Formalized processes
Autocracy/Direct Control (6.6%)	Skills	Money	Direct monitoring
Aberrant (33.1%)	Various	Various	Various

and economic trends. This is how the organizational blueprints correlated with key outco,mes:

> *Commitment* startups tended to reach an IPO fastest. They were also the least likely to fail. Conversely, *Autocratic* startups perished at the highest rate.
> *Star* startups were among the least likely to make it to an IPO, but if they managed to cross that hurdle, their growth in market cap was strongest. *Autocratic* startups had the worst growth in market cap—12 percent lower. While *Commitment* startups did well at making it to an IPO, they didn't do nearly as well post-IPO.

> *Star* startups tended to have a lot of attrition—some intentional as they weeded out underperformers, some unwanted as key people got bored after early challenges were solved.

> *Star* startups relied on company stock as the main compensation, which meant that when they did well, people were inclined to cash out, and when they struggled, people were inclined to give up.

> *Commitment* startups were the most reliable—they got the job done and avoided outright failure—but they had limited upside. It's as if building a team that prioritizes cultural fit helps keep it focused on the big milestone of an IPO, but then the lack of diversity becomes a liability post-IPO, when a startup needs to expand into new markets, new business units, and new talent pools.

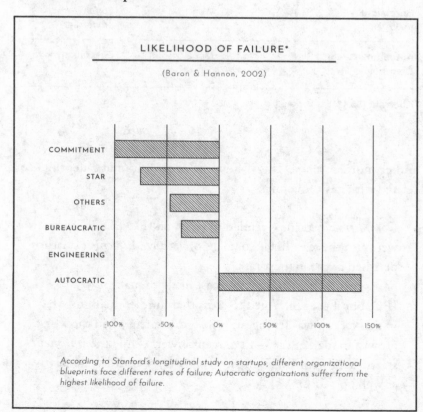

LIKELIHOOD OF FAILURE*

(Baron & Hannon, 2002)

According to Stanford's longitudinal study on startups, different organizational blueprints face different rates of failure; Autocratic organizations suffer from the highest likelihood of failure.

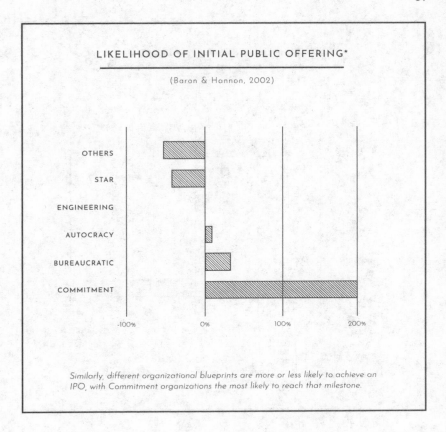

LIKELIHOOD OF INITIAL PUBLIC OFFERING*

(Baron & Hannon, 2002)

Similarly, different organizational blueprints are more or less likely to achieve an IPO, with Commitment organizations the most likely to reach that milestone.

"Although the *Commitment* and *Star* models might have a higher upside, they are also, in some respects, more fragile, unstable, and difficult to manage," concludes the study. Both were more likely to see a departure of their founder-CEO, often followed by highly disruptive changes.

If you're already spinning your wheels wondering whether you need to retrofit your team to a new model, the study offers a word of caution. The study found that shifting models midstream was very damaging, often leading to an exodus of disgruntled employees, which badly hurt financial results. This conclusion should convince leaders that they really don't have the luxury of waiting to play the long game.

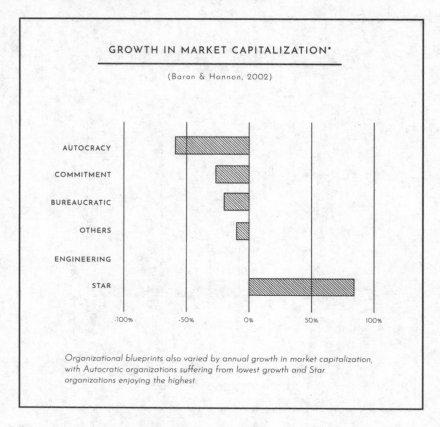

GROWTH IN MARKET CAPITALIZATION*

(Baron & Hannon, 2002)

Organizational blueprints also varied by annual growth in market capitalization, with Autocratic organizations suffering from lowest growth and Star organizations enjoying the highest.

Be Vigilant against Executive Magnification

Your team culture starts to get built on day one, not when you decide to get around to it. How you show up, make decisions, set boundaries, and favor some habits over others will build the culture, whether or not you're aware of it. So you can either actively shape it or passively leave it to be shaped by your unconscious behaviors.

Mary, the founder of an enterprise solutions startup in Australia, struggled to figure out why her team kept needing to run fire drills. For each new customer, they would struggle with the early planning, waste a lot of time on less important parts of the work, and then have to sprint to the final deadline. They always hit it (barely) with good results, but the process was frustrating and exhausting. Then, a few weeks later, it would happen again. She asked us for help in solving their culture of procrastination.

After a few questions, we learned that after each of these last-minute saves, Mary would pat the team on the back and take them out for beers to celebrate the successful project completion. She thought this was what good leaders were supposed to do. But by rewarding those frantic sprints, she was inadvertently encouraging the very procrastination she hated. Her team was simply giving her the heroic saves that she seemed to appreciate.

When we suggested that Mary stop the celebratory beers after each deadline, she worried that such a change would make her look cold and ungrateful. Sure enough, her people weren't happy to lose those celebrations. But then Mary replaced them with new ways to reward forward planning and meeting early milestones. This relatively small tweak changed the entire culture, and fire drills became a thing of the past.

Stanford professor Robert Sutton calls these unintended outcomes of a leader's behavior *executive magnification*.[14] Most good leaders will communicate clearly and temper their tone to match their intention. They try to be consistent about what they do and what they say. But perhaps one out of ten times, when they're tired, hungry, sleep-deprived, or just in a rush, they react in anger, look past bad behavior to smooth things over, or make a throwaway comment. These thoughtless actions or omissions then get misinterpreted as a dictate. They waste the team's time, money, and effort, and become defining moments of your culture.

Leaders like Mary can begin to beat the trap of speed by becoming more mindful of executive magnification.

Don't Wait for a Crisis

Now let's consider another founder, Mark, who observed early on that his team's culture was suffering as they staffed up, and found an unconventional way to address it. He was leading a Singapore-based startup, developing a payments app targeted to India, Southeast Asia, Latin America, and Africa. Their premise was that the next billion users to get on the internet for the first time would come from those parts of the world, and they would have very different needs and expectations than users in North America or Western Europe. So Mark, who had family roots in Southeast Asia but grew up in Silicon Valley, hired software engineers from those developing markets who would understand the target users firsthand.

Mark and his team were under intense competitive pressure to launch their product, making them vulnerable to the trap of speed. But he was growing increasingly concerned about the deference to authority he's started to notice. Most of his team had grown up in cultures where workers always deferred to their bosses, never disagreed with them in group settings, and expected them to make all decisions.

Mark wanted to create a meritocracy of ideas, where his people would feel psychologically safe to challenge the boss when they had a better idea. He was willing to accept the best solution even if it came from the most junior person on staff, and he didn't want his position as founder to suppress good ideas. Mark noticed some small, troubling signals. During product meetings, for example, he noticed junior engineers taking a quick glance at their manager before speaking, as if to ask for permission. Subtle, but insidious.

This culture had to change before its weaknesses were magnified— but how? Under so much pressure to launch, the simplest thing to do would be to power through product meetings, lecturing people not to be afraid to share their ideas. He could also outsource the problem by hiring trainers to help his team speak up with confidence. But Mark knew neither would work. At best, nothing would change. At worst, he would frustrate and alienate his team.

So Mark came up with a crazier idea, with the help of his senior engineers. He asked them to connive with the junior staff and play some elaborate pranks on the big boss. The goal was to humanize the founder, making him more like an approachable peer. Over the next few months, many pranks ensued, including a fake mass resignation and a fabricated front-page newspaper article reporting the leak of their project. Perhaps the best was the time Mark's car was completely covered in cling wrap—from hood to trunk—in the parking lot. Random onlookers had a good laugh at that one! But such antics really worked. As people saw Mark laughing too, instead of raging, they became much more willing to share their opinions openly and honestly in and out of work meetings.

Ultimately Mark was able to launch a great product, but only by confronting people issues instead of deferring them indefinitely.

Speed Creates Drag, Which Reduces Speed

What Liran Belenzon and Larry Page knew by intuition, what the Stanford research study confirmed, and what Mary's and Mark's culture hacks demonstrate is that when leaders don't invest time in the long game early on, their success at the short game may end up being inconsequential. Perhaps the best metaphor for this phenomenon is the physics of drag.

Engineers who build Formula 1 race cars know that a really fast car needs more than a strong engine. It also needs an aerodynamic body to reduce and redirect the drag that high speeds create. Drag increases exponentially—not linearly—relative to speed. At 70 mph, a car is pushing against four times more drag than at 35 mph. So without eliminating drag, you would have to burn much more fuel to run at top speed. This paradox is as true of race cars as it is of startups: speed creates drag, and then drag in turn reduces speed.

This is what *team drag* looks like at your startup: misaligned decisions, miscommunication, wasted work, unnecessary rework, and the need to fill gaps left by departing key players. These will all drain your precious time, money, and energy. Every team has limited energy, and you can either waste it on drag or use it to build the startup. If you take it for granted, team drag will make it harder for you to hit your milestones—or those expected by your investors.

How do you know that you're wasting too much energy on team drag? Look out for how often you get pulled into small decisions that should be handled by your team. Check if you yourself are micromanaging decisions. Reflect on whether you're spending too much time resolving ego-based disputes within the team. Look for zombie projects—efforts that you've tried to kill but somehow live on. Look for deliverables that take too long for their complexity level, especially if their quality is also disappointing. If you tolerate the leaders and teammates who create drag, you'll soon see your A players walk out the door to escape your culture of mediocrity and dysfunction.

Twenty Critical Sources of Team Drag

To help you see where your startup might be struggling with team drag, we asked founders to share the things they wished they hadn't ignored early on that created a lot of drag down the line. Think of these questions as foundations for the future that teams can easily rush past while focusing on the short game. Fortunately, you can fix many of them, as you'll see in the chapters ahead.

In part II of this book, we'll have much more for you to chew on about avoiding the trap of speed. But for now, you might want to pull out a notebook and scribble down your reflections. Read through each question set, and for every item that your team hasn't spent time on, mark it as a red flag. Our unscientific reckoning is that startups with five or more flags will tend to struggle with team drag.

Initiation:

1. **Mission.** Is our work trying to solve an important, meaningful problem, and has that higher mission been clearly articulated for the team?
2. **Skills and networks.** Do the people on our team have mostly overlapping skills or networks? Do we have enough diversity to open a wide range of prospective employees, customers, and funding?
3. **Equity splits.** Did we make the easy choice of distributing equity in equal shares, since we started as a tight-knit group of peers? If so, what will we do in the future if contributions to the startup start to

vary widely and people perform at different levels of quality? What will happen if a pivot makes some cofounders' skill sets less essential?

4. **Colocation.** How do we feel about having everyone based in the same city, working from the same physical space, or taking advantage of options for remote work? How often do we expect people to be physically in the same place? How flexible will we be when making exceptions?

5. **Representing the team.** Who will be the face of the startup when a media outlet or conference allows only one cofounder to represent us? Will it always be the same person? How do we prevent any of us from feeling invisible?

Operation:

6. **Decision-making.** Will we make important decisions based on data, intuition, or a combination of the two? In scenarios when there isn't good data, whose intuition do we lean on?

7. **Raising money.** What kinds of investors are we willing to work with? Are we clear about the pros and cons of receiving money from family or friends? Whom are we going to turn down for financing? Will those guidelines change if we get desperate?

8. **Spending.** How much will we spend on non-revenue-generating expenses, such as a nice office? Are we aligned on whether certain kinds of expenses help attract talent or build confidence with customers, or if they're empty ways to feed our egos?

9. **Running out of money.** If we're ever about to run out of money, what are we prepared to do? Do we ask friends or relatives for help, put in our own money, and/or take no salary? Should we make exceptions to salary cuts based on personal circumstances?

10. **Hiring and firing.** Will culture and values be a key part of our hiring decisions? Are we willing to turn away highly credentialed people who fail those tests? Should we fire people who undermine the culture, in addition to firing for underperformance? How much time should we give people to address constructive feedback?

Interaction:

11. **Time commitment.** What hours will we keep? Are we expecting everyone to work part-time, full-time, or all the time? If we started off working part-time (as many startups do), are we aligned on who will later be willing to go full-time and at what point? How will we handle deviations from this time commitment?

12. **Conflict.** How do we handle conflict in the team? What are the rules of engagement for resolving issues without damaging relationships?

13. **Expressing stress and anger.** What are acceptable expressions of stress and anger? Will we tolerate profanity, yelling, incivility, or property damage? What are we prepared to do to enforce our norms?

14. **Gossip.** What will we do when gossip starts to spread within the team? What is each team member's responsibility when they hear one colleague complain about another? When does gossip cross the line from harmless to damaging?

15. **Mental health.** What will we do when someone on the team is struggling with their mental health?[15] To what extent are we ready to support our teammates, especially if they need to take temporary breaks from work?

16. **Friendship outside of work.** Is spending time in social activities with colleagues outside working hours optional, encouraged, or expected? Are we mindful that certain activities (such as drinking at the pub, playing soccer on Saturdays, or doing recreational drugs) might put some people in an awkward position? Will we allow participation in these social events to define the inner circle of the startup?

Separation:

17. **Personal stagnation.** If one or more cofounders aren't building their skills fast enough to keep up with the growing business, what are fair actions to move forward without them?

18. **Resignations.** What do we consider fair reasons for one of us to resign from the team? Will we support teammates who can't stay due to family responsibilities or financial needs?

19. **Exit plans.** Are we aligned on possible exit plans for the startup? If a large company offers to buy us out before we intend to exit, will we consider selling? Under what conditions would we reject a serious offer?

20. **Failure.** At what point will we decide this startup is a failure? What metric do we use: bankruptcy, or a success hurdle such as "*x* users in *y* months" or "*x* dollars in revenue by year *y*"? What will we do if some members of the team want to keep fighting while others have already mentally moved on?

If you find that your team has rushed past many or most of these questions while playing the short game, don't despair. The Bonfire Moment will help you get back on track.

tl;dr

The Problem

Startups need to win at both the short game and the long game. But they often fall into the trap of speed, making them hyperfocused on the short game. People are instinctively biased toward urgent, burning issues (like launch deadlines and investor pitches) and take for granted important team issues that have longer-term payoffs (like partnering with the right cofounders, shaping the team culture deliberately, and resolving conflicts).

The Evidence

Hyperbolic discounting, a phenomenon studied by behavioral economists, helps explain why this happens: we tend to undervalue long-term investments, while accurately valuing immediate benefits. Yet a longitudinal study by Stanford University researchers revealed that to be a risky approach; the decisions you make regarding how you build the team and manage its culture are strongly linked to your likelihood of failure, your likelihood of making it to an IPO, and your growth in market capitalization.

The Solution

First, recognize that your team culture will get built whether you shape it or not. Be careful about executive magnification, when the team misinterprets a leader's actions or inactions, which unintentionally shapes the team's culture. To gauge how badly your team is struggling from the trap of speed, go over the twenty sources of team drag and find out what's likely to slow you down. This compilation was drawn from founders sharing their regrets about overlooked early decisions that later caused problems.

Chapter 3

The Trap of the Inner Circle

MIT systems scientist Peter Senge, a pioneer in the field of organizational learning, reached a surprising conclusion: the collective intelligence of a team is usually lower than the average intelligence of the team's members.[1] We've found this insight to be true from our work with startup teams around the world. And we have a theory about why it happens—a very common phenomenon that we call the trap of the inner circle.

It usually begins in the earliest days of a startup, when the cofounders share a common origin story, whether as personal friends, family members, or long-standing colleagues at a prior company. The strong, familiar bond they bring to the startup has many advantages, but it also tends to nudge the inner circle toward groupthink. A big challenge for most teams is how to make the most of the individual talents of their members, without pressuring them—either openly or subconsciously—to go along with the biases and preferences of the inner circle.

Many experts besides Senge have recognized this challenge. As Harvard professor Cass Sunstein wrote, after years of studying decision-making in teams, "Do groups usually correct individual mistakes? Our simple answer is that they do not. Far too often, groups actually amplify those mistakes."[2] Comedian George Carlin had a simpler way of putting it: "Never underestimate the power of stupid people in large groups."

In this chapter, we will explore some strategies that great teams use to beat the trap of the inner circle and minimize groupthink. Through the stories of the founders who developed the early versions of the internet and personal computing, and, more recently, the founders behind one of the COVID vaccines, we offer ways to spot the unhealthy dynamics of inner circles.

When Teams Make Life-or-Death Decisions

In a previous iteration of our workshop, we put teams through a social experiment to test how they'd work together on a high-stakes, high-pressure challenge. This exercise shows how quickly and invisibly the trap of the inner circle can arise.

Our activity was based on a real news event: on August 5, 2010, a century-old copper and gold mine in northern Chile caved in, trapping thirty-three miners more than two thousand feet underground. These survivors jammed into a tiny safe room, just five hundred square feet, with only two days of emergency supplies. By carefully restricting their consumption, they all stayed alive for the next seventeen days, until rescuers could drill a shaft large enough to deliver food, medicine, water, and communication devices. The rescuers then drilled a larger rescue shaft so that they could retrieve one miner at a time via a narrow, cable-pulled capsule. There was no guarantee that this hastily built mechanism would keep working long enough to make thirty-three round trips, which would take about an hour each way.[3]

The test we gave our workshop teams: Imagine you're the team in charge of the operation. How would you decide the order of rescue? Which miners would you select to exit the collapsed mine first, knowing that the men at the back of the line were most likely to perish if the mechanism failed?

We shared a brief bio of each miner, reduced to twelve to simplify the exercise, and with some names and details altered. Here are examples:

> Claudio Ojeda, forty-seven, a widower with no children who had diabetes.
> Jose Yáñez, thirty-four, a drill operator who requested cigarettes be sent down while awaiting rescue and expressed disgust at the nicotine patches he received instead.
> Edison Galeguillos, fifty-five, who had been injured in at least two earlier mining accidents. He had thirteen siblings and required medication for hypertension. Recently, his marriage had ended due to his infidelity with a fellow miner's wife.
> Victor Peña, thirty-four, married and suffering from severe depression.
> Omar Zamora, thirty-four, an auto mechanic and laborer who had worked at the mine for five years. He sent up poems to his pregnant wife and four-year-old son.
> Carlos Espina, forty, the most engaging personality in videos sent up from underground. Known for his ability to solve tough technical challenges, he had a wife and two girlfriends awaiting his rescue.
> Esteban Ticona, twenty-eight, whose wife gave birth to their second daughter while he was trapped underground. They named the baby Esperanza, which means hope. He led daily prayer meetings to keep hope alive among his fellow miners.

Imagine you were handed this information and you had to decide who would get to survive and who might get permanently trapped. How would you go about it?

The workshop teams, each five or six people, were given thirty minutes to hand in both their individual order of rescue lists (listing the miners 1 through 12) and a group list representing the entire team's decision. No other instructions. During this exercise, we would always overhear similar comments:

> Oh my gosh, a wife and two girlfriends?
> He has a new little baby!
> Should the ones with medical conditions go to the front of the line or the back?
> Should the ones with kids get priority, or is that unfair to those without kids?
> We have no right to play God—we should just randomize the order!

After the lists were handed in, we'd reveal what had happened to the miners as everyone leaned in and listened intently. The room would always be relieved to learn that all the miners had been successfully rescued, without any panic or fighting.

The decision-makers aboveground faced two separate risks: mechanical and social. They needed to keep a skilled mechanic underground to the end, in case the mechanism jammed and needed a repair from below. They also needed an emotionally strong leader to stay, to hold everyone's spirits up for another thirty-two hours, and to prevent panic in case the mechanism failed. And they wanted two strong and healthy men to go first, to troubleshoot the mechanism if necessary and then reassure the others if it worked.

Other than the first two and last two miners (whose names we announced), the leaders allowed the other miners to decide their own order. There was a strong feeling of support and community, with many volunteering to let others go ahead. No one got any preferential treatment based on their age, marital or parental status, or personal indiscretions like infidelity.

We graded the submitted lists by giving one point each for matching the first two and last two names. The other eight names would get one point each if they appeared anywhere between slots 3 and 10. So the maximum possible score was 12.

Here's where things got really interesting. We handed everyone back their scores and asked each team to read out:

> The average of the team members' individual scores (we called this the *individual average score*)
> The highest individual score of any one team member (we called this the *individual best score*)
> The score of the list that the team agreed on (we called this the *team score*)

As these three numbers for each team were posted on the whiteboard, a pattern tends to emerge: individual average scores usually beat the team score, and the individual best score almost always beat the team score. Very rarely does the team score beat the individual average or individual best. In the odd case when that happens, we'd say the team had "synergy." If the team score outperformed the individual average but not the individual best, we'd call that "some synergy." For instance, here are the scores on our whiteboard from a few years ago:

	Team 1	Team 2	Team 3	Team 4	Team 5	Team 6	Team 7	Team 8	Team 9	Team 10
Individual average	6.4	6.5	6.5	6.7	8.2	6.7	7	8	6.3	6.8
Individual best	8	7	10	8	10	7	8	10	7	8
Team	7	5	6	7	8	8	8	7	9	6
Synergy	Some	None	None	Some	None	Yes	Some	None	Yes	None

Senge's observation seemed to be confirmed, as only 20 percent of these teams achieved synergy, while half did worse than they would have if their contributions had simply been averaged. Synergy—making a team more valuable than the sum of its parts—was an elusive goal.

Or as one participant exclaimed after studying the whiteboard, "Teams make us stupid!"

How Inner Circles Amplify Errors

The social experiment based on the Chilean mine rescue was, of course, artificial, with unrealistically limited information and an arbitrary time limit. But it still shows how hard it is for teams to achieve synergy while grappling with complex problems. Having A-level players won't guarantee you an A-level team. To understand why, let's look more closely at how the teams in our experiments decided on their team lists.

Most teams said they had started by asking each person to share their individual list, along with the criteria that led them to that order of rescue. There was almost always a wide range of responses, based on how people thought about profound moral questions, such as whether people with serious health problems should go first or last. As team members spoke in turn, alliances would quickly form between people who agreed with one another. These subgroups would build on each other's ideas, get excited, and more confidently advocate for related ideas. This process created a confirmation loop that cemented and emboldened some members into an inner circle. Those who disagreed with this inner circle would either lose confidence in their own ideas or dig their heels in, asserting their opposing opinion.

These dynamics became clear whenever we questioned the no-synergy groups. We'd ask whoever had the highest individual score, "Why did you fail to convince the team of your superior point of view?" The typical answer was something like, "I didn't know it was right, so I second-guessed myself. Then when several others got excited about their idea, I reconsidered and went along with the group."

In that moment, the team lost the brainpower of that individual. This was the most common result.

The second most common result was an impasse between two or three conflicting approaches. With the deadline looming, someone would usually call for a majority vote. It's an efficient way to lock in a choice quickly, and it feels like a fair, democratic process. But voting was a losing strategy in this experiment, because it silenced minority views and ignored their potentially superior insights. These groups achieved limited synergy at best.

In contrast, the roughly 20 percent of teams that did achieve synergy usually worked harder to encourage each member to try to convince the others by asking questions like, *Why do you want to put the older miners last? Why do you think we should ignore health and mental health problems? Did you consider* x? *Why? Why not?*

The most successful groups worked to build consensus. This approach rarely led to a 100 percent consensus, but it worked well to surface diverse perspectives and help the teams find common ground. It invited everyone to have "strong opinions weakly held."[4] Consensus building slowed down the formation of inner circles and the marginalization of minority opinions.

Which leads to an obvious question: If consensus building is so effective, why is it so rarely seen in team dynamics?

The short answer is that consensus building is very time consuming. In real-life decision-making contexts, teams rarely have the luxury of discussing or debating issues for days or even hours. In a real-world best-case scenario, leaders listen to everyone with an open mind, surface all relevant information, frame points of disagreement, and debate them honestly. If consensus remains elusive, time constraints eventually require the team to "disagree and commit"—a phrase coined by Andy Grove, the legendary former CEO of Intel. The leader ends the debate and makes a call, which the full team commits to implement. Despite the failure to achieve consensus, the dissenters feel like they were heard and respected, not bullied or outvoted. Morale stays high, and so does the team's willingness to implement the decision.

Why Startups Are Especially Vulnerable to Inner Circles

Inner circles hurt a team's success, and they exist at all kinds of companies. Startups, however, are especially vulnerable, because most startups begin with a small, tight-knit group of two to five friends or family members. Some are colleagues at a big company who break away to launch a startup, such as PayPal alums Steve Chen, Chad Hurley, and Jawed Karim, who founded YouTube. Some are college friends, such as Snapchat founders Evan Spiegel, Bobby Murphy, and Reggie Brown. Some are business school classmates, such as Rent the Runway's Jennifer Hyman and Jennifer Fleiss, or Warby Parker's Neil Blumenthal, Andrew Hunt, David Gilboa, and Jeffrey Raider. Some are siblings, such as Stripe founders Patrick and John Collison. Some are even child and parent, such as Rand Fishkin and his mother, Gillian Muessig, who built Moz.

These kinds of partnerships are appealing because preexisting trust is hugely valuable. When all you have at first is a dream and a work ethic, it will be hard to recruit strangers to join your effort. Building a team with family or close friends can grease the wheels of decision-making. And these are the people founders feel the most comfortable sharing the risks and rewards of starting a business with.

As Noam Wasserman points out in his book *The Founder's Dilemmas*, teams that start out as family and friends are the least stable business partnerships.[5] This type of inner circle will tend to resist healthy conflict, disagreement, and unpleasant conversations—all of which are essential. The cost of conflict becomes significantly higher because of the personal relationships at stake. See below how Wasserman graphs these dynamics based on studying thousands of technology startups.

Inner circles blur important boundaries between private and professional relationships. For instance, Marty built a fintech startup with his close friend and former university classmate Marco. Their idea was hatched in their dorm room during a series of drinking-and-dreaming sessions. They launched their company as peers who saw eye

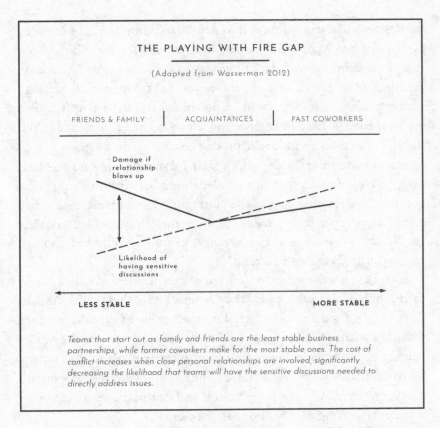

THE PLAYING WITH FIRE GAP

(Adapted from Wasserman 2012)

FRIENDS & FAMILY | ACQUAINTANCES | PAST COWORKERS

Damage if
relationship
blows up

Likelihood of
having sensitive
discussions

LESS STABLE   MORE STABLE

Teams that start out as family and friends are the least stable business partnerships, while former coworkers make for the most stable ones. The cost of conflict increases when close personal relationships are involved, significantly decreasing the likelihood that teams will have the sensitive discussions needed to directly address issues.

to eye on most issues and still enjoyed each other's company long after graduation.

But then Marty assumed the role of CEO, while Marco, who was interested only in his area of expertise, became user experience (UX) lead. It was probably too soon for the startup to have a dedicated UX lead, but Marty was loyal to Marco and wanted to keep him on the team in whatever role he wanted. Besides, they agreed that titles were mostly arbitrary at an early-stage startup. CEO or UX lead—it didn't matter; they were equal partners. Friends first, coworkers second.

Tensions started to build when Marco missed some big deadlines, and Marty matter-of-factly followed up. In most professional settings, asking someone why they've missed a deadline is trivial. But in this case, Marco saw Marty's following up as a challenge to their egalitarian friendship and partnership, as if Marty was pulling rank. The tensions escalated when Marty hired a new head of engineering. Throughout this time, drinking-and-dreaming sessions continued to happen on Fridays, but the head of engineering was kept out of these strategy conversations, instead receiving a download from the two founders on Monday. The head of engineering left soon after, feeling like he did not have the space to influence product road map decisions.

Here's another example, with a family dynamic. Simone was running an e-commerce startup that she'd founded with her aunt, who became CFO. After a year of the aunt's poor performance and office gossip that she was untouchable, Simone reluctantly decided to let her go. Nearly two years of awkward family gatherings followed, most of which the aunt refused to attend.

Former coworkers tend to manage interpersonal conflict better than family and close friends. They've seen each other's work ethic in a professional setting and selected each other based on skill sets they need to get the startup going. The professional behaviors they practiced at the companies they came from transfer easily to the startup. So when there's a need to resolve conflict, or challenge each other's thinking, they tend to be more honest and forthright with each other without triggering deeply personal emotions.

If you founded your startup with college friends or close family, it's important to know that instability and failure are not inevitable. But you should be ready to put in the hard work to prevent the dynamics of your inner circle from derailing your company.

Inner Circles Form around Positional *or* Personal Power

Even if you're not part of a startup like the ones we've just described, your company is not immune from the trap of inner circles. They can form and threaten quality decision-making anywhere, due to two forms of influence: *positional power* and *personal power.*

Positional power is more obvious because it's based on job titles and reporting structures. In extreme cases, teams adopt what has been called the Jim Barksdale rule (named after the former CEO of Netscape): "If we have data, let's go with the data. If all we have are opinions, let's go with mine." That's a recipe for an inner circle formed around the CEO, and for widespread resentment among those who are excluded.

Personal power arises when someone (not necessarily the CEO or another senior leader) has exceptional personal traits such as verbal skill, confidence, likability, or persuasiveness. Even if this person isn't high up on the org chart, they can quickly build a coalition around their ideas, which can develop into an inner circle. People with personal power can seemingly bend others to adopt their positions, even when those positions might lead the team off course.

Some teams wind up with multiple inner circles in conflict with each other, perhaps one around the CEO/founder and another around a department head or more junior leader. As you evaluate your own team for the trap of the inner circle, remember to look for informal coalitions that might not be obvious on your formal org chart.

Spotting the Symptoms

As we saw in the mine rescue experiment, teams with strong inner circles are prone to self-censor their disagreements and suppress healthy contention. The result is groupthink, which can emerge in any kind of organization, from a startup to an established company, a nonprofit, or a government. Researchers have even found that groupthink helps explain heinous crimes such as the Holocaust, the Nanjing Massacre, and the Jonestown tragedy. Others have suggested that groupthink explains the chain of decisions that led to the explosion of NASA's space shuttle *Challenger*, and the failures of UK companies Marks & Spencer and British Airways.

To diagnose groupthink in teams, we use the following list of symptoms inspired by research by Yale's Irving Janis,[6] as well as by Cass Sunstein's work a few decades later. Some of these symptoms are easier to spot than others, but all are clues that your team might be on the road to serious problems:

1. **Illusion of invulnerability.** Team conversations become dominated by excessive optimism and "happy talk," leading the group to take abnormal risks. "Don't pay any attention to the haters and doubters out there; we will eventually succeed" is a typical red-flag comment. Another is "No one else has done this, but we can be the first." A founder's grit can be an asset in tough times, but too much grit can silence important perspectives. It's healthy to explore *why* no one else has been able to do what the startup is attempting.

2. **Unquestioned beliefs.** Teams suffering from groupthink will ignore, discount, or rationalize warning signs, negative feedback, or outright bad behavior within the group. In some competitive markets for ride-sharing, for instance, startups have engaged in industrial espionage, having employees sign up as drivers to report on their competitors' onboarding protocols, incentive plans, or driver-facing app features. The startups then justify these ethical gray areas by saying, "It's a competitive market and we're just trying to survive."

3. **Self-censorship.** This happens when a group latches on to the first idea that's shared, or to the most easily accessible information. Someone might have a dissenting opinion but holds back, waiting to see if anyone else will speak up first. But others in the room may be equally afraid of sticking their necks out, since they don't realize how many of their peers secretly disagree with the apparent consensus. Silence during meetings is a strong indicator of self-censorship.

4. **Stereotyping the enemy.** Groupthink that positions a common enemy (whether a competitor, a regulator, or another team within the same company) with simplistic, stereotypical representations risks fostering careless decision-making. If you hear straw man arguments in meetings, such as "They're not smart enough to come up with this killer idea," watch out.

5. **Illusions of unanimity.** People's energy and excitement around the mission can create a sense that the team is unanimous about the direction they're taking. But in these

high-energy teams, there's often a loud faction (maybe but not necessarily a majority) that treats the silence of others as a sign of agreement.

6. **Direct pressure.** Some leaders pressure team members with dissenting opinions by making them feel disloyal or dumb, with comments like, "You don't get it now, but eventually you will." Smart leaders need to be careful not to turn into intellectual bullies, lording their presumed superiority over the team. At times, the condescending language isn't intentionally aggressive, just a sign of interpersonal insensitivity or social obtuseness.

7. **Psychological shields.** Some leaders shield the group from problematic information that will challenge their views, decisions, or cohesiveness. We often see this when a CEO hides the true financial situation of the company. If you're close to running out of money, it's natural to not want to alarm people about possible layoffs or pay cuts. But trying to prevent panic by hiding bad news is usually less effective than being honest and getting the team working toward solutions.

8. **Polarization.** Polarization happens when people take up more extreme positions than those they held before being challenged. As in a game of tug-of-war, the stronger your opponent, the deeper you have to dig in your heels to win. This instinct leads even highly intelligent and rational people to cherry-pick data or make dubious arguments to support their opinion. Yale's Dan Kahan and his colleagues even found that more intelligent people are more likely to selectively reshape their interpretation of data to the result most consistent with their point of view.[7]

Escaping the Trap of the Inner Circle

If your startup tends toward inner circles, whether due to blood ties, long-standing relationships, or alliances formed around personal influence, you will need to go the extra mile to overcome groupthink and encourage productive debate. It's worth studying a few teams who figured out how to beat the trap of the inner circle.

Founders Uğur Şahin and Özlem Türeci (both German scientists with Turkish roots) married in 2002, then launched BioNTech in 2008, with Uğur as CEO and Özlem as chief medical officer. For the next twelve years, they researched cancer immunotherapy, developing monoclonal antibody treatments and later mRNA-based therapeutics. But the latter proved to be unstable, and their research was underwhelming to the global anti-cancer community.

Then, eighteen years after BioNTech's founding, came the fateful Friday of January 24, 2020, when Uğur read one of the first scientific papers describing the SARS-CoV-2 outbreak in China. Since the evidence pointed to asymptomatic transmission, he became concerned that the outbreak would become a global pandemic "very, very quickly."[8] The following Monday, he pivoted his team toward the crash development of a COVID-19 vaccine, which they called Project Lightspeed. By early March, when Germany entered its first lockdown, BioNTech had already developed twenty vaccine candidates.[9] One would later become the BioNTech-Pfizer mRNA vaccine—the first to be approved by the FDA, the EU, and the WHO. This previously obscure startup played a central role in saving millions of lives around the world.

You might assume that as a married couple, Uğur and Özlem would be the ultimate inner circle, leading to dysfunctional team dynamics, especially during the high-pressure scramble for a vaccine. But somehow they enjoyed the advantages of being married partners, such as the ability to have round-the-clock conversations about work, without the typical drawbacks.[10] Those who know them have identified a few key reasons why.

First, their skill sets are complementary. According to Rolf Zinkernagel, a Swiss Nobel Prize laureate who once employed both Uğur and Özlem in his lab, "he is an innovative scientist, and she is an amazing clinician with a great sense for running a business."[11] This difference helped them have unique perspectives and mutual respect for each other's skills, while they each focused on different parts of the work.

Second, they shared an obsession over BioNTech's mission. In many inner circle partnerships that we've observed, the commitment of the partners can vary widely. A deeply shared purpose gives partners the internal drive to work through their challenges.

Third, they shared a scientific commitment to evidence over ego or hierarchy. After the vaccine made them famous, one interviewer asked them, "Who decides if you both have a completely different opinion on an important issue?" Uğur replied, "If I'm wrong, I admit it, even though I am technically the boss."[12]

This commitment to healthy debate extended to the whole company, not just the two founders. BioNTech staffers engaged in many vigorous debates, without turning them into personal conflicts or power plays—and without letting the inner circle win every argument. As Uğur told another interviewer, "In lab meetings, scientists don't have a hierarchy. Science is not about hierarchy. It's really about understanding. That means it is not important who says something, but what is said."[13] Startup leaders can benefit from thinking like scientists.

Invite Disagreement

To avoid the trap of the inner circle, leaders need to communicate their eagerness for dissenting points of view, as BioNTech's founders did. We also saw this in our own research on behalf of Google for Startups (a summary can be found in appendix A).[14] When we asked startup leaders whether it was important to invite disagreement, a mere 3 percent said yes. But when we asked their peers and teams, 42 percent said yes—fourteen times more. As we looked closer at the data, it became clear that most leaders did value having their ideas challenged, but they expected their teams to take the initiative to raise concerns and objections. If no one pushed back, most leaders assumed the team was in agreement.

Leaders need to *invite* disagreement, not just expect it. When the invitation to offer their opinion is not clear, teams will assume you don't want it. Leaders often don't realize that their status can unconsciously silence dissent. No matter how often leaders stress that no one will be punished for disagreeing, their own zeal, conviction, intelligence, and energy can be intimidating.

The classic American "open-door policy" isn't enough to draw out dissenters. Leaders need to create conditions that empower their teams to speak up. When it has been the cultural norm to be deferential to power, or when disagreeing has been conflated with being disagreeable, leaders need to work even harder to change the norm.

One leader we worked with in Singapore, Mei Chen, developed a creative way of drawing out her people's best ideas, even when they contradicted her own. Mei had received some bracing feedback during her Bonfire Moment. Her team said that she always responded to objections with defensiveness. We could see that she was brilliant but very measured in how she shared ideas. As we discussed these issues, Mei realized that some of the behaviors that had made her effective in her prior job as an analyst were now hurting her ability to lead. She would take a few days to develop any new proposal before bringing it to the team. She had so much of herself invested in her ideas that when they got any pushback, it felt like a personal attack on her capabilities.

Mei recognized that she needed to change before the most talented people on her team quit in frustration, and she found two tactics that worked very well. First, she committed to come to meetings *less* prepared, despite her perfectionist instincts. She found that when she put less prep work into her own ideas, it didn't sting as much when people raised questions and outright disagreed. Second, to further encourage honest exchanges, she started having more one-on-one conversations. In private with a single team member, she would lay out her idea and the reasoning behind it. Then she'd say: "I'm pretty sure I'm missing out on important things here. What's missing? What don't I see?"

Mei's approach aligns with the conclusions of researchers from Singapore Management University and UC Berkeley. Their study suggests that when leaders frame conflicting ideas as expressing disagreement, team members assume the leader isn't really open to dissenting opinions. This assumption tends to shorten conversations and reduce the exchange of important information. But when the leader frames a conflict as a debate, with fair treatment for all sides, people assume that dissenting opinions are wanted and expected. In the study, the amount of shared information increased fourfold when the leader simply changed their language.[15]

The good news is that it really is possible to escape the trap of the inner circle. Anil Sabharwal, who led the team that built Google Photos into a multibillion-user app, describes his approach this way: "Debate. Argue. Get into it. The best results come from passionate, constructive, positive contention. Encourage it. Even force it. But know it requires a foundation of trust, honesty and respect. If you don't have that, you just get pure contention, and that ain't good."[16]

Improving the Quality of Your Disagreements

Tech pioneer Bob Taylor, who built one of the dream teams of the computing revolution, was a master at fostering productive disagreement. In the late 1960s, he played a key role at the Pentagon's Defense Advanced Research Projects Agency (popularly known as DARPA), which launched the earliest version of the internet, connecting computers at the Pentagon, MIT, UC Berkeley, and a research lab in Santa Monica. Then in the 1970s, he led the team that invented the world's first personal computer at the Xerox Palo Alto Research Center (PARC). As former Google CEO Eric Schmidt observed, "Bob Taylor invented almost everything in one form or another that we use today in the office and at home."[17]

Visitors to Xerox PARC were often shocked at the intensity of arguments among Taylor's researchers. They didn't try to win debates for the satisfaction of proving each other wrong; the goal was always to illuminate each other's ideas. Criticizing a colleague's personality or character was not allowed. Taylor saw his main role at the lab as preserving this collaborative culture and protecting it from the lone-wolf tendencies of some of his smartest researchers. He frequently quoted a Japanese proverb: "None of us is as smart as all of us."

Taylor liked to explain that there are two kinds of disagreements. In "Class 1" disagreements, neither party truly understands each other's point of view, so they resort to straw man arguments—distorting an opposing opinion into an exaggerated, easily rebutted version of itself. Class 1 disagreements erode morale and degrade a team's effectiveness over time.

During "Class 2" disagreements, in contrast, people take the time to fully understand each other's point of view, to the standard that "I can explain your point of view to *your* satisfaction." By doing a deep dive into someone else's position, finding the strongest aspects of it, explaining it back to them, and only then formulating a rebuttal, you have to create a "steel man" argument instead of tearing down a straw man.

Taylor saw his role not as judging disagreements but as moving his people from Class 1 to Class 2 disagreements.[18] He was able to bring together brilliant minds representing a vast array of expertise

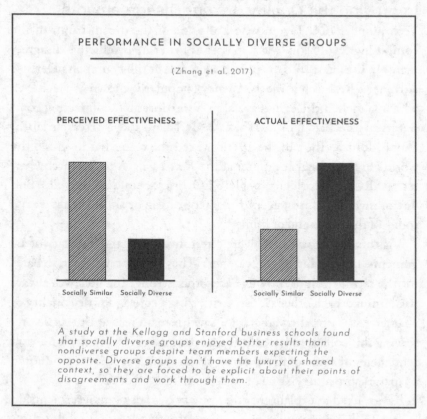

PERFORMANCE IN SOCIALLY DIVERSE GROUPS

(Zhang et al. 2017)

PERCEIVED EFFECTIVENESS   ACTUAL EFFECTIVENESS

Socially Similar   Socially Diverse   Socially Similar   Socially Diverse

A study at the Kellogg and Stanford business schools found that socially diverse groups enjoyed better results than nondiverse groups despite team members expecting the opposite. Diverse groups don't have the luxury of shared context, so they are forced to be explicit about their points of disagreements and work through them.

and backgrounds. More impressive, he created an environment that maximized the benefits of that diversity and essentially took himself out of the inner circle.

Taylor's instincts a half century ago confirm what we know today about high-quality disagreements and the power of diversity. In an experiment by the Kellogg and Stanford business schools, respondents were put in socially diverse and nondiverse teams. At the end of a team-based performance task, they were asked to predict how well they did. By comparing each team's self-perceived effectiveness with its actual performance, the researchers found that we incorrectly assume that working with similar people will lead to better results. In fact, socially diverse groups had better results, even though they found it harder to debate their opinions because they didn't share as many references and vocabulary.[19]

Stop Over-Relying on Adult Supervision

When some founders find themselves struggling with the trap of the inner circle, they try to delegate the hard work of leading teams and managing conflict. They hire more seasoned executives to join the C-suite, taking their cue from high-profile success stories such as Google's Eric Schmidt, Facebook's Sheryl Sandberg, Airbnb's Belinda Johnson, and Dell's Mort Topfer. All were hailed by the business media as "the adults in the room" who could help less experienced founders solve their management problems.

But research at the University of North Carolina challenges this strategy.[20] It turns out that adult supervision rarely serves its intended purpose, because founder CEOs tend to resist the guidance of those adults. Researchers found that when a startup is run by a professional CEO, the quality of the top management team has a major impact on results. But when a founder CEO retains the top role (and especially when dual-class equity conveys unbeatable voting power), it almost doesn't matter who gets hired for other key roles. The founder remains the core of the inner circle and continues to set the tone and call most of the shots. The adults in other key roles have little material impact on the startup's performance.

Andrew Mason, the founder of Groupon, is one example the researchers cite. Mason had plenty of adult supervision; every member of his management team was at least a decade older. But less than two years after their 2011 IPO, Mason was fired by the board because of his antics and controversial accounting techniques, all discouraged by his team.

For a more dramatic case, look at Adam Neumann, of WeWork infamy. He was surrounded by seasoned executives when WeWork was celebrated as a unicorn startup and then went public in 2019. But he was forced to resign when the stock price tanked soon after the IPO, and reporters then exposed his extravagant lifestyle, misuse of company funds, raucous office parties, drug and alcohol abuse, and other misbehaviors despite "adult supervision."

As the UNC researchers concluded, if founder CEOs want to benefit from the adults in the room, they have to actively relinquish some control and allow the executive team to make real decisions, not just execute the founder's vision. A founder CEO, like any other leader, needs to learn to invite dissent—and, just as important, rethink decisions in light of quality objections.

In part II, you'll learn more detailed techniques for building (or rebuilding) a culture that values constructive disagreement and honesty over happy talk and groupthink led by the inner circle.

tl;dr

The Problem

Synergy—the expectation that every team should be greater than the sum of its members—tends to be very hard to achieve, in large part because of the trap of the inner circle. Many teams find their cultures dominated by an inner circle that forms around the founders or other strongly opinionated, charismatic leaders within the organization. The positional or personal power of those in the inner circle often leads to groupthink and an inability to create positive disagreement and constructive conflict.

The Evidence

In the Effective Founders Project at Google for Startups, we found that leaders consistently undervalued inviting disagreement within their teams, while their teams were fourteen times more likely to value it. Academics from Yale and Harvard have studied the phenomenon of groupthink in teams, surfacing a range of symptoms you need to look out for when trying to diagnose the trap of the inner circle. Other researchers have documented the value of diverse teams, constructive debate, and getting founders to relinquish some of the perks of having a strong inner circle.

The Solution

Pay attention to behaviors that result in the silencing of diverse opinions. Instead, actively invite disagreement into your conversations. Recognize that while seeking out clashing perspectives may feel laborious and time consuming, you are much more likely to end up with better decisions. For high-quality disagreements, aim to convert Class 1 disagreements (featuring straw man arguments) to Class 2 disagreements (where all parties feel their points of view are fully understood and respectfully challenged).

Chapter 4

The Trap of the Maverick Mindset

Many entrepreneurs are inspired by romantic conceptions of how great startup life can be, and are looking for an exit path from the typical culture of a big company. They dream about getting rid of bureaucracy, hierarchies, irrelevant policies, unfair inequalities, and all the other corporate irritations. The appeal of reinventing all this is especially strong for founders who see themselves as maverick disruptors. If you believe that it's possible to reinvent a product, service, or industry, it's easy to extend that thinking to reinventing the way people are managed. Many corporate practices can seem as outdated as a VHS machine in the age of streaming.

The problem is that humans are a lot more unpredictable and nuanced than code, and there are universal challenges to working in groups that defy quick fixes. As frustrating as many traditional business processes can be, keep in mind that they've endured, at least to some extent, because they make it possible to build large, successful organizations. To be clear, there are many things about corporate practices that are broken, and we are *not* apologists for old-school management. But we've seen founders go too far in the other direction, ignoring the fundamentals of human dynamics and the hidden wisdom behind seemingly arcane customs.

It's relatively easy to be a management maverick in the early days of a startup, when a handful of cofounders and early hires share the same passion, goals, and energy. You can throw out all those corporate practices and run the startup as an egalitarian, non-bureaucratic, highly effective team. And you might congratulate yourself for being a management disruptor as well as a product or service disruptor.

But sooner than you think, your anti-corporate vibe will become hard to sustain. If you insist on clinging to maverick leadership as the startup grows, the result can be a dysfunctional and unhealthy culture, which can breed deep conflicts among the cofounders and the team.

In this chapter, we lay out evidence that explains why certain maverick ideas can lead startups into trouble. We will explore the six most common maverick management beliefs, whose drawbacks are frequently overlooked. These beliefs would be wonderful if true, yet the evidence shows otherwise. As a company grows, these beliefs can lead to misaligned expectations and strained partnerships:

1. **The myth of equal equity:** Cofounders should receive equal equity in return for equal commitment and equal contributions.
2. **The myth of shared command:** Power and decision-making should be shared equally among cofounders.
3. **The myth of scaling without hierarchy:** Layers of management should be avoided as the company grows, because they create bureaucracy and slow progress.
4. **The myth of structural harmony:** Disputes between functional roles represent a failure point that should be fixed.
5. **The myth of conflict-free growth:** A strong culture should be able to minimize or even prevent all interpersonal conflict, even as the team grows.
6. **The myth of sustained heroics:** Heroic extra effort is necessary for the long haul, not just during the startup's earliest months.

Let's see how these myths can become a damaging or even fatal trap for startups.

The Myth of Equal Equity

One of the most common mistakes first-time founders make is to split the equity equally on day one, in the overly idealistic belief that it creates the conditions for 100 percent (and therefore equal) commitment and contribution.

The largest-scale compensation survey ever done with privately owned tech startups shows that equal splits are most common when all the founders are first-time entrepreneurs with about the same level of industry experience.[1] In these situations, the decision to split equity equally is often locked in before the newly formed team is able to gauge the skills and contributions of the individual founders.[2]

These founders don't realize that equal splits (whether in halves, thirds, quarters, or more pieces) predict a lower chance of business success. According to management professor Jason Greenberg, who's taught entrepreneurship at Wharton, NYU, Cornell, and Columbia University, replacing an equal equity split with clear agreements about expected contributions and fair, variable rewards makes startup teams *four times more likely* to achieve viability.[3] Cofounders are better off setting up a dynamic, variable allocation of equity, or a balance of equity and salary that will be easier to adjust when everyone's actual contributions become clearer.

Why is splitting equity equally so common? Mainly because it feels like the best way to drive equal commitments and contributions. It's an idealistic, maverick rebuke to the tedium of calculating, corporate-style careerism. *We're focused on building something amazing and changing the world, not bickering about compensation*, founders tell themselves. And who could be opposed to fairness?

Equal splits are also a way to avoid the uncomfortable discussion of expectations. *What do I contribute? What do you contribute? What standards of quality and speed do we agree on? How much of our personal time, effort, and resources are we expected to give?* Without an explicit discussion of expectations, it becomes virtually impossible for everyone on the founding team to meet everyone else's standards. It is guaranteed that the cofounders won't make identical contributions. How can you, when you each bring to the table varying skills, networks, and resources? If you imagine a metaphorical ledger that tries to balance implicit expectations with explicit rewards, someone (if not everyone) is bound to be disappointed.

When expectations are not explicit, team members jump in with their own assumptions, as our research with startup founders showed.[4] We assessed hundreds of founders on thirty-three leadership capabilities, including their ability to get things done, deliver high-quality output, collaborate effectively, mentor and grow their team members, and keep them motivated. Founders in our dataset felt it was only important to be truly outstanding at just one capability: to be an inspiring leader to their team. But when cofounders assessed each other, expectations were much greater: they expected excellence at seventeen of the thirty-three capabilities. Put differently, the typical founder's expectations of others were seventeen times greater than the expectations they held themselves to. That's a huge gap between the minimalist expectations founders tend to set for themselves and the multifaceted expectations they set for their peers, even if unconsciously (see an overview of the study in appendix A).

You can imagine the vicious cycle caused by this gap. You master one leadership capability and think you're doing great, while your cofounders silently fault you for not meeting their vastly higher implicit expectations. As time goes on, the cofounders keep disappointing each other, and blame and bitterness increase.

Zola and Makena, cofounders of a healthtech startup, learned this the hard way while working to solve the inefficiencies of emergency ambulance services in Johannesburg. Zola, the technical cofounder, grew up in Ghana as an exceptional student who loved gaming and set her sights on a computer science degree. As she sat in her first programming course at a local university, and her first line of code—"Hello, World!"—was successfully executed, she felt a rush of excitement, realizing this was her true calling.

Zola met Makena at a university in Canada in 2019 while completing a master's degree in entrepreneurship and technology. Makena had grown up in South Africa and earned a master's degree in global health and development to pursue her dream of improving healthcare in her home country. She was working on a business plan for an app that would allow South Africans to get emergency medical help more quickly and efficiently. Makena needed a technical cofounder to balance her own skills at managing, developing partnerships, raising funds, and marketing.

Zola, who became CTO, and Makena, who became CEO, split the equity fifty-fifty and got to work. As Zola recalls, "The differences in our skill sets made us a dynamic duo. Makena understood public health. I could build the tech." Zola pulled in a few Ghana-based developers on a bootstrap budget, and they worked for months toward product-market fit. But Zola felt that Makena kept expanding the feature requests to the development team, pushing them to make the product more appealing. Zola started to dread her weekly meetings with her partner, where the unspoken message was "Do more and more, faster and faster."

Zola remembers the moment when it became clear that her cofounder didn't understand the challenges of developing software. Makena said something like, "Let's add a button in this part of the app—that should be easy, right?" Zola tried not to lose her composure as she explained how hard that addition would be, especially on top of all the other feature requests that had piled up from their last five meetings.

We often see this problem emerge between startup CEOs and CTOs. CEOs are typically in front of clients and investors, selling a bright future with their cool new tech. CTOs are hustling to deliver on those grand promises, while trying not to incur too much technical debt along the way. CEOs tend to live in the future; CTOs need to remain fully in the present to get the product shipped. Both tend to make assumptions about a cofounder's knowledge, skills, and commitment. A CEO will often assume that the CTO knows everything about how to build the product, while a CTO may assume that the CEO knows how to access all the resources the startup needs.

Makena and Zola were able to repair their partnership by being open and honest with each other about their frustrations and expectations, rather than keeping them hidden. Makena shared openly with

Zola: "I don't know enough about the technology. So if you don't tell me about the challenges in developing these features, I'll never know."

Looking back two years later, Makena notes the value of their honesty: "It's been incredibly useful for us to uncover and discuss our expectations, then one by one confirm or discard them." More than having the discussion about how to split equity, founders need to make sure expectations are clear and openly discussed. You are nearly guaranteed to violate unspoken expectations.

The Myth of Shared Command

In late 2010, two cofounders in their early thirties were knocking on doors along Sand Hill Road, the legendary heart of Silicon Valley's venture capital community. Behind every door were deep-pocketed VCs looking for the next big idea to invest in—and Garry Tan and Sachin Agarwal thought they had one. Two years prior, they had launched Posterous, an easy-to-use microblogging platform that was similar to Twitter but offered a better user experience. It now had a cult following and a user growth trend line that pointed steeply upward. Garry and Sachin were now trying to raise a few million dollars in a Series A round, so they could keep growing Posterous toward mainstream adoption and then monetization.

The cofounders were impressive when pitching investors about their early victories. But their pitch meeting with VC legends Marc Andreessen and Ben Horowitz took a bad turn when Horowitz asked, "Which of you is the CEO?" They responded with "Both," in the tradition of equal leadership teams like Google's Larry Page and Sergey Brin. But "both" was the wrong answer for Horowitz. The meeting ended abruptly, and the firm declined to invest.

Horowitz later explained his opposition to "shared command" in a blog post, which wasn't specifically about Posterous but might as well have been:

Shared command always seems really attractive to the people at the top of the organization like the CEO and the board: "We have two world-class people, this gives us the best of both worlds! We shouldn't get caught up in the conventions of years past. We're all adults. We can get along." It looks much less attractive to those who do all the work in the organization. To them it looks more like frustration, chaos, and delay.

As a company gets big, the information that informs decision-making gets massive. Depending upon the prism through which you view the business, your perspective will vary. If two people are in charge, this variance will cause conflict and delay. Every employee in a company depends on the CEO to make fast, high quality decisions. Often any decision, even the wrong decision, is better than no decision. . . . Sharing command almost guarantees that the CEO position will perform poorly in this dimension.[5]

Horowitz also noted that he and Andreessen did not share command at their firm, despite what many assumed. And he reiterated the advice that Marvin Bower, the principal architect of consulting firm McKinsey & Company, had famously given: "Power sharing never works."

Garry and Sachin were able to raise their Series A funding, but they then realized that they couldn't continue as co-CEOs. Sachin was the "idea guy" who had written the code for version 1.0, and was 100 percent focused on Posterous. Garry was the "product guy" who had shaped the super-simple user experience, but he also had many goals beyond the startup. So they agreed that Sachin should become the sole CEO. After all, titles were mostly a formality, right? What really mattered was that they were equals.

Unfortunately, this decision would lead to the unraveling of their partnership. Soon after the Series A round, user growth hit a plateau, exposing the limitations of the Posterous platform relative to its competitors, especially Instagram. The cofounders failed to see eye to eye on crucial decisions, the biggest of which was how to pivot. Being successful had previously masked the problems hidden in their partnership, because a startup that's growing by ten times per year doesn't generate much conflict. Garry recalls: "I learned the hard way that if you haven't prepared for conflict in your cofounder relationship, you'll be at each other's throats right at the moment when you most need to be working well together."[6] He and Sachin rarely spoke directly and honestly. Then, as the company struggled, they were thrown into a seemingly life-or-death battle without protective gear, training, or rules of engagement.

It all came to a head when Garry realized he had to move on. "In the weeks before I resigned, I couldn't sleep, I couldn't eat, and my heart rate felt pegged at 120. I had reached a point where I couldn't agree with my cofounder on the future of the company. I had to step away from the startup for which I shed blood, sweat, and tears. I didn't want to do it, but I had reached a point, physically and mentally, where I couldn't handle the stress anymore."[7]

Posterous was acquired by Twitter in 2012 and shut down in 2013. A decade later, Garry regrets letting his partner take the CEO title, not because of the lost prestige but because Garry thinks he could have fixed the startup's problems and steered it to success. "I didn't think being CEO mattered. I discussed it with my cofounder after our Series A, when he became the CEO. And if I'm being honest, I regret that. It took me too long to realize that I needed to be CEO. . . . If it was broken, I needed to be able to fix it."[8]

Garry now applies the lessons of this experience to help other founders avoid similar mistakes. As of this writing, he is the CEO of the startup incubator Y Combinator, invests in startups via an early-stage VC fund, and runs a popular YouTube channel with startup advice. He and Sachin eventually reconnected and put their conflict behind them. But Garry looks back with some disappointment on his overly idealistic, maverick belief that they could still be equal cofounders even when they were no longer co-CEOs.

The Myth of Scaling Without Hierarchy

It's no surprise that maverick founders hate the very idea of hierarchy. What could be a bigger drag on creativity and boldness than a chain of command, requiring permission from above before anything gets done? Hierarchy seems to spawn bureaucracy. Leaders at the top tend to lose touch with the realities of the work and the needs of users or customers. Decision-making slows down, and teams get stuck in a loop of overexplaining to deflect blame and paperwork to keep management appraised. Who would want their exciting new startup to become that kind of organization?

One of today's leading thinkers in organizational design, INSEAD's Phanish Puranam, studied the often unspoken reasons why hierarchy is unpopular.[9] Hierarchy contradicts the egalitarian ideal that everyone is equal, and implies that some people deserve more power and autonomy than others. It forces people to take narrower and more specialized roles, creating deep dissatisfaction among those who value variety in their work. It forces managers to create reporting systems to coordinate and integrate a team's efforts, but people experience these management reports as drudgery and red tape, not as an essential tool. And hierarchy forces managers to do intangible work that's hard to measure, relative to the more visible and quantifiable work of writing lines of code, closing sales, or completing projects. Tangible output is widely seen as more valuable, so people who aren't managers start to resent them as unnecessary.

People often conflate hierarchy with bureaucracy—for good reason, because they tend to expand in tandem. All other things being equal, a company with fifty people with a layer of managers will have more meetings, documentation, and approval processes than a company of five. Nevertheless, it's possible to reap the positive aspects of hierarchy to help a growing startup achieve its goals without suffering from the downsides of too much bureaucracy. Maverick managers get into trouble when they ban hierarchy in the hopes of minimizing bureaucracy but create chaos instead.

In Google's early days, Larry Page and Sergey Brin experimented with a nearly flat organization, eliminating engineering managers and having a few hundred people report directly to a single VP of engineering, Wayne Rosing. Their goal was to break down barriers to rapid idea development and to replicate the collegial environment they'd enjoyed in grad school. But this maverick management experiment lasted only a few months. Too many people were going directly to the founders with minutia, such as questions about expense reports and minor interpersonal conflicts. Projects that needed resources didn't get them, while redundancy of projects became an issue. The engineers craved feedback and guidance on their career development. Everyone soon realized that at least *some* hierarchy is useful.[10]

Other maverick startups such as Valve, Zappos, GitHub, Medium, and Buffer have also attempted flat organizations. Tony Hsieh, Zappos's founder, implemented a radical self-management fad known as "holacracy" in 2014, to widespread grumbling. Holacracy decentralizes authority and decision-making in dramatic ways: employees raise their hands to work on a task, then fluidly assemble a working group that has full authorization to make decisions. Holacracy's proponents call it self-management, but its critics have called it undermanagement. Two years after adopting the system, Hsieh gave everyone an ultimatum to either commit to holacracy or take a severance package; a third of the fifteen hundred employees quit. (Ironically, that move was a dramatic use of power and hierarchy.)[11]

Within three years, Zappos was unwinding holacracy and recreating some amount of hierarchy. They found that as the company continued to grow, teams craved rules and guidance in the face of what felt like anarchy—especially for important business functions such as budgeting and setting priorities. Self-managed teams also spent a lot of time negotiating with each other, instead of having a manager to make quick decisions so everyone could move forward. John Bunch, who coled the rollout of holacracy, recounted that the business metrics started to get shaky, and the company's reputation for exceptional customer service was at risk.[12]

The evidence is clear that a healthy hierarchy with effective managers can help reduce operational ambiguity. It can help align the team around shared goals, resolve conflicts, speed up progress, and ensure that people's development and well-being are looked after. Columbia professor Adam Galinsky showed in several studies that if you need a collaborative team to solve complex problems, you're better off with a boss in the mix instead of a group of equal friends.[13]

Similarly, Saerom Lee of Wharton studied the impact of hierarchy on a large sample of video game studios, responsible for more than 190,000 games. He found that every additional layer of management correlated to a decrease of about 1 percent in the average customer ratings of a studio's games, attributed to some reduction of cross-pollination of ideas when managers divide large groups into smaller teams. On the other hand, adding one extra layer of management correlated with a 14 percent increase in global sales, attributed to a reduction in aimless exploration and dysfunctional conflicts. That's a big gain in commercial success in return for a very small decrease in perceived product quality.[14]

Puranam put it well: "Hierarchy has its discontents, as it seems to violate basic human preferences for egalitarianism, autonomy and task variety. . . . For this reason, non-hierarchical forms of organization may sometimes enjoy a popularity that exceeds their direct economic significance."[15]

Hierarchy doesn't have to devolve into bureaucracy. Applied within reasonable limits, it can add speed and clarity within your team, driving measurably better results. Startups need not fear hierarchy.

The Myth of Structural Harmony

As your team grows and members start taking on more specialized roles (e.g., operations, finance, product development, sales), you will begin to see a different kind of conflict emerge. We call this structural conflict, in contrast to personal conflict, which has been more widely written about. When two people are frequently at odds because of clashing values, personality traits, communication styles, or behavior, that's personal. Leaders need to address the root causes of that kind of conflict, swiftly and decisively. This might require clearing up misunderstandings, fostering more empathy, removing one of the parties, or some other kind of solution.

Structural conflicts, in contrast, emerge naturally from the roles people play within an organization, including the competition for limited resources, the desire to steer the team's strategy in one direction or another, and a built-in system of checks and balances between functions. Here are some common structural tensions that emerge from the roles people play:

> CEOs and CTOs see timelines and execution risks differently. CEOs frequently get impatient for product launches, because they've already made big promises to investors, the board, or the public. CTOs feel pressure to make every product as good as possible before it launches, without accruing excessive technical debt.
> Product management often argues with engineering about speed and quality trade-offs. Product teams will typically want to launch features quickly to keep competition at bay, while engineering teams want the fewest possible bugs before exposing something to users.
> Finance almost always tries to restrict spending by marketing, human resources, and other functions, which in turn almost always feel their budgets are too low.
> Sales VPs often push to give discounts to new customers to drive new revenue, while CFOs will hesitate because discounts hurt profitability.
> Hardware teams clash with software teams over timing, because hardware faces much tougher deadlines from suppliers and manufacturing partners, and hardware doesn't have the luxury of doing rapid postlaunch updates.

These tensions are built into various roles, and often the individuals in these roles don't recognize the upside of facing checks and balances from other departments. There's genuine value in creating silos of focused activity for complex work to get done; representing the needs of varied stakeholders such as employees, investors, customers, and users; and having internal controls to ensure that the company runs effectively, with a transparent use of resources. A successful, growing startup must be able to do all of that well, and these tensions are a natural outcome of that growth.

Maverick managers get in trouble when they try to solve structural conflicts as quickly and decisively as they do personal conflicts, usually by blaming one of the individuals involved. They seldom stop to think that if, for example, the CFO and sales VP traded jobs, they would simply start arguing about discounts from the opposite perspectives.

You can think of this dilemma using the metaphor of a soccer team. Suppose you ask a team to vote on whether they'd rather win a game 5–4 or lose it 0–1. You might assume that, of course, everyone wants to win. But the goalkeeper might actually prefer losing 0–1, to make her personal goal-preventing statistics look better. And if you flip the options around to a 1–0 victory or a 4–5 defeat, the team's star striker might prefer the defeat, to improve her scoring statistics. Ideally, all players will focus on simply winning the game, but you can see how other incentives can push and pull at one another. Neither player needs to be labeled difficult, disagreeable, or uncooperative because they instinctively want to optimize their statistics. The coach's job is to keep both goalkeeper and striker focused on the team's success over their personal accomplishments, while acknowledging that when each player does their best, they make the team better.

Unlike soccer teams, startups don't always enjoy tight feedback loops and a clear definition of what it means to win. But a leader's strategy for dealing with structural conflicts is the same: acknowledge them, use the structural conflict to clarify priorities, and accept that you can never fully resolve the perpetual, built-in tensions between functional roles. Allow the product team to turn up the heat on sales, and vice versa. Allow finance to have an honest debate with marketing about their budget. But then remind everyone that, in the end, the goals of the overall organization come first.

The fatal mistake many startups make is to marginalize and disempower one function over another, in an effort to resolve the conflict.

The Myth of Conflict-Free Growth

Another hallmark of maverick management is the attempt to suppress conflicts in pursuit of an idealized vision of perfect harmony. We just saw that suppressing structural conflicts can be extremely damaging. But even the more destructive kinds of *personal* conflicts are inevitable as any startup grows. Growth always creates complexity and reduces the founders' ability to control what happens.

Consider a fairly typical tech startup journey. They start with a very small, tight-knit group that's totally in sync during the frantic early days. They achieve success and hire more people to get more done. This cycle repeats several times—hit a milestone, add more staff—but the per capita output never again seems to match what the original team was able to accomplish. Getting work done feels harder each time the head count grows, even if everyone is hardworking, collaborative, and great at what they do.

To understand what drives this common phenomenon, we can use a model that calculates the effect of the dynamics within a large system. It's a rigorous way to test our intuitions. Let's build a model!

Imagine a two-person team, Andrea and James. They're great collaborators who engage in productive debates and agree on key priorities—the textbook definition of an A team. But sooner or later, personal conflict will inevitably crop up between them. For the sake of this simple model, let's say they have a 1 percent chance of a personal conflict on any given day. Maybe one of them is having a bad day, or some disappointment leads one to blame the other. Maybe an innocent miscommunication triggers a strong reaction. By multiplying the chances of a conflict (1 percent) by the number of relationships in the team (1), we get the total expected daily conflicts for the team (0.01). Here's the formula, where p is probability:

$$p \text{ (conflict)} \times \text{(relationships in the team)} = \text{(number of expected conflicts)}$$

Now suppose Andrea and James hire Lucia, and the dynamic is still very strong. So let's say the chances of a conflict between any pair on a given day are still just 1 percent. But now there are three relationships: Andrea/James, James/Lucia, Lucia/Andrea. Using the formula, we get:

1% chance of conflict × 3 relationships = 0.03 expected conflicts

Then the team hires a fourth member, José, and suddenly there are six relationships. (If you're good at statistics, you can say that as total head count increases linearly, total relationships increase exponentially. Some call this a "quadratic explosion.")

1% chance of conflict × 6 relationships = 0.06 expected conflicts

To make it easier to do the math as this hypothetical startup grows, let's replace "(relationships in the team)" with a formula that uses n for total members of the team:

$$p \text{ (conflict)} \times [(n) * (n - 1)/2] = \text{(number of expected conflicts)}$$

Assuming that this startup still has a perfect hiring record, and the probability of any two people falling into personal conflict is still only 1 percent, watch what happens:

Team members	Number of relationships	Expected conflicts
5	10	0.10
10	45	0.45
15	105	1.05
20	190	1.90

Even with a very small chance of personal conflict between any two colleagues, our model predicts this startup will have personal conflict once they grow to just fifteen people. And they can expect nearly two conflicts per day once they grow to twenty people!

So if anyone complains that your growing organization now has a depressing number of conflicts, unlike in the good old days when the culture was focused and strong, you can point out that the conflict was inevitable. As any team grows, the probability of conflict grows exponentially. It's probably not true that your culture has gone down the drain, and it might not be a personal failure by anyone involved. It's just math!

Of course, real companies often see their p (conflict) increase as structural differences develop, as we saw earlier. Sometimes the natural tensions between two departments will boil over into personal animosity. The more people involved, the more likely that someone will misinterpret a structural disagreement as a personal attack.

Regardless of whether you have a tight, low-conflict team or a distressed, high-conflict team, the critical point is this: *team growth creates more opportunities for conflict, and even the world's best leaders*

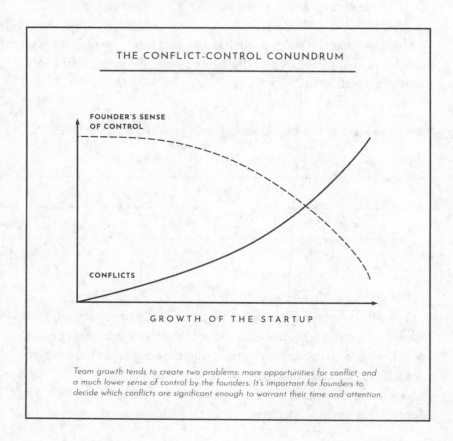

THE CONFLICT-CONTROL CONUNDRUM

FOUNDER'S SENSE OF CONTROL

CONFLICTS

GROWTH OF THE STARTUP

Team growth tends to create two problems: more opportunities for conflict, and a much lower sense of control by the founders. It's important for founders to decide which conflicts are significant enough to warrant their time and attention.

can't prevent it. Even more frustrating for leaders with maverick management beliefs: just when they feel most compelled to step in and resolve all those conflicts, their ability to control relationships within the company will be lower than ever.

Instead of lamenting what feels like growing conflict within your team, ask yourself which conflicts are most in need of your attention and invest your limited time in those. Pick your battles to intervene when conflicts become so visible that they set the wrong cultural tone for the team, or when they cross a boundary that violates your core values, or when they have an outsize impact on the performance of the startup.

It can seem like a cruel twist of fate, working so hard and so long to grow a startup, only to find it harder than ever to manage. But that's the trap of maverick management beliefs. You will have to come to terms with the fact that you can't resolve every conflict.

The Myth of Sustained Heroics

Maverick founders love heroics—the insane hours and dramatic efforts that are often required in the early months of a startup, when the demands of the new company on the cofounders and early hires are magnitudes greater than the typical workload. We tend to celebrate stories of such heroics, especially in the tech industry, because they reinforce cultural norms such as hard work, ingenuity, and resilience in the face of obstacles. Years or even decades later, some founders still brag about the time they worked twenty-hour days for a month to hit a product deadline, perhaps while sleeping on the office floor and eating nothing but cold pizza.

It feels great to the hero. The adrenaline that comes from intense focus and unlocking that elusive epic win (in gamer slang, something amazing that you might not have even thought possible) can be addictive. So are the accolades of colleagues and friends after an episode of heroics. So it's not surprising that some leaders try to sustain that intensity. But trying to perform such heroics consistently, month after month, is extremely dangerous, for at least three reasons.

First, heroics create a single-point dependency that is guaranteed to break down, sooner rather than later. When the hero repeatedly swoops in to save the day, others on the team have less incentive to build their own skills and take ownership. Because one person's heroics nudge others toward learned helplessness, the fire that the hero puts out today will contribute to a new fire that will flare up later. Psychologists have started to look at the downsides of prolonged patterns of heroics, or what they call "overfunctioning" behavior. Over time, overfunctioning is reciprocated by others with underfunctioning; colleagues become passive, resistant to taking on tasks or responsibilities and dependent on the hero to hold the quality bar high or even do their work for them. This response then frustrates the overfunctioning hero, who often ends up suffering from resentment and burnout.

Hero culture creates inefficiencies over time from underskilled teams and unreliable systems. Liz Wiseman, author of *Multipliers*, offers the example of Richard Palmer, the founder of a startup that built systems for business process reengineering in the 1990s.[16] He was the chief genius of his company and insisted on making all the key decisions, even after stepping back as CEO to become chair.

In one executive meeting, his general counsel presented a recent update of their corporate governance code. Palmer subjected her to a battery of tough questions, and after finding her answers unsatisfactory, bought a six-hundred-page book on that code, which he stayed up all night to read. The next day, he called an urgent meeting to announce that he was now an expert on governance and would take any questions about it going forward. Whatever marginal value Palmer might have added was far outweighed by the damage he caused by undermining his general counsel, terrorizing his other executives who feared the same treatment, and misallocating his time as chair. Palmer unknowingly turned himself into a single-point dependency.

The second problem with heroics is that the hero will inevitably start to look at the rest of the team as weak, lazy, and in need of rescuing. Alex Komoroske, a successful product leader at several Silicon Valley companies, told us how his impulse toward heroics shaped his perspective of his colleagues: "I thought the others weren't as strong or capable as me. I came to resent the people who weren't also constantly heroically sprinting, who it seemed to me were just being whiny or lazy. Over time I found myself pointing fingers, or pushing those people away, closing myself off to their perspective or insights."[17] Komoroske eventually realized that these opinions were distorted and unfair, and ultimately the reason why fires kept needing to be put out.

Third, an addiction to heroics can lead heroes to start thinking, "I do so much more than my peers, so I deserve more." Daniel and Kyle were the cofounders of a multibillion-dollar European fintech company, with distinctly different management styles. Daniel, the CEO for the startup's first ten years, focused on assembling strong teams and wrestling with the most important problems, while delegating day-to-day decisions. He wasn't easy to work for, often calling out people in public for their poor judgment, but he would always give them a chance to come back with better ideas or a stronger plan.

Kyle, after holding several executive roles over that first decade, eventually succeeded Daniel as CEO. He was much more prone to heroics because he had a rare gift for mastering new disciplines quickly—he was a coder, a data scientist, a strong operating executive, and a corporate finance whiz who orchestrated their IPO. Because people loved working with Kyle, and he loved getting into the weeds on all kinds of details, he soon became the chief problem-solver for relatively minor issues that Daniel would have delegated.

In a conversation with us shortly after he stepped down as CEO, following a long and successful run, Kyle reflected on the joys and pains of his journey. "I always felt Daniel didn't work as hard as I did to build this company. But he was the face of the company, and the public loved him. . . . I only realized lately that I constantly overworked myself because I was trying to prove to people that I deserved to be recognized just as much. Things would have probably been better for me if I had realized that sooner."

Creating a hero culture is not the way to build an enduring business. Instead, think of heroics as a "Break Glass in Case of Emergency" option, and engage in it selectively. This is *not* meant to diminish the value of deep commitment to the mission or the hard work needed to make progress. Just be mindful that disruptively solving problems that others on your team were hired to address will have unintended consequences and can undermine all your hard work. So invest your time and energy in building a stronger team and effective systems, to help your people solve most of their own challenges without needing you to save the day.

Not all maverick ideas about running an organization are doomed to result in negative unintended consequences. We are always excited to see companies find success via unconventional management methods. (Yes, many exist, as you will see in other chapters.)

But if you're tempted to try the specific maverick practices described above, the data is clear: proceed with caution. Perhaps you can redirect your instincts toward the rigorous use of evidence, as you experiment with new ways of working with old human technology.

tl;dr

The Problem

Entrepreneurs choose to build a startup to disrupt norms and industries, but they risk falling into the trap of the maverick mindset when they also challenge certain management practices. They may force egalitarianism with equal equity splits while leaving expectations unclear; create fuzzy power-sharing arrangements; resist introducing hierarchy to avoid bureaucracy; over-rely on heroics; or strive to eliminate all conflicts, including the healthy or inevitable ones.

The Evidence

A number of rigorous studies have shown the serious but often hard-to-see downsides of some of these maverick practices. For instance, while many founders dive into equal equity splits, clear agreements about expected contributions and fair, variable rewards make startup teams four times more likely to achieve viability. In another study, adding an extra layer of management correlated with a 14 percent increase in commercial success, with hardly any downside in product quality. And a simple agent-based model demonstrates that as teams grow, personal conflict becomes inevitable.

The Solution

Assess to what extent you've fallen into these maverick management practices, and then, if necessary, replace them with proven systems and structures more likely to lead to an enduring company. If some of those practices are unappealing simply because they remind you of big companies, that doesn't necessarily mean that they aren't worth adopting. Keep an open mind and follow what works—chase the evidence relentlessly, whether that leads you to a bold management innovation or a tried-and-true best practice.

Chapter 5

The Trap of Confidence

In 2018, Gojek CEO Kevin Aluwi and his leadership team spent a few days with us at Google's Singapore campus, to learn Google's approach to people and culture. Gojek is an Indonesia-based super-app that started as a ride-hailing service but soon expanded into payments, deliveries, on-demand massages, salon services, and much more. Gojek was at that point one of the most successful startups in Southeast Asia, with a rare $10 billion–plus valuation. So we assumed they had gotten a lot of things right and wouldn't have much to learn from us. Up to that point we had been supporting only earlier-stage startup teams, who frequently came to us with little idea of how to lead people or build a healthy culture.

As we explained how Google's culture had scaled in Asia (including all the mistakes along the way), Kevin's team listened intently, took notes, and asked thoughtful questions. At the end of the sessions, we thanked them for their eagerness to learn despite all the great success they had already achieved.

Kevin responded, as if to brush off the compliment, "We're not a seed-stage startup—we know we need help!"

Kevin's unassuming remark has stuck with us ever since, and made us rethink what we believed about confidence in startup founders, especially the ones who are very successful. We had known plenty of brash, overconfident founders. We had also known plenty of anxious, self-doubting founders who took setbacks very hard. But this was something different: a hybrid of the two that we'd later call *confident humility*.

Most if not all founders are plagued by either overconfidence or underconfidence. Either can destroy their startup's journey, yet both tend to serve some use. Navigating between these two extremes can be incredibly hard, as the many challenges of startup life keep nudging them toward one side or the other. The most capable startup leaders are able to travel through a treacherous, narrow strait with the six-headed monster of overconfidence on one side and the deadly maelstrom of underconfidence on the other side. These are the Scylla and Charybdis of the startup journey.

Our research with hundreds of startups for the Effective Founders Project[1] has shown us how much damage can be caused by both overconfidence and underconfidence. Some founders mostly face the danger of just one of these monsters, while others swing back and forth, becoming overconfident when things are going well but then underconfident when problems arise.

On one side—especially in the early stages of a startup's journey—*overinflated confidence* creates the excitement and energy to take bold risks. That kind of energy is virtually a prerequisite to getting started. But while it's helpful to founders early on, overconfidence is almost exclusively a liability later in the journey, as it can lead to a host of problems, including underpreparation or overestimating financial forecasts.

On the other side—especially when startups inevitably encounter obstacles and setbacks—many founders experience *perfectionist self-doubt*. They become overwhelmed with self-criticism and fear about their ability to succeed, often after comparing themselves to other founders who seem to set an impossibly high bar of excellence. This can tempt them to give up.

And some, like Kevin Aluwi, eventually achieve an equilibrium of *confident humility*, with a more realistic grasp of their strengths and weaknesses, and an appropriate confidence in their ability to handle challenges, but not the kind of confidence they had at the beginning of the journey. The data shows that the strongest startup leaders display this kind of humility. We don't mean being meek, soft-spoken, or docile. We're talking about leaders who accept that they will always have more to learn, no matter how much they've already achieved, and don't feel threatened by colleagues or advisors whose knowledge and skill far exceed their own. They embody the ancient wisdom of Aristotle: "The more you know, the more you know you don't know."

A lot has been written about confidence and self-doubt, especially the supposed virtue of visionary, charismatic confidence. But we think there are deeper lessons to be explored. In this chapter, we offer evidence about the folly of overconfidence, the prevalence and danger of self-doubt among even the most successful founders, and the case for confident humility as a secret weapon. Examples that illustrate these states include some of the rawest, most revealing stories in the book.

The Psychology of Confidence

Like many in the startup world, we used to assume that competence and confidence were strongly correlated, and therefore high confidence could be taken as an indicator of exceptional competence. When we started digging into the data, we did uncover a correlation, but in almost the inverse direction. In reality, founders who scored highest on effectiveness tended to *underrate* their skills and abilities —as long as they didn't underrate them so dramatically as to fall into the paralysis of perfectionist self-doubt.

There is a wealth of psychological literature about overconfidence and hubris, as well as about self-doubt and insecurity. And what we found in our data was not unique to startup founders. Two Cornell psychologists, David Dunning and Justin Kruger, found in 1999 that people who act highly confident are generally perceived as highly competent, at least at first. But their actual competence is often much lower than they estimate it to be, thanks to what Dunning and Kruger called "illusory superiority." On the other end of the competence

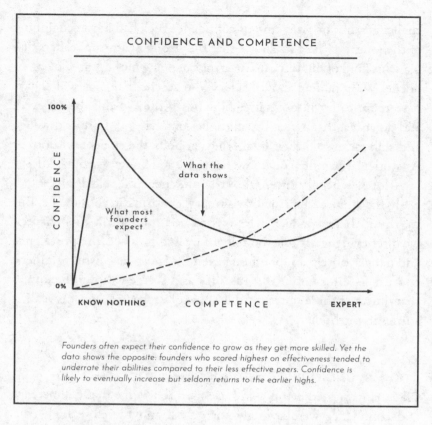

CONFIDENCE AND COMPETENCE

Founders often expect their confidence to grow as they get more skilled. Yet the data shows the opposite: founders who scored highest on effectiveness tended to underrate their abilities compared to their less effective peers. Confidence is likely to eventually increase but seldom returns to the earlier highs.

scale, the psychologists found that those who displayed the highest levels of skill tended to underestimate their own abilities.[2] This paradox became known as the Dunning-Kruger effect.[3]

Dunning and Kruger theorized about the origins of overconfidence when someone takes on a new skill or role, in business, sports, academia, the performing arts, and so on. Early on, a novice is unable to avoid mistakes and, equally important, is also unpracticed in recognizing mistakes. For instance, the researchers asked respondents to first take a difficult trivia quiz with questions like, "What is the diameter of the moon?" At the end of ten such questions, they asked how well the respondents thought they had done. These studies invariably found that people overestimate their performance. When something similar happens in real-life situations and the individual is never given the chance to see how poorly they actually performed, their confidence stays high.

That's why incompetence tends to be invisible to those who suffer from it. And as writer Robert Hughes put it, "Perfect confidence is granted to the less talented as a consolation prize."[4]

Those who diligently practice a new skill eventually learn just how far they are from high-performers in that field, which can lead to a new phase of discouragement and self-doubt. As their overconfidence gets punctured, quitting feels like a reasonable response, on the (usually false) assumption that the task is too difficult and continued failure is inevitable. But if they stick with it past that trough of self-doubt, most people find that their self-confidence increases as their skills improve, though probably never all the way back to the overconfidence they felt as novices.

The most dangerous examples of the Dunning-Kruger effect are people who never go beyond their initial stage of ignorant overconfidence, because they never put in the work necessary to improve their skills. They remain stuck in the upper left corner of the graph: less effective yet more confident than their peers. When those people are running a startup, they can repeatedly create havoc.

The Peak of Overinflated Confidence

If founders knew the real cost and difficulties of building a startup, many would never even begin.

As a twenty-three-year-old Swedish engineer in 2004, Daniel Ek was invited to join a startup that claimed to have a revolutionary new idea. "They said, 'People can sit in front of their computers and make phone calls,'" Ek recalls. To which he smugly replied, "Nah, never going to work."[5] That startup turned out to be Skype, the pioneer in internet telephony, which was bought by Microsoft in 2011 for $8.5 billion.

In his youthful overconfidence, Ek felt he could build something equally revolutionary. He realized that about half a billion people were consuming music through sharing (i.e., pirating) services like Napster, Kazaa, and the Pirate Bay. The only legal way to consume digital music in 2006 was via iTunes, which sold a limited set of songs under strict protections that made it hard to play them anywhere, or at high-level audio quality. Ek wondered how to combine the better quality and limitless variety of piracy sites with the legality of iTunes, so musicians could be compensated and no one would file lawsuits to shut the sites down.[6] And so Ek and Martin Lorentzon founded Spotify.

Their overconfidence was an essential asset in the early days, when getting Spotify launched was much harder than they'd imagined. Ek recalls that he initially thought he wouldn't have to make deals with giant record companies like Universal Music Group, Sony Music, and Warner Music Group. He believed that the new platform's quality would convince artists to upload their music directly to Spotify. He didn't even realize that the vast majority of musicians sign over their rights to the major labels, which wouldn't allow Spotify to play a note without licensing agreements. So Ek's team set out to negotiate those deals. "That can't be too hard; surely they'll be up for that," he recalls thinking.

What followed was two and a half years of grueling negotiations, followed by a tense relationship with the major labels that remains fragile to this day. The labels still feel threatened that Spotify might try to compete with them by offering artists better terms if they go independent. Ek would later admit that if he'd known in advance how hard the business side of Spotify would be, he wouldn't have started the company.[7] Instead, he eagerly but ignorantly charged forward, exemplifying what computer scientist Larry Wall once called "the three great virtues of a programmer: laziness, impatience and hubris."[8] (Later in the chapter, we'll see how Ek overcame his hubris.)

The Three Forms of Overconfidence

Harvard economist Albert Hirschman called this kind of foolish overconfidence *the principle of the hiding hand*. After years studying companies that committed major effort and capital to unpromising projects, Hirschman suggested that some hidden force must be nudging innovators to underestimate challenges. By the time they grasped the true magnitude of the obstacles they faced, it was often too late to abandon a project. Hirschman concluded: "The only way in which we can bring our creative resources fully into play is by mis-judging the nature of the task, by presenting it to ourselves as more routine, simple, undemanding of genuine creativity than it will turn out to be."[9]

He was talking about overprecision, one of three types of over-confidence, according to UC Berkeley professor of organizational behavior Don Moore.[10] *Overprecision* is an excessive certainty about your ability to plan and forecast something that can really only be guessed or estimated. The second type is *overestimation*, the inaccu-rate belief that you are better than you are. And the third type, *over-placement*, is an exaggerated belief that you are better than others.

Startup founders often show signs of all three kinds of overcon-fidence. They become *overprecise* about the difficulties and risks ahead, *overestimate* their ability to take on those risks, and *overplace* their own competence relative to peers, including other startups.

All three forms of overconfidence can sabotage your efforts. For instance, overconfident athletes tend to inadequately prepare for a competition, resulting in a poorer performance than they could have achieved with more prep time. In one experiment where researchers manipulated the subjects' levels of self-confidence, they saw a nearly 20 percent increase in effort among those with less confidence.[11]

Overconfidence in CEOs has been studied by economists Ul-rike Malmendier of Stanford and Geoffrey Tate of the University of Pennsylvania. Using public data on the investment decisions of major corporate CEOs, the researchers classified CEOs as overcon-fident if they took on high levels of company-specific risk, overes-timated the returns of their acquisition projects, and overpaid for acquisitions in a competitive bidding situation. They found a statis-tically significant correlation: cumulative stock market returns after an overpaid acquisition by an overconfident CEO were lower than those of their peers.[12]

One Antidote: Hard Feedback from a Respected Partner

While the Bonfire Moment will help you get your overconfidence under control, another solution is to surround yourself with levelheaded advisors who will give you hard feedback. One Silicon Valley advisor who knew how to tame overconfidence was Bill Campbell, nicknamed the "Trillion Dollar Coach." He spent many years working with tech luminaries Larry Page, Sergey Brin, Jeff Bezos, Jack Dorsey, Eric Schmidt, Sundar Pichai, and Sheryl Sandberg, to name just a few.[13]

One of Bill's mentees in the 2000s was Jonathan Rosenberg, the Google product executive who first oversaw Search, Ads, Gmail, Android, Apps, and Chrome. His great strength was technical and strategic brilliance; and his approach to keeping the quality bar high was to show no patience for incompetence. When he was included as number nine in a clickbaity article, "The 10 Most Terrible Tyrants of Tech," Jonathan took it as a badge of honor. He thought he was in good company next to Apple CEO Steve Jobs, Microsoft CEO Steve Ballmer, and Salesforce CEO Marc Benioff. The article listed him as "Google SVP Jonathan Rosenberg: He'll yell at Larry and Sergey, too." As he later recalled, "That was pretty cool . . . I sent the article to my staff. Wouldn't you?"[14]

A week later, Jonathan was waiting in Bill's office for their usual one-on-one. Bill was uncharacteristically late, but on the table in front of Jonathan was a printout of the article. When Bill finally arrived, fifteen minutes late, he picked up the article, threw it down, and turned to Jonathan: "What the f— is this?"

"Well, that's me in an article with Steve Jobs and Marc Benioff and Steve Ballmer," Jonathan replied. "I'm the ninth most terrible tyrant of tech."

Bill shot back, "I work with Steve Jobs. I know Steve Jobs. You're no Steve Jobs. You don't get to behave this way."[15] And he walked out, refusing to do their usual coaching session. Bill then canceled all their sessions for the next month.

When they finally met again, Jonathan began by "vomiting out" an apology. Bill responded by giving him a big hug, saying, "I don't need to hear what you learned. I delivered a lesson, and I know it got through. What's on your list today?"

When we asked Jonathan about that experience fourteen years later, he noted that people who didn't carry the same level of confidence he had at that time struggled with his critical feedback. He learned that his style could cause some talented colleagues to be "much more reticent to participate, less likely to share their views." And he appreciated the disincentives now in place that make his former management style far less common.[16]

Jonathan was especially grateful to have had someone as respected as Bill Campbell set him on a better path—gratitude that he later expressed by cowriting a *New York Times* bestseller about Bill, *Trillion Dollar Coach*.

The Crash of Perfectionist Self-Doubt

By the time we meet many founders, their initial overconfidence has been squashed by the brutal challenges they've been facing. Some slide all the way from overestimating their talents to underestimating them, perhaps thinking in despair: "People will soon find out that I'm not as good as they think I am. I don't know how to do this. I'm likely to fail!"

These impostor thoughts stem from what psychologists call *pluralistic ignorance*, a phenomenon where individuals hold beliefs different from those they express publicly, because they mistakenly assume that their views are different from those of the majority of the group.[17] In other words, a person's outward behavior will sometimes contrast with their private thoughts, out of their desire not to stick out as an outlier. When this kind of masquerade happens across an entire community of founders, it makes any newcomer who's figuring things out feel even more alone in their self-doubt. But in reality, such feelings are extremely common, just not easily visible in others.

There are gender differences in this kind of self-doubt, but not as many as most people assume. When the impostor phenomenon was first studied in the 1970s, by clinical psychologist Pauline Clance, she first observed it among her female patients and thought it was much more common in women.[18] We now know that it's nearly as common among men but harder to detect because men are far less likely to talk about it. This is one area where cultural expectations of what it means to be a man have really hurt men.[19]

Studies suggest that women generally suffer more from the life-limiting consequences of impostor thoughts; self-doubt tends to lower their performance on a given task and chip away at their self-image, resulting in a lower sense of well-being. Men, on the other hand, will generally tend to struggle to sit with negative emotions and would rather take strong actions to address them. It's important to remember that not all men or women will conform to these general tendencies.

High-achieving individuals are just as prone to self-doubt, and were in fact the very first subjects when the impostor phenomenon was spotted.[20] A survey of Google employees, for instance, found that nearly half regularly experience impostor thoughts, despite getting through a hiring process that screens out 99 percent of all job applicants.[21] (We're both included in that half, and it took a while until we were willing to admit it.)

Australian entrepreneur Mike Cannon-Brookes, nicknamed the "accidental billionaire," told a 2017 audience, "Most days I still feel like I often don't know what I'm doing. I felt that way for fifteen years." He added that it wasn't just a fear of failure but "more a sensation of getting away with something, a fear of being discovered, that at any time someone is going to figure this out." Despite the success of his collaboration software startup Atlassian (known for Jira, Confluence, and Trello), his impostor thoughts were strong and persistent. "People think that successful people don't feel like frauds. Knowing a lot of entrepreneurs, the opposite is more likely to be true."[22]

A recent study by management scientist Sana Zafar suggests that almost 80 percent of founders experience impostor syndrome at least sometimes, with potentially damaging consequences: "As impostor phenomenon in entrepreneurs increases, the likelihood that ventures led by these entrepreneurs receive no funding or only receive personal funding also increases."[23] It's also common to see these founders resort to self-handicapping actions: pitching only less prominent VCs, delaying actions that feel intimidating, or scaling back their ambitious goals.

The Cycle of Perfectionist Self-Doubt

After years of listening to founders share their deepest insecurities, we've identified a consistent, cyclical pattern among those plagued by unjustified self-doubt. We created a framework to make it easier for people to recognize this pattern and have language to describe it and break out of it. As with any framework, ours is somewhat simplified. But we find it helpful to show founders that they are far from alone in their struggles.

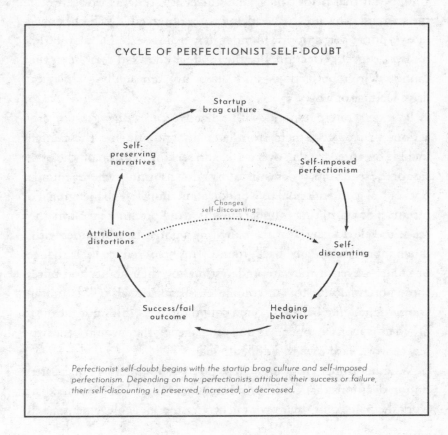

CYCLE OF PERFECTIONIST SELF-DOUBT

Perfectionist self-doubt begins with the startup brag culture and self-imposed perfectionism. Depending on how perfectionists attribute their success or failure, their self-discounting is preserved, increased, or decreased.

This cycle starts with the brag culture of the startup world, where entrepreneurs face pressure not merely to create a profitable new company—which is hard enough!—but also to disrupt an entire market, attract major investors, and achieve an eye-popping valuation. The pressure to play up their ambitions and early milestones is exacerbated by the tech media, which is always looking for the next larger-than-life founder to spotlight. Alongside those external pressures, startup founders often hold themselves to extreme standards of perfection, shaped by their families or early school environments.

When impossibly high standards collide with the harsh reality of startups, founders often begin to undervalue their own capabilities. This in turn triggers increased feelings of short-term worry or persistent anxiety. As Jared Fenton, founder of the Reflect Organization, a nonprofit that helps college and university students work through the extreme pressures of academic life, observed: "Whether accurate or not, a perfectionist founder may believe external players, like funders, expect perfection. But the founder knows in their heart they cannot deliver perfection—and surely not repeatedly—which can drive feelings of worry."[24]

Founders often respond with what we call *hedging behavior*—actions that protect them from later disappointment. These might include overpreparation, overwork, and seeking help, or, on the other side of the spectrum, procrastination or downshifting, where a founder opts out of a difficult goal to work on something less challenging. For instance, downshifting founders might avoid pitching investors they see as too elite or shy away from inviting a potential cofounder with a much more credentialed background. This helps reduce their chances of failure—even if they are underestimating their ability to impress those potential investors or cofounders. Fatalistic self-talk is another common hedging behavior, often sounding like, "If it's not meant to be, then it won't happen." It dulls the agency they would otherwise feel to work hard toward a difficult goal.

Whether things are going well or poorly, a founder will make attribution decisions that credit or blame one or more basic factors: hard work, help, luck, or their own talent. In times of achievement, a self-doubter who overprepared will tend to credit hard work; a help-seeker will credit those who helped; a self-handicapper will credit dumb luck; and all three will discount their own capability. Conversely, in moments of failure, any kind of self-doubter will tend to blame their own inadequate capability, rather than the lack of effort they put in, a lack of support, or bad luck.

All of these attributions distort reality to some extent. In almost all situations, a combination of varying degrees of luck, talent, work, and help contributes to your success or failure. But underconfident founders would rather tell themselves and others a more comforting narrative after a failure, one that allows them to save face.

These self-preserving narratives tend to come in three varieties.

The founder might project positivity, conveying false optimism to look quickly ahead to new challenges and reassure the team and investors that all is well. If others respond with equal positivity and validation, that's emotional fuel to keep going.

The second narrative is to project strength; the founder focuses on their many other successes so far, brushing off any sign of weakness. This may lead to a tendency toward arrogance or abrasive criticism of the team or outsiders, to deflect any self-blame.

Finally, there's a narrative of detachment; the founder fades into the background and goes into incognito mode. *Keep calm and carry on.* The resulting silence can unnerve the team or investors, who want to analyze whatever went wrong instead of sweeping it under the rug.

When Underconfidence Becomes Almost Fatal

For a haunting example of the consequences of extreme self-doubt, consider a woman we'll call Valerie, a UK founder we interviewed who struggled with burnout and severe depression.

Fresh out of college in 2010 and working late nights at a telecom company, Valerie yearned to connect with others without the oversexualized vibe of the popular dating sites of that era, like Match.com. So on a whim, she decided to code her own social-connection service, which caught on faster than she could have dreamed. She had to spend £500 of her meager savings to upgrade her servers and get help from a UX designer.

Her project caught the attention of an accelerator program that invested in very early-stage startups. "It was a time when everyone wanted a female founder, and there just weren't many of us," Valerie recalls. She felt like an impostor because it was so easy for her to raise capital, after hearing how hard fundraising was for other founders.

She joined a community of founders who tended to be highly assertive, charismatic men, some of them veterans of Silicon Valley. Valerie, in contrast, was a quiet twenty-two-year-old from a humble town in the UK. "I couldn't speak the same lingo, and I was not as confident." She was pushed by the accelerator to name herself CEO, which she reluctantly agreed to. But her only real interest was in building the product, not the leadership responsibilities of a CEO.

In retrospect, Valerie realizes that she was hedging and self-handicapping her ambitions. By trying to avoid the CEO title, she was trying to escape the pressure of other people's expectations. She felt like other founders she met were silently judging her, not realizing that many of their own startups would flop, despite all their bluster.

As Valerie told us with a deep sense of disappointment, "People would offer help and tell me they were there for me. But when I reached out to share how things were getting difficult, their response was basically, *You did that wrong*. Mentors were more mansplaining than helping. There was no empathy." One mentor's response to an earnest question was a condescending, "Just read *Zero to One* by Peter Thiel."

Valerie started to feel like she was doomed to fail in a man's world, where the glass ceiling for women founders was just too thick. Her struggles reached a crisis point when, after she'd burned through the accelerator's seed capital, her investors pushed her to cut costs and borrow additional capital on her own. She had to lay off two of her six team members, one of whom was fighting cancer. It crushed her spirit. She then turned to friends and family to borrow money, which she found shameful despite assurances from other founders that this was just part of the gig. She didn't come from family wealth and lacked the financial cushion that her peers seemed to enjoy.

Soon, Valerie couldn't even pay her rent and had to beg her land-lord not to evict her. She felt like she was letting everyone down and was doomed to fail. "It reached a point where every night, I'd be awake late staring out the window, thinking that I should just jump out and end it all."

This kind of anxiety and depression is far from rare. A 2015 study by researchers from UC San Francisco, UC Berkeley, and Stanford suggests that entrepreneurs are 30 percent more likely to experience depression than the general population.[25] (If you're in this group, we urge you to seek help from a professional therapist.)

Fortunately, Valerie survived the darkest part of her journey by con-fiding in her sister, who spent lots of time with her and convinced her to see a therapist, despite her fear of the stigma of therapy. Soon, she began to feel less compelled to display false confidence, and both her team and her customers appreciated it. For instance, she would an-swer some customer service tickets herself, responding to complaints with something like, "Sorry, we're a startup; we're still learning a lot."

With her company on the verge of bankruptcy, Valerie accepted an offer to sell 51 percent of the equity to a San Francisco investor and serial entrepreneur. It was for only about a half million dollars—not enough to make headlines in the tech media—but enough to pay off her debts, including some delayed salary payments. The company was saved, and the new majority owner became a true mentor and coach, at least at the beginning.

Until this point, Valerie had been stuck in the cycle of self-doubt, unable to trust her own instincts or stand up for her convictions. Her self-preserving narrative was positivity: she was too agreeable and overly accommodating to the wishes of her investors. But now she was building confidence and learning to stand up for herself. Those skills became essential when her new majority owner got enmeshed in alle-gations of serious wrongdoing, including drug dealing and immigra-tion fraud to bring his girlfriends into the country.

When it was finally time to move on, Valerie was proud of having built a stable company with 30 million users and then leaving on her own terms. Today, she supports other women founders, focusing both on product development and building their self-confidence. "People should realize that building a startup is a hard job. And many times, the problem isn't the product; it's making sure founders learn to trust their instincts."

Along with having the support of a hard-honesty relationship with friends or a coach, lifting others up is one of the most effective ways to build your own confidence and protect yourself from self-doubt. It's a good reminder of how far you've come on your journey.

The Equilibrium of Confident Humility

Now that we've seen the potential dangers of both overconfidence and self-doubt, we can turn to the narrow path of safety between those two monsters: confident humility.

In controlled doses, self-doubt can be beneficial. Wharton researcher Basima Tewfik found that investment professionals, medical students, and military academy cadets who sometimes felt like impostors were not necessarily any worse at their jobs—and sometimes performed better—than their peers. Subjects who second-guessed themselves took extra time to seek input from others, which led to better decisions and more collaborative behavior. For instance, the medical students in this study who experienced impostor thoughts were more likely to check in with their patients and ask if there was anything else they could help with. By displaying more compassion and care, they earned rave reviews from their patients.[26]

Our own research and several academic studies have concluded that the most effective leaders seem to combine confidence in their mission and their ability to lead a team with humility about their own weaknesses and their need to rely on their colleagues. Although confidence and humility might seem like an unlikely combination, leaders who exhibit both tend to foster greater creativity, productivity, and commitment in their teams.

We can see this even in one of the most famously self-confident and demanding CEOs of all time, the previously mentioned "tyrant"

Steve Jobs. Researchers have suggested that during his second stint as CEO of Apple, which began a dozen years after he was humiliatingly fired from his own startup, Jobs was notably less narcissistic. Those who worked with him closely confirm that he had become more open to other people's ideas, more willing to acknowledge his own mistakes, and more grateful for his immensely talented colleagues, such as Tim Cook, Jony Ive, and Tony Fadell. As a result, his people felt a much greater sense of loyalty to Jobs than they had during his first era as CEO.[27] By balancing his narcissistic tendencies with a new measure of humility, he was able to lead Apple to unprecedented heights of success.

Organizational psychologists in China describe similar behavior in Jack Ma, the mega-successful founder of Alibaba. He was able to temper his innate narcissism with credit sharing and self-deprecating moments. He spoke confidently about Alibaba's bold plans but also about the risks of ego inflation. One observer described him as "crazy yet charmingly humble."[28]

Studies that compared humble leaders with overconfident, narcissistic leaders have shown a clear performance advantage for the humble leaders. Their teams were more collaborative, more open to sharing information, better at making joint decisions, and more committed to collective success above individual success. But leaders who combined humility with high confidence did even better than the humble but low-confidence leaders—and nearly 30 percent better than the overconfident leaders.[29]

Of course, striking the right balance is easier said than done—just as it was hard for sailors in Greek mythology to sail between Scylla and Charybdis. Marc Porat, a serial entrepreneur turned investor, described this challenge:

> *There's a paradox that I've never figured out how to close. On the one hand, people want authenticity, truth telling, a sense of commonness, that you're part of them and that there's empathy, and even vulnerability. But, at the same time, they want to hear a story*

that's optimistic and positive and forceful and resolute and directionally correct, and that, "We're going to win." So, as the CEO, I felt that duality had to coexist at the same, at the same exact moment. And that was a tough state for me to keep in equilibrium.[30]

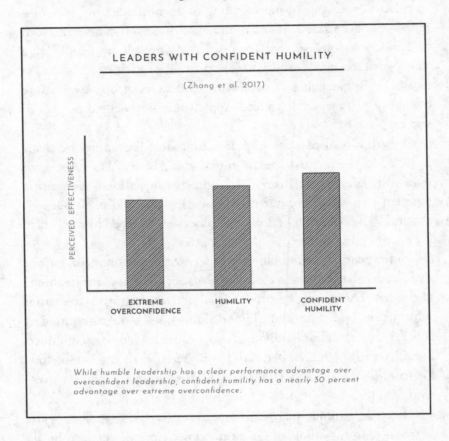

LEADERS WITH CONFIDENT HUMILITY

(Zhang et al. 2017)

While humble leadership has a clear performance advantage over overconfident leadership, confident humility has a nearly 30 percent advantage over extreme overconfidence.

What Confident Humility Looks Like

Bradley Owens, an organizational psychologist at Brigham Young University, describes three distinct advantages of humility.[31]

First, it helps leaders see their strengths and limitations accurately, which distinguishes true humility from false modesty. If you overestimate your skills, you'll tend to underinvest time and effort in important tasks, resulting in blown deadlines and underperformance.

Second, humility creates openness to feedback, enabling leaders to learn from their mistakes and get better over time. Humble leaders embrace feedback from wherever it may come, whether they choose to act on it or not.

Third, humility helps leaders appreciate the strengths of others, without feeling threatened by their brilliance or skills. This helps leaders learn more while encouraging their people to contribute as much as possible to the team's success.

A great example of a founder who eventually found the sweet spot of confident humility is Spotify's Daniel Ek, whom we met earlier, when he was single-handedly taking on the giants of the music industry. This formerly overconfident CEO now consults his team rather than trying to make every major decision unilaterally. Ek still has strong, confident opinions about what might or might not work, but he has created a culture where his people know he will listen to their ideas and feedback. Crucially, they also know that it's safe to challenge his positions.

Ek has described a great example of the business advantage that stems from confident humility. In 2015, Spotify launched its Discovery Weekly personalized playlist, using an algorithm to understand each user's preferences and generate a unique playlist of new music they might enjoy. By 2021, users were spending 2.3 billion hours streaming these customized playlists. Ek called Discovery Weekly one of Spotify's "most loved product features."[32]

But here's the interesting part: prior to its launch, Ek wanted to stop development of the feature. As he told an interviewer, "I never really saw the beauty of it. I questioned them two, three times: Are you sure you really want to do this? Why are we spending all this time and energy?" Yet Ek still allowed his team to launch Discovery Weekly, and he was happy to be proven wrong. He added, "There are lots of things in this company that I didn't think were good ideas that turned into some of the best things."

He also tells a story about the moment when his head of product gave him some very direct and unpleasant feedback: "I'll just be very honest: no one enjoys the meetings that you're having, because you're not actually adding anything to the meeting." Ek's immediate reaction was extreme defensiveness; he was tempted to fire his VP. But instead, he decided to sleep on it. Then he tried sitting out the next few product meetings, to see how they went without his presence in the room. "It turns out that they did incredibly well without me."[33]

A former Spotify manager shared with us their up-close assessment of Ek: "If you look at the group of leaders he's assembled over the last ten-plus years, you'll see he has retained a mix of very tenured people who've grown with the company who have a very high level of candor with him, as well as people from the outside who have brought him expertise he's lacked himself, who are also encouraged to be very open with him."

Unlike his younger self, Ek now shows a deep appreciation for his team's talents and expertise. "My firm view is that the best talent in the world is at least ten times better, if not fifty times better, than the average person. I'm incredibly fortunate to come in and learn from some of the smartest people in the world."[34]

Whether you are starting from a default setting of brash overconfidence, like Ek, or facing the pain of perfectionist self-doubt, like Valerie, you too can learn to sail safely past both monsters. The tools of the Bonfire Moment, which we'll now explore in part II, will help you reach the calmer waters of confident humility.

tl;dr

The Problem

Founders must find a balance between overconfidence and underconfidence. While overconfidence is often necessary to get started, it can later result in underpreparation and prediction errors. Underconfidence, often triggered by startup brag culture and self-inflicted perfectionism, can lead founders to quit or engage in self-discounting and hedging behaviors that chip away at their potential success. Effective startup leaders must travel a narrow strait between these two extremes.

The Evidence

A global dataset on founders shows that confidence is inflated among the least capable, while the most capable tend toward humility. Studies reveal that overconfident CEOs take more risks, overpay for investments due to overestimated returns, and end up with lower stock market returns. Underconfidence is just as common among high achievers, with 80 percent of founders experiencing it at least sometimes. This tempts them to self-handicap: pitching less prominent investors, delaying actions that feel intimidating, or limiting their ambitions. Leaders who exhibit humble confidence are 30 percent more effective than overconfident ones.

The Solution

Pursuing confident humility means learning how to feel confident in your mission and your team's ability to achieve it, while embracing hard feedback about your strengths and weaknesses. With practice, as we saw from the examples of Steve Jobs and Daniel Ek, leaders can learn how to celebrate the strengths of others without feeling threatened by their brilliance. A great coach or mentor can help you hone these skills, as can the tools of the Bonfire Moment.

Part 2 /

...AND
WHAT TO DO
ABOUT IT

Chapter 6

The Bonfire Moment

Workshop Overview

If you've decided to get your team to do a Bonfire Moment, congratulations on taking this important step!

This chapter will give you an overview of what your team's day will look like, whether you plan to be a participant or serve as facilitator. It will also explain some of the key ideas that informed our design of the Bonfire Moment, based on academic research in psychology, organizational behavior, and related fields, plus our own experiences with many startup teams around the world. These concepts will help your team get into the right mindset for a productive day.

If you're planning to serve as facilitator, this chapter will also introduce you to the skills you'll need to bring to that role—especially the most critical skill of leading conversations that feel safe to the participants. There will be more detailed instructions for facilitators in appendix B, including checklists that will make it easy to DIY this workshop.

A few years ago, one of us visited the workspace of a small e-commerce startup in Stockholm, with about fifteen people. Stacked boxes lined the walls, and colorful scraps of ribbon and paper littered the floor. A few people sat on cheap plastic stools, wrapping products to be shipped out as gifts. Ram,[1] the solo founder who had spun up this highly profitable operation, gave me the warmest introduction to his team. He spoke briskly and with a stutter—the kind of stutter that's usually evidence of a bright mind that works too fast for the low bandwidth of human speech.

As Ram showed me around, he whispered, "Martin, thank you. You're the reason I'm less of an asshole lately!"

That was the best compliment I'd ever heard from an alumnus of our program. It was also not surprising if you knew the kind of wake-up call he'd had during his Bonfire Moment.

Ram had received very tough written feedback from his team at the workshop. Here are a few snippets:

› You have a condescending tone, especially with new hires.
› Micromanage less; take what others say into real consideration.
› Think of people as people, not fungible objects.
› Be more empathetic to people's feelings and situations.
› Be conscious of your comments about other people's abilities when speaking to team members.
› Be less defensive and interrogative in your approach at meetings.
› When you disagree, try not to do it by attempting to be the smartest person in the room.
› Stop being so selfish!

Ouch!

But as unpleasant as it had been for Ram to read this feedback during the workshop, the impact was exactly what we had intended. He and his team had a transformative experience that cut through the usual startup vibe: no bragging, no bullshit, no ego.

Left to their own devices, it might take the average startup a year or more to realize they had fallen into any one of the traps we discuss in part I. This was true of Ram's team, and it might be true of yours. Our intense eight-hour workshop provides participants a unique opportunity to slow down, expose hidden conflicts, anticipate future conflicts, and share their biggest fears and insecurities about the work. It's a chance to connect at the most human level, by stepping away from the daily grind; to stop feeling like they're drowning in the daily work, and instead reflect on the work itself; to disentangle themselves from the people problems that slow them down.

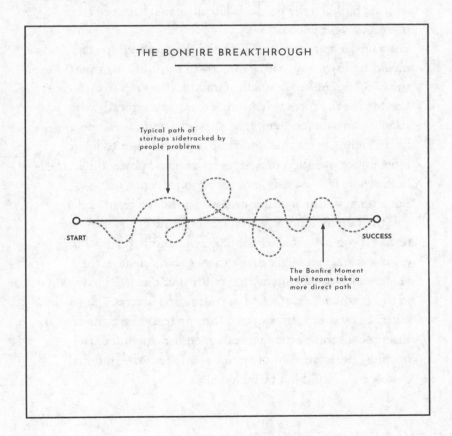

THE BONFIRE BREAKTHROUGH

Typical path of startups sidetracked by people problems

START

SUCCESS

The Bonfire Moment helps teams take a more direct path

Getting the Team Together

The team is the first critical ingredient. To maximize the day, each team member should prepare to dedicate time and attention to this work. But who is *the team*? In some situations, there's an easy answer: it's everyone working tirelessly on the startup. Other times, it's more complicated. Here's a cheat sheet.

WHO SHOULD BE THERE?

› **For an early-stage startup:** Everyone working full-time or a large portion of their time, which includes all the cofounders, the CEO, CTO, and any other C-level execs. In some early-stage startups, this might simply be the small team of friends who are building the product. Usually you'll have between three and eight people.

› **For a larger startup:** The CEO and their leadership team, including anyone reporting directly to the CEO. At times, the CEO might have a smaller circle of direct reports who are regarded as the core leaders of the company, typically with sizable teams under them. If so, this small senior team would be the right size for this workshop. Be careful not to invite more junior members of a larger startup; the power differential in the room will make it hard for people to open up.

› **For a team within a larger organization:** The team leader and their direct reports, which we sometimes call "the intact team." If you have close collaborators in another part of the organization, you might invite them to participate if they (1) have day-to-day interactions with your team, (2) have skin in the game and are invested in your team's success, and (3) are regarded by your team as peers, with no real power differential. Examples of these extended team members might be your people/HR, finance, or operations partners. Any "internal customers" should not be included.

WHO SHOULDN'T BE THERE?

› **Investors or board members** who are not involved in running the team. The presence of major investors or VCs can complicate the workshop dynamic, making the team feel worried about airing dirty laundry to people who control their cash reserves. We strongly recommend that investors sit this one out. In a scenario where a major investor asks the leadership team to do this workshop, the investor should still sit it out, and be happy to receive a summary with the team's explicit permission. (See below on creating psychological safety in the workshop.)

> **Mentors**, for the same reason as investors, unless the mentor is helping the startup on people matters and will be the facilitator of the workshop.
> **Interns** who won't have a long-term outlook on their work with the team.
> **External or internal customers** who may induce performative behavior by the team during the workshop.

We wrote the following chapters assuming you will do the workshop with just one team, but you can scale up to include multiple teams.

Choose a Facilitator

You'll need to designate a facilitator to run the workshop, which includes being responsible for managing time and getting any pre-work completed. This person will play the role of orchestrator of the day, explaining what needs to be done and why, and setting a hard stop when it's time to close a discussion and move on. You don't need a professional trainer or facilitator to do this well. The next few chapters will make it easy for anyone committed to learning the material to start facilitating a Bonfire Moment. (We've also included in appendix B a Facilitator's Playbook with instructions for the entire process, including prep work.)

The role of facilitator is very important, but that doesn't mean it should automatically go to the most senior person on the team. In fact, you're better off if the facilitator is not the boss but someone who is widely trusted by the team and respected by its leaders. There may be times when the facilitator will have to contradict or overrule the boss, so they need to be willing and able to do so.

Part of the challenge is that the facilitator has to simultaneously be an unbiased referee and a biased participant. If you think that combination of roles is too much to ask of anyone on your team, you can bring in a trusted outsider. The process is designed to run successfully whether the facilitator is an insider or outsider, as long as the person is trusted by the team.

There are at least two situations where an outside facilitator is especially helpful:

> **If you have a large group,** especially if you have multiple teams participating in one big workshop. The logistics can get complicated, and you might need to deviate from the usual flow of steps.
> **When the team already has a lot of open conflict,** and the workshop is serving as an intervention for a toxic team dynamic. In this scenario, a trusted outsider who isn't party to the conflict is essential to direct the group in an unbiased way.

Be Ready to Spend an Entire, Focused Day

The average workday is marked by constant interruptions that attack our ability to concentrate: fifteen-minute stand-up huddles, ninety-second pings, sixty-minute all-hands meetings, thirty-minute video chats, quick emails, Slack questions. As summed up by Jake Knapp, author of *Sprint*, "Fragmentation hurts productivity."[2]

Your Bonfire Moment will be nothing like that. Instead, you will create focus and intensity by blocking off an entire day, for real, with no exceptions. Every phone, tablet, and laptop will be checked at the door, to minimize distractions (you'll need one of those screens for one portion of the day, but they can otherwise sit in a device parking lot).

We find that most teams do best if the workshop is held on a Friday (or at the end of the workweek). The energy we're looking for flows when you're less beholden to your task list, less likely to face incoming demands, and more likely to be able to think expansively. The best time of all would be soon after a milestone event or big deadline, when the team feels there's finally some space to take a deep breath. In contrast, the worst possible time would be right before a big product launch or investor meeting.

Some people will probably grumble that you're asking them to block eight full hours, 9:00 a.m. to 5:00 p.m.[3] They may see it as an eternity to spend on "soft stuff." But that's the trap of speed. You can reassure everyone that the eight hours usually fly by, and many participants end up wishing the day had been even longer. But we don't recommend scheduling any more than eight hours, because the time constraint will force people to focus on what they really need to say, and prioritize what's most relevant.

You might consider splitting up the four blocks, perhaps doing one every week on a Friday morning. Such variations are possible, but for maximum impact we recommend doing the full workshop in a single day. You can always revisit parts later on for reinforcement. Think of the one-day experience as a carefully choreographed four-course meal, with each dish building on everything that came before. It would be a lot less memorable to spread out those restaurant courses over several weeks.

Find the Right Space

Your choice of space is critical to the success of your Bonfire Moment. The least effective space is probably your day-to-day work area, whether it's your office cubicle, your kitchen table, or your favorite café. It will be incredibly hard to think beyond the daily grind if you're surrounded by reminders of that grind.

A new, well-chosen space, in contrast, will focus everyone's attention, encourage quality conversations, and minimize distracting thoughts such as "Oof, I forgot to respond to that email!" We've successfully facilitated these workshops in many types of spaces, including:

> Someone else's office space, rented or borrowed. If you can call in a favor, that will save you money.
> Someone's home, provided that your host won't feel compelled to wait on you as if you are social guests. This option can also save you money.
> A rented meeting room at a coworking space.
> A hotel conference space, if you want to be fancy.
> Outdoors on a hiking trail or campground, maybe even with a real bonfire!

What if your startup or team works virtually and is widely scattered? We are big believers in the value of holding your Bonfire Moment in person. Until video conferencing services are able to convey simultaneous talking or laughter, a virtual workshop will not give you the same experience. (Worse, you can't get a real high five, sans emojis.) But we recognize that remote teams are increasingly common, and it might be cost-prohibitive to transport everyone to the same location. (If it's *not* cost-prohibitive, do it. An in-person gathering can deliver a huge ROI.)

For a team that truly has no option other than going virtual, here are some guidelines:

> Ask each participant to find a spot that *isn't* their day-to-day workspace. It might be another part of their home, or a rented or borrowed space somewhere else. Anywhere with minimal distractions and a change of scenery, where they will feel comfortable for a full day.
> Test for high-quality Wi-Fi connections. The workshop will deteriorate significantly if people's video cameras have to be switched off because of weak Wi-Fi.
> Delay the workshop if necessary, until every participant has lined up a place that meets the above criteria. If you can't afford a bunch of plane tickets, you can probably afford some day passes to shared workspaces with strong Wi-Fi.

> Set strict expectations about multitasking and electronics, other than the computer running the video connection. This should be a fully analog experience since, well, humans are analog. Insist on having participants print out the materials they'll need, and use paper and pen. Phones and tablets should be hidden away, on the honor system.

An Overview of the Day

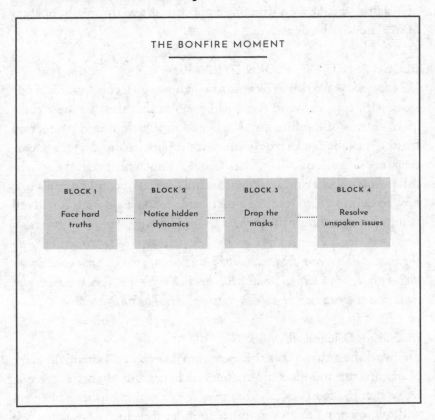

THE BONFIRE MOMENT

BLOCK 1	BLOCK 2	BLOCK 3	BLOCK 4
Face hard truths	Notice hidden dynamics	Drop the masks	Resolve unspoken issues

Now that you have all the ingredients in place, here's an overview of how the workshop will run. The day will consist of four blocks, each ranging from 60 to 180 minutes.

BLOCK 1: FACE HARD TRUTHS

There's rarely any chance during your daily grind to pause and reflect on how well you're doing and how you contribute to your team dynamic. So we offer a self-assessment tool based on a global study on founders. Through a questionnaire available on our website, you'll spend time reflecting on your capabilities as a founder and learn how you stack up against a global dataset of founders. You'll find details in appendix C, including an expanded option to collect feedback from your team a few weeks in advance. After you reflect on a rich summary of insights, you'll have a structured opportunity to troubleshoot areas of weakness with your team.

BLOCK 2: NOTICE HIDDEN DYNAMICS

We then ask you to hit a reset button on how you'll collaborate. In our work with teams around the world, we find that the two most common sources of conflict are misaligned motivations and simmering frustrations about a lack of fairness in the partnership. So we ask participants to work on their "User Guide," a document that will establish norms of behavior, anticipate future sources of conflict, and show how to defuse them. Just like a user guide for a new device, it will tell you important things about your team: *Why are they here? What do they care about? How can you get the best (or worst) out of them? How do they want to receive feedback and resolve conflict? What expectations do they have of you, their peers, and themselves? What breakup scenarios do they anticipate, and how can those scenarios be mitigated?*

BLOCK 3: DROP THE MASKS

The workshop then takes the team into a deep and potentially dark place. Startup founders are masters of hype, and almost every one we've met has felt privately that they're just making it up as they go, without knowing that every other founder feels just as insecure. We give each member of the team a chance to talk about their greatest insecurities and worries, as a reminder that *everyone* comes into this work with at least some fear alongside their excitement. This block also offers a chance to reflect on the coping mechanisms you rely on, the kind of mask you wear, and the bullshit you put out into the world. We fondly call this process the Bullshit Circle.

BLOCK 4: RESOLVE UNSPOKEN ISSUES

With the level of candor you've built up with your team through the first three blocks, you'll now have a chance to dialogue about some of the hard, unspoken issues you face, and make decisions to move the team forward. We invite you to consider a list of questions that point to sources of team drag, as discussed in chapter 2. As you talk through this list, you'll make a plan to avoid the most common failure points. In this final block, you will pay attention to some of the key long game decisions you might be ignoring or downplaying under the pressures of your day-to-day, short game obligations.

The Foundations of the Bonfire Moment

Now that you have an overview of what the day will look like, let's back up to explain the design principles we used to architect the day, and the psychological research that guided us.

When we set out to design this workshop, we knew we were dealing with time-starved, ambitious, smart people. They would have no patience for a drawn-out process that wasn't immediately valuable. So we asked ourselves: What strategies would be minimally viable to turn A players into an A team? What approaches would work even if the participants had no initial interest in changing how they worked and collaborated? What would be transformative and enduring?

These questions led us down two paths.

Startups Are a Wicked Learning Environment

First, the research of Gary Klein helped us understand the most important mechanisms world-class individuals use to hone their expertise. Klein is an acclaimed pioneer in expert intuition, the ability of some people with deep expertise to make quality decisions quickly, under time pressure and uncertainty. He spent decades studying the decision-making powers of people like chess masters, seasoned fire-fighters, and tennis champions. His surprising conclusion: high IQs, above-average spatial reasoning, and better short-term memory *do not* distinguish the fastest and most accurate decision-makers.[4]

Instead, Klein concluded that people develop the most effective expert intuition when two things are true of their learning environment: it's highly predictable (which he calls a "high-validity context") and it provides the opportunity to make repeated attempts with timely feedback.[5]

An environment conducive to learning needs to have recognizable patterns of cause and effect, creating a high-validity context. For instance, chess feedback is clear and instantaneous; you make a move and quickly find out if it was effective or a mistake. If you're serious about improving, you can add this move and its consequences to your mental database for future reference. Trading stocks, in contrast, is a much harder learning environment, because the outcome of every decision is affected by countless external factors, including insight into the company that isn't easily discoverable and the emotional state of everyone else who is trading the stock. Any outcome that seems to be the result of a pattern might simply be a random fluctuation.

The second key aspect of the expert's learning environment is the opportunity to make repeated attempts and receive timely, accurate feedback.

College admission professionals make decisions whose consequences (e.g., graduation rates, career success) can't be confirmed for many years. This makes it hard to recognize key patterns at the application stage, which means there's limited opportunity to develop expert intuition. You can see this reflected in one study that attempted to predict the grades of first-year college students. It found that an algorithm outperformed nearly 80 percent of the human judges—by this measure, they were far from experts.[6] Another study found that radiologists tend to do worse than other medical specialists when making predictions, because it takes much longer for them to find out if, say, a shadow on a screen is really a cancerous lump. Anesthesiologists, in contrast, get immediate feedback on the patient's vital signs during surgery, so they can adjust dosages immediately, with a much better success rate.[7]

Building a team is a lot like stock trading, college admissions, and radiology: an inherently low-validity environment with poor feedback accuracy and frequency. In other words, it's pretty much impossible to develop expert intuition in this domain.

As Ben Horowitz wrote in his bible for startup founders, *The Hard Thing About Hard Things*, "There's no recipe for building a high-tech company; there's no recipe for leading a group of people out of trouble; there's no recipe for motivating teams when your business has turned to crap. That's the hard thing about hard things—there is no formula for dealing with them."[8]

This is why the founder's journey feels messy, painful, and circuitous. Founders operate in what psychologists Emre Soyer and Robin Hogarth call *wicked* learning environments, which lack recognizable patterns and accurate, timely feedback loops.[9] In a *kind* learning environment, in contrast, you can learn much more easily from your experiences.

The Bonfire Moment is designed to teach teams that their day-to-day dynamic is a wicked learning environment, with no simple formulas. Therefore, teams can't assume that their own experiences offer universal lessons. Instead, they should approach people problems with curiosity and the assumption that they don't already know the answer. Meanwhile, the high-quality feedback provided at the workshop helps establish a *kinder* learning environment for the team.

Engineer for Crucible Moments

Another path led us to Warren Bennis, the scholar who is widely regarded as the pioneer of leadership studies. His research over several decades helped move the corporate world away from regarding military heroes as paragons of great leadership, toward a more humanistic, less hierarchical, more adaptive model.[10] Bennis called this reframing a shift "from macho to maestro."[11] He taught at major universities like Harvard, UCLA, and USC, and wrote about thirty books interrogating such questions as *What sets great leaders apart from the rest of us?*

Are they born or made? What formative moments set them on a path to true leadership?

Bennis took an archaeologist's approach to exploring the inner worlds of prominent leaders, excavating their life stories and looking for patterns. He found that every great leader could point to "intense, often traumatic, always unplanned experiences that had transformed them and had become the sources of their distinctive leadership abilities."[12] He called these experiences *crucibles*, after the vessels used by medieval alchemists to make gold out of base metals.

Some crucible moments took the form of a trial, a do-or-die test, or a life-threatening event. Others were less dramatic, such as an episode of self-doubt, a microaggression, or a discovery of data that created cognitive dissonance. All crucible moments led Bennis's subjects to deep self-reflection, as they questioned assumptions about their values, their identity, or their worldview. They emerged with more self-confidence and clarity of purpose.

Yet a crucible moment alone was not enough, Bennis found. Great leaders work through their painful experiences, eventually reframing them in a way that moves them forward. For instance, one founder had initially seen her country of origin as a disadvantage. She had limited access to quality education, didn't have a chance to build an affluent network, and spoke in a dialect of English that was a personal source of embarrassment. But she eventually realized that all these insecurities were the reason she hustled harder than others.

With all this in mind, the Bonfire Moment is designed to be an uncomfortable, often jarring experience—a crucible moment, on demand. And to complete Bennis's leadership formula, we created a space for startup teams to reflect on, and then reframe, the worst moments of their journey so far.

We *didn't* want it to be a day of teaching, in which students were passive recipients. Disturbance was our theory of change. Disturbance offers participants the chance to fundamentally reconsider how they lead and work. And these smart, driven individuals intuitively know how to change, with hardly any help from some expert in the room.

You'll see this mechanism at play throughout the day. We designed the process to deliver high-quality and often revelatory feedback, to show people the differences and similarities among their teammates, and to surface the unspoken expectations team members have about each other. We created a structured space where it feels safe to share self-doubts and coping styles.

Creating Psychological Safety

When crucible moments are the goal, there is nothing more critical for facilitators to learn than how to create a psychologically safe environment for the group.

The process asks teams to be not just open but wide open. You'll be sharing your challenges, weaknesses, frustrations, and newly discovered hidden gaps. You'll talk about your self-doubts and how you tend to mask them. This is very personal stuff, the kinds of disclosures people might share only with a therapist or a very close friend. Only a psychologically safe environment will make such disclosures in front of their colleagues possible.

Before the day starts, participants need to be assured that anything they share will be received with empathy and gratitude, not hostility or defensiveness. They need to believe that nothing they say will be turned against them, and that there will be no consequences—overt or subtle—for admitting to weakness or questioning the work of the startup.

Even if your team is already showing signs of internal strife, they can still come together and have a psychologically safe Bonfire Moment, with the help of a strong facilitator. Here are some of the most effective strategies that we've used as facilitators to create an environment of psychological safety:

> **Don't come in cold.** The facilitator should meet with each
> team member, one-on-one, before the workshop. If there
> are too many participants to meet with all of them, home in
> on those who seem most likely to be contentious, to create a
> hostile atmosphere, or to feel unsafe. Help them feel heard,
> and try to build trust before the workshop. If you connect

with empathy in advance, they will hopefully trust you to be a neutral, unbiased guide for the group.

> **Reduce performance pressure** by acknowledging that some of these topics are gnarly and difficult, with no easy solutions. Questions will be asked that have no easy answers. Stress that because these challenges are hard, you need everyone's best ideas and energy to solve them, and no one will be judged for speaking up and asking questions.

> **Help the team find common ground,** ideally by showing them that everyone is committed to improving the group's dynamic. During your one-on-ones with participants before the big day, try to gauge their willingness to tackle the challenges facing the team. During the workshop, you can demonstrate that everyone in the room is there with good intentions, even those who might appear to be sources of conflict. You might say something like, "I'm feeling nervous because I anticipate that today will surface a lot of hostility and defensiveness. But I have faith that we can work together to find good solutions." Then you might invite everyone to share, on a scale of 1 to 10, how difficult they anticipate the day's conversations will be. And on the same scale, how willing they are to work to make the team stronger. Showing the group that they're all in roughly the same mental state will help normalize the awkwardness and de-escalate any nervousness.

> **Model curiosity by asking a lot of questions.** Become the most ignorant person in the room. Ask people to explain themselves if they're using vague language. Ask for an example when someone drops a broad statement such as, "We just aren't delivering quality code on time." Share what you think you just heard in your own words, and ask, "How well did I understand that?" When you sense an accusatory tone being used, ask a naive question: "It sounds like you're assigning blame to X; did I hear that correctly?" or "I wonder if you see yourself contributing to this challenge as well?"

> **When challenged by big egos, think like a judo master.** You can always spot a big ego in statements such as, "I've launched fifteen products in my career, and it doesn't work that way," or "I graduated at the top of my Wharton class. I'm correct." These kinds of comments expose underlying insecurity; the speaker is asserting their power as a response to feeling threatened. In that moment of threat, they have little capacity to listen or engage productively. Instead of trying to block them or challenge them head-on, use their own weight against them. Invite them to share more about their experiences and point of view. Then acknowledge something you agree with, even if it's small. De-escalate the tension by reducing the threat they're feeling, while steering them gently back into the group discussion.

> **Watch out for the "parent voice."** The definition of a parental voice varies from culture to culture—it might be firm and kind, or tougher and more authoritative. Either way, try to stop yourself if it feels like you're talking to kids, or if you sound the way your own parents did when instructing you. Remember that your role is not to be what cognitive psychologist Alison King calls the "sage on the stage" but rather a "guide on the side."[13] Try not to let the group become dependent on you for problem-solving, a quick answer, or a way out of a jam. If you slip into the role of assertive, all-knowing parent, some members of the group may reciprocate and regress to helplessness.

Our Four Cornerstone Principles

With the ambitious goals and intense psychological demands of the workshop in mind, we consulted the most seminal studies in cognitive and behavioral science, leadership, and organizational behavior to develop four cornerstone principles for the Bonfire Moment:

1. **No bragging; no bullshit.** This is the first rule of the Bonfire Moment. You are not allowed to talk about your fancy degrees, your CXO title, or how successful your startup has been so far. We care only about the honest, gritty, painful challenges you and your team are facing. We don't waste time on tactical skills (e.g., how to craft a pitch deck). Instead, you'll zero in on structured feedback from the people you work with, which will give you unambiguous insight into how you act as a teammate and where your blind spots are. This is why investors are not allowed in the room: so the team won't have to worry about looking bad in front of them.

2. **Diverse perspectives.** We give the team an opportunity to hear each other out, and to share perspectives on the work or the team that leaders rarely hear. These fresh opinions will give you a chance to reconsider your own. You'll talk about potential failure scenarios and how you might mitigate those risks. Throughout the day, you will surface hidden misalignments within the team and anticipate future conflicts. Think of this process as a vaccine—a low-risk exposure to small doses of conflict that can immunize your team from big conflicts in the future.

3. **Making intangibles concrete.** Our process will allow you to turn intangible concepts, frustrations, desires, and disagreements into artifacts that you can examine in an analytical, objective way. It's like the difference between feeling the pain of a broken bone (intangible, hard to describe) and looking at an X-ray (tangible, clearly definable). Turning abstractions into specifics will make it much easier to work through your team's challenges productively.

4. **Slowing down.** Workshop day will feel slower than the typical frenetic day at your startup. That's deliberate—but slower doesn't mean easier. Although the tasks may seem simple, many people who've experienced the Bonfire Moment say it was a tough experience. Don't worry; we've crafted the workshop activities so that the experience is safe and rewarding.

Getting the Team into the Right Mindset

After running the Bonfire Moment for thousands of people, we've seen all kinds of behaviors from participants, from extreme enthusiasm to open hostility. Here are three behaviors to look out for that might cause problems if you don't spot and address them early:

1. **Vacationing.** Often found in participants who are happy to have a day off from the daily grind and see the workshop as an opportunity to kick back and chill out. Their bodies are in the room, but their minds are having cocktails on some beach. It's important to give them the benefit of the doubt: perhaps they're coming off a really intense period that culminated in a big milestone. But as you empathize, you have to set expectations about the importance of the workshop. It's not a day off—it's serious work, perhaps even harder than their usual work. If you sense that they still aren't taking it seriously, pull them aside during a break and check in on their energy. Ask what they need from you to be able to lean in fully.

2. **Absenteeism.** You'll spot this in participants who come back late from every break, sneak peeks at their phones whenever they think they can get away with it, and ask to step outside for a "really quick, really important" call. In addition to doing what you can to set expectations in advance, if you have several absentees, you can offer the entire group an extended break, so that those who seem too focused on their daily work can respond to nagging texts, emails, or voicemails. You can also pull them aside to ask what's preoccupying them and remind them of the importance and benefits of this work.

3. **Hypercriticism.** You want your people to be mentally engaged enough to question any aspects of the process that create mental dissonance for them. But hypercriticism goes beyond questioning specific ideas or emotions that come up in the room. Hypercritical participants challenge the whole premise

of the workshop, preventing the team from moving forward. They nitpick about minor details and waste the group's time. If you notice someone with this mindset, pull them aside during a break and ask why they seem to be hostile to the workshop. Allow them to vent their frustrations, and if possible, offer to make some tweaks that honor their valid objections. You can try to meet them halfway: "If we do X, will you be ready to go all in?"

We once had a participant who was absent during some parts of the day and hypercritical during others. We were hosting a large group of forty, with several startup teams in the room. Due to a last-minute change, he ended up attending without his cofounders, which we'd never recommend. He was frequently disruptive, saying things like, "I'm not learning anything here, but if any of you want advice, I'm happy to talk." He approached us at one of the breaks, laying out the reasons why he didn't want to finish the day.

After hearing him out, we agreed with him that leaving the workshop would be a better use of his time. It would also be better for the rest of the participants. At face value, some of his feedback was useful. Maybe we could have been clearer in defining the criteria for participation and preparing people for the experience. But we later found out that his negativity actually had nothing to do with our workshop. He had recently received scathing feedback from his team, and earlier that week one of his cofounders had quit the company after a rough, explosive argument.

The moral of the story is that we sometimes don't know what battles people are fighting; how they show up in a workshop might just be their way of coping. So whenever possible, give people the benefit of the doubt, and don't blame yourself for being an ineffective facilitator. Another lesson: Your responsibility as a facilitator is to protect the experience of the whole group. Empathy for a struggling individual is great, but not at everyone else's expense.

You now have the basic guidelines you'll need to jump in and start planning your Bonfire Moment. If you're going to be a facilitator, please see the Facilitator's Playbook (appendix B) for a detailed checklist of things to do prior to the big day, starting as early as four weeks ahead.

Before we dig more deeply into the four time blocks, let's get into the room with a real team that's going through their own Bonfire Moment.

Chapter 7

Inside a Startup's Bonfire Moment

We now invite you inside an actual Bonfire Moment, so you can see how a fairly typical startup team goes through our process to confront their toughest challenges. You will witness the profound obstacles this team faced and how the Bonfire Moment helped them unlock important realizations and move forward. Names and identifying details have been changed for confidentiality, and dialogue has been simplified, but the basic story is that of a real startup we worked with.

Not every team that experiences a Bonfire Moment will begin at this level of dysfunction; many do the workshop before such problems get out of hand. We're sharing this particular story to show that the workshop can help any team, even one nearing a point of crisis.

You'll meet Jacob, their facilitator, who learned to run the workshop with the guidance you'll find in the chapters that follow this. He had done this several times before, so he'd had practice. But don't be intimidated by his Jedi Master–like skills—you'll get there too with this book. We'll make it as easy as putting together a Lego set; it'll take effort and focus, but if you follow the step-by-step instructions, you'll end up with something sturdy.

It's 9:00 a.m. on a Friday, and five people are sitting in the spacious living room of a nice house in Kuala Lumpur. Four of them are the executive team of Fisk, an agritech startup. Fisk is building smart devices for fish ponds, which will enable fish farmers to maximize their harvests and minimize waste. The startup is working to improve food security in Malaysia, with a goal to scale across Thailand, Vietnam, Indonesia, the Philippines, and beyond.

Jon (the CEO) and Miguel (the CTO) cofounded Fisk together and are now in their late twenties. They were buddies in college, then started their careers in different global tech companies. They built Fisk in the evenings and on weekends, and when they got some early funding for their project, they decided to quit their day jobs to go all in.

Over the past few months, Miguel has been struggling to recruit enough good engineers; he recently missed a launch deadline, despite working insane hours to make up for the staff shortage. Fisk's investors are losing patience, which has put Jon on the firing line. Miguel feels like Jon might be throwing him under the bus instead of defending him when he talks privately to their investors.

Meanwhile, Jon has secretly been taking on consulting projects on the side, to earn extra cash and hedge his bets. Now word of that has gotten back to Miguel, making him even more bitter. He wonders why they are splitting the equity fifty-fifty if Jon isn't all in as CEO while Miguel works nonstop.

Tensions got even worse when TechCrunch asked to interview one of the founders. Jon grabbed the opportunity without trying to include Miguel, since he was so busy working toward that aggressive deadline. Miguel felt like Jon was hogging all the credit, and he himself was becoming an invisible founder. He never confronted Jon directly about any of this, but his bitterness has been seeping into all of their recent interactions.

The barely suppressed tension between the founders has created stress for the other two Fisk team members who are also in the room this morning: Farah (the VP of operations) and Kelly (the VP of sales and marketing). Both VPs are in their mid-twenties and were the first two hires of the startup. Both have seen their check-in meetings with Miguel turn into venting sessions about his grievances. Farah and Kelly have tried not to take sides, but they're tired of feeling like collateral damage in a cold war between the founders.

The fifth person in the room, Jacob, doesn't work for Fisk. He's a successful entrepreneur in his mid-forties who volunteers part-time to advise new founders. He met Jon and Miguel at a local startup accelerator where he was a mentor. After helping them through their struggles for a few months, Jacob offered to facilitate a Bonfire Moment, a workshop he's led several times after experiencing it himself as part of Google's Startup Accelerator program. He's welcomed the group into his home, where they now sit.

Through prior conversations with the Fisk team, Jacob has learned that it's been an eighteen-month grind for the startup, which now totals fifteen people. While early tests of their technology have gone well, morale is low and continuing to deteriorate. Gossip and whispered complaints are crowding out productive conversation at the office. Several people have been thinking about quitting.

During one of his mentoring conversations with Jacob, Miguel said under his breath, "I should have been the CEO." Meanwhile, Jon complained privately to their new mentor that Miguel was being unfair and unreasonable. "I'm an MBA, not a tech guy. I don't know how to screen new engineers or solve engineering problems. That's on his plate as CTO. And our VCs would still have been pissed no matter what I told them!"

Instead of agreeing with either cofounder, Jacob urged them to set aside a day for a Bonfire Moment. Both were skeptical but trusted Jacob's judgment. Farah and Kelly were up for anything that might improve their miserable work situation.

Jacob is an entrepreneur, not a professional facilitator, let alone a therapist. But with the facilitator playbook we provided, he is confident that he can guide them through the day, creating the open and disarming conversations they badly need.

Block 1: Face Hard Truths

Now the five are sitting on chairs arranged in a circle, with no table. As the facilitator, Jacob kicks things off with a review of the ground rules and the process for Block 1. Tensions are already rising.

Jacob says, "I'm looking at a team that's done some great work together. But I know you're all exhausted. Each of you have told me separately that you're thinking about quitting. Before you take that drastic step, consider all that you've achieved, and take a moment to feel good about it. If you're willing to get back on track, I can help you have some tough yet productive conversations today. It won't be easy, but it's the way to save this company."

They all nod because they all trust Jacob. He spent time privately with each of them over the previous week and understands their individual perspectives. They trust him to keep the details of their conversations to himself as he helps the team get unstuck.

They begin the day reflecting on how effective they've been in the roles they play at Fisk. Jacob invites them to take out their phones (the only time in the whole day they will do so) and work through a self-assessment based on research on hundreds of founders around the world. The self-assessment prompts participants to reflect on more than thirty probing questions, pushing them to take an honest look at themselves. For some, this feels like an incredibly high bar to set for what they need to do in this team. For others, it's a relief to finally understand what good looks like in a tangible and structured way.

Jacob gives the team time to reflect and do the self-assessment. The four colleagues move to separate corners of the living room.

Jon is restless as he goes through the questions. He steps outside and paces for a bit, realizing that he's fallen short on many of these criteria: *I lead by inspiring people. I am not distracted by new ideas and projects. I try to resolve conflict by openly talking about disagreements with those involved. I am not discouraged by major challenges or failure.* And so on.

At the end of this battery of questions, the assessment tool gives Jon a summary. His face scrunches up as if he's in pain. Clearly he's been distant or even absent with his colleagues, both physically and mentally. Jon is starting to see how his fading confidence in the startup has made him ineffective at many of his CEO responsibilities. And perhaps that has demoralized the others.

After about ten minutes alone with their self-assessments, the colleagues return to the circle. They find it hard to make eye contact, with each feeling some combination of vulnerability, disappointment, self-blame, and defensiveness, as well as some hope that they can fix things.

Jacob explains that they'll each have a chance to address one—only one—area of improvement. They might choose something that was especially frustrating because they were already aware of it but found it hard to improve. Or they might choose a new revelation that had never occurred to them before. This next step is called "peer coaching" because everyone will come together as peers, not collaborators or competitors, to help each of the others process their realizations. Jacob encourages them to take turns asking questions, to listen with empathy, and to brainstorm solutions.

Jon volunteers to take his twenty minutes of coaching time first. Jacob reads him the first question: "What area of your self-assessment do you want to work on today?"

Jon takes a deep breath. "I realize I haven't been the best CEO lately. I've been hard to pin down for a while. I guess I haven't been as excited as I was in the early days."

Jacob quickly says, "Thanks for bringing that up. But let's make sure: Do you really want to spend your twenty minutes on this topic?"

Jon says, "Sure. It's important to me because I hate being insincere. I still believe in our mission, but I feel beaten down by the deadlines we've set for ourselves and how hard it is to hire good engineers. Miguel, I know you're doing your best, but maybe it was a mistake to build here in Malaysia? Maybe we should have started in Singapore?"

Jacob steps in again to keep the process on track: "Okay, pause there. We're not looking for solutions yet. We're trying to understand your goal. So what do you want to work on with this group? In a single sentence."

Jon ponders this for a few seconds. "I want to figure out how I can show more confidence in our mission to our team." Satisfied, Jacob reads the second question: "What have you tried so far?"

Now Jon begins to meander. He says he tried to prepare better for Fisk's company-wide meetings. He tried to bring back their Monday morning stand-ups, where he used to give pep talks in the early days, when the team was much smaller. He's sorry that lately those pep talks have devolved into sermons about discipline and reliability. Jon also mentions a few intense calls with Francis, one of their disgruntled investors, and how upset he feels during and after those calls.

Miguel seems annoyed at that last point and asks, "Have you considered pushing back against Francis?" Jacob jumps in again because this question is out of bounds; it skips to solutions. Miguel replies, "Sorry. Let me ask it differently. What do you say during those calls?"

Jon explains: "I get grilled for details about our progress. And I feel like I'm always on the back foot. Miguel, I know you're swamped, so I never pull you into those calls. I also know you'd be much better at explaining the tech stuff."

Jacob reads the third question. "Would you be open to suggestions?" This strikes everyone as strange, because anyone would have to say yes. Jon says, "Yes!" with a bit of a laugh, hoping to relieve some of the awkwardness. Then Jacob asks Jon to turn his chair around and listen to the next part of the discussion as if he isn't in the room. He can take notes, but he cannot participate. This feels highly unnatural, but Jon soon realizes how much more he can absorb when he's not allowed to interrupt.

Miguel says he didn't realize that Jon was taking so much heat from the investors and protecting the team from them. And that he's always willing to help by providing technical updates and explanations.

Kelly observes that all this time, she'd assumed Jon had lost faith in their mission, and she'd had no idea how much pressure he was under. "I think a lot of people assume CEOs put pressure on everyone else but don't have much on them. If Jon can make it clear that he's still very inspired by the vision and still believes we can get there, that would really help morale."

Farah adds, "I agree with Kelly. Also, I figured Jon didn't really care about the mission and the farmers we're trying to help. I thought he was just in it for the money. I was really surprised to hear his passion a few minutes ago. I guess I joined the company after Jon's inspiring stand-ups lost their spark."

A few more ideas are exchanged, as Jon shifts in his seat, increasingly uncomfortable that he can't respond. But finally, Jacob invites him to turn his chair around and rejoin the group, then asks the final question: "Which of these ideas interest you enough to act on in the next thirty days?"

Jon says that from now on, he will talk to them honestly about the pressures he's facing. He realizes that bottling up his stress and anxiety was a terrible strategy, since his nonverbal signals were obvious, and everyone's assumptions were worse than the truth. He also tells Miguel that he will include him on future investor calls, so they can present a united front as cofounders.

PEER COACHING QUESTIONS

GOAL	What challenge do you want to work through in the next 20 minutes? Why is that important to you?
REALITY	What have you tried so far? What are you thinking of doing?
OPTIONS	Would you like suggestions from the group? (while coachee turns their back to the group)
WILL	Which of these ideas interest you enough to act on in the next 30 days?

Adapted from the GROW coaching model, developed in the 1980s by John Whitmore, Graham Alexander, and Alan Fine.

Jon's twenty minutes are up. Kelly, Farah, and Miguel get their turns next, each using their time to address one piece of feedback. Their peer coaching sessions fly by as well.

Finally, Jacob calls a fifteen-minute break, and everyone sighs with relief. Block 1 was intense for each of them, and, at times, awkward and challenging. And yet the process has given them hope for a clear way forward.

Block 2: Notice Hidden Dynamics

After the break, it's 11:20 a.m. Jacob suspects that Jon, Miguel, Kelly, and Farah are still privately mulling over Block 1, so he reassures them that over time, the painful bits will lose their sting. In the meantime, they need to begin Block 2.

Jacob explains the User Guide, a powerful tool to use in anticipating and working through points of conflict. Each team member will answer multiple pages of questions to help the others work with them more effectively. Once completed, these pages function just like a user guide for a new and unfamiliar piece of technology. Without such a guide, it's easy to get frustrated when a device isn't delivering on its promised features. But with one, a seemingly impossible problem might be solved in seconds.

The four skim through the questions with curiosity and a bit of anxiety, as Jacob describes the guide's three distinct sections. Section 1 is about their personal motivations. *Why did you join the startup? What aspects of it make you excited? What do you care about a lot, a little, or not at all?* And so on.

Section 2 is about working style. *What strengths do you bring to the team? What gaps do you need help with? What's the best way to give you feedback? How do you prefer to resolve conflicts? What's your favorite (and least favorite) way to communicate?* And so on.

Section 3 is the toughest, Jacob warns them, because it goes to deeper and darker places, exploring the team's expectations. *What expectations do you have of yourself in your role? What contributions are you making or do you plan to make to help the startup succeed? What expectations do you have of each member of the team? What expectations do you think others have of you?* Then it delves into how each team member feels about their contribution compared to that of others, which we call *interpersonal equity* and which often represents a primary source of conflict. *On a 10-point scale, how satisfied are you with what you contribute compared to what your teammates contribute? How satisfied are you with what you receive compared to what your teammates receive? How fair do you feel your arrangement is overall?* Finally, it turns to the future, asking about hypothetical crises that we call breakdown scenarios. *Suppose our startup fails within the next twelve months because of interpersonal challenges. What are the three most likely reasons for that failure? What can we do now to minimize those risks?*

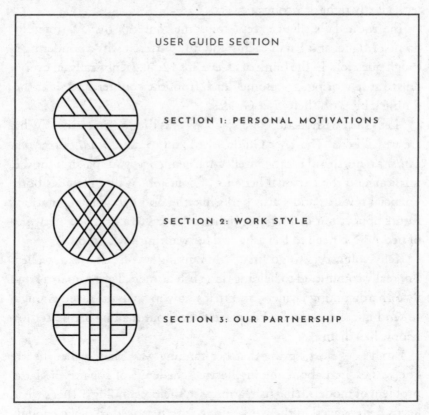

USER GUIDE SECTION

SECTION 1: PERSONAL MOTIVATIONS

SECTION 2: WORK STYLE

SECTION 3: OUR PARTNERSHIP

Jacob adds that he knows he's asking them for a level of openness and vulnerability they haven't had to summon before. But he urges them to take advantage of this structured opportunity to work through the team's challenges.

"You'll be tempted to duck the uncomfortable questions or sugarcoat your responses. But there's a big payoff if you're brave enough to be honest. This is a rare chance to truly listen to each other with respect and an open mind. So as you fill out your User Guide, remember that *clear is kind, unclear is unkind.*"[1]

Jacob sends them off to different corners of the room to get started, warning them that an hour may seem like a long time to complete the User Guide, but they'll likely wish they had even longer. It will require thoughtful reflection, not snap responses. It's not a standardized test with clearly right or wrong answers.

The room falls silent except for some muted sighs. At different points, Miguel and Farah each stand up to stretch while pondering a tough question. In the blink of an eye, it's 12:30. Jacobs calls on everyone to stop writing, grab some lunch from the counter, and sit at the dining table with their User Guides.

"Let's start with section one," Jacob says as they begin eating. "Why are we all here? The User Guide asked you to rank *head, heart, and wallet* as shorthand for the intellectual challenge, your passion for the mission, and the personal benefits of your job. Wallet includes both financial rewards and status perks like the boost to your reputation, future opportunities, bragging rights, or access to a cool new network of people. No need to feel ashamed for wanting any of those."

Kelly volunteers to go first. "My ranking was heart, head, wallet. I'm really committed to helping these fish farmers. I grew up in a family of hardworking farmers, and that's how my parents saved enough to send me to college. So I'm passionate about making life better for people like them."

Farah goes next, saying that her ranking was head, wallet, heart. She was excited about the intellectual challenge of solving the hard problem of modernizing fish farms with their technology. That's what keeps her engaged in the work, along with her need to make enough money to support her parents and a younger sibling she is putting through school.

Miguel then talks about why he put wallet first, for both the financial and status aspects, followed by heart. "My dream is to be a serial entrepreneur, and I see Fisk as a great opportunity to build the reputation I need to make that happen. I don't want to sound arrogant, but I love telling people that I'm the CTO working on this really cool mission. It makes me proud of what we're building and the progress we're making."

Finally, Jon says he struggled to decide if his top choice was heart or wallet. "On one hand, I care deeply about lifting up the families who work for these farms. On the other hand, I'd really like Fisk to thrive over the next five years to support my growing family. I have a toddler and another baby on the way, and I worry about my financial responsibilities."

Jacob then asks the next question: *Where do we differ the most? What conflicts do we expect to have as a result of our differences?*

This time Miguel starts. He says he suddenly realized that Jon's nervousness about Fisk's viability is probably what pushed him to take on outside consulting work. He also realized why it agitated him so much when Jon did that TechCrunch interview solo—it was a missed opportunity for Miguel to build his own profile as a founder. But Jon didn't even consider the "status wallet" and just saw that interview as a way to help the product ship faster. The team was starting to see that they could have saved themselves so much trouble if they had talked about their motivations sooner.

The lunch session continues briskly as the team answers questions about how they prefer to collaborate and resolve conflict. But then they reach the third section of the User Guide, about the partnership itself. Jacob reads the first question in that section: "What expectations do you have of each person on the team?"

Miguel shifts nervously in his seat, then turns to Jon: "I wrote that I expect honesty." Everyone knows that he was referring to Jon's undisclosed outside consulting gigs. "When we agreed to do this full-time, I left a job that felt really secure. And when you do your side projects without letting me know, I wonder if you think I can't handle an honest conversation about the state of Fisk. I wish we were more honest with each other about things like that." Miguel is visibly flustered but trying to maintain his composure.

Before Jon can respond, Jacob steps in: "Miguel, that seemed really hard for you to say, so thank you." He then motions to Jon, who doesn't explode in anger, as Miguel had feared. Instead Jon says, "Yes, thanks, Miguel. I wrote in my User Guide that I expect myself to stay focused on our work, and to communicate more with you all on what I've been thinking. So I agree with you, we have the same goals."

Kelly then offers her expectations of the cofounders: "Miguel, I feel a lot of emotional burden when you unload your angst about Jon on me. I always listen, but it drains my mental energy and makes it harder to do the important things our teams need from me. So my request is that we all find a way to deal with our conflicts without dragging other people into them." The others are surprised to hear Kelly speak so directly about her frustration.

By 1:50, they've finished discussing their User Guides, and Jacob calls a ten-minute break. The four colleagues all seem drained as they clear their lunch plates and step outside to stretch or use the bathroom. But while Block 2 was exhausting, it has laid the groundwork for navigating even deeper conversations in the future.

Block 3: Drop the Masks

At 2:00 p.m., the group reconvenes in the living room. The curtains have been closed and the lights are off, so the room is mostly dark—except for the glow coming from four laptops on the floor, in the center of a circle of pillows. The screens, pointing in four directions, depict a bonfire along with the familiar sounds of crackling, hissing, sizzling, and the occasional snap of a breaking branch. Jacob gestures for them to sit on the floor around this digital bonfire.

Jon, Miguel, Kelly, and Farah aren't sure what to make of this new setup. They still trust Jacob, but this feels a little weird. Still, they each find a comfortable position on a pillow and stare into the dancing flames. Then Jacob breaks the tension with a joke. "It got cold, so I built us a fire," he says, while rubbing his hands rapidly in front of one of the screens. There are some snickers. Then he declares: "Welcome to the Bullshit Circle!" The team is intrigued as he warns them that this part of the day is when they will feel the most vulnerable.

"Have you wondered why we call this process the Bonfire Moment? Every day, you're under an incredible amount of pressure, some of it self-inflicted, and there's no end in sight. In some ways, you might say, you're constantly inside the fire. Today presents an opportunity for you to step out of the fire and gather around it—to examine it as a team, reflect, reconnect on a human level, and determine what you want to change. So far, we've delved deeply into your startup's fire and addressed some issues that often remain unspoken. At this particular moment, we'll be focusing on one specific, and possibly painful, part of the journey."

Jacob then explains the trap of confidence (see chapter 5): "Almost any startup's journey will include ups and downs—a mix of confidence and self-doubt, excitement and fear. Setbacks will be inevitable and can easily lead to discouragement. On this roller coaster, you need to remember two things that psychologists have confirmed.

"First, your most confident days are usually at the start of the journey. Paradoxically, the more you build this startup, and the more skills you develop, the more likely you are to lose confidence. That's because the better you get at this, the more you realize what greatness would look like, and the more clearly you see how far you are from it. But this insecurity can keep you striving and working toward that goal. Don't take it as a sign of inevitable failure. Don't quit. Don't lower your standards so they feel more achievable. The self-doubt you feel is not a signal of failure, it's a signal of growth. So keep going!"

Jacob pauses to let this sink in. "Second, when you start to feel overwhelmed and discouraged, you can easily fall into something we call the bullshit zone. That's where people consciously or unconsciously mask their insecurities with a false front, to protect their egos. These self-preserving narratives are common in startups because of the brag culture encouraged in our world. Almost all of us have perfectionist tendencies—we want to reach for excellence and be seen by others as excellent."

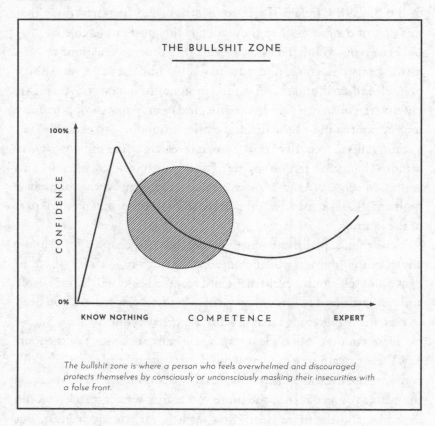

The bullshit zone is where a person who feels overwhelmed and discouraged protects themselves by consciously or unconsciously masking their insecurities with a false front.

Jacob then explains the three types of self-preserving narratives we described in chapter 5:

1. **False optimism:** Assuring the team and investors that everything is fine.
2. **False strength:** Emphasizing past achievements with arrogance, while downplaying signs of vulnerability.
3. **False detachment:** Pretending to be calm and indifferent to problems, often using silence or absence to deflect attention.

He then issues a challenge: "Over the next few minutes, I invite you to reflect on and share the most painful parts of Fisk's journey so far. Think about the self-doubt, insecurities, and fears that weigh you down, and what self-preserving narratives you might be using to cope. It's a chance for your team to hear your innermost thoughts and help them begin to understand what they see on the surface." He gives each person a piece of paper that reads:

The bullshit I project to others is _____,
because what I'm really afraid of is _____.
The experience that first caused me to feel this fear or insecurity was
_____.

He then lays out a few ground rules using the acronym JOIN: no *judging*, no *offering* advice, no *interrupting*, and *nothing* leaves the Bullshit Circle.

Jacob goes first by filling in his own blanks. He knows that if he digs deep and models vulnerability, he will set the wheels of reciprocal self-disclosure in motion.

Then Jon follows his lead. "The BS I project: I push myself to be the most outspoken person in the room with smart ideas. It's because I'm really insecure about not being an engineer, and I know VCs prefer to work with technical CEOs. I also don't have any fancy degrees from a top school like Stanford or Harvard, and I never worked at an elite company like Google or Amazon. So all I really have is my street smarts and instincts. When I get questions about the product, I think I'm able to explain it decently enough, but I really struggle with most everything else."

Jon pauses for a few seconds, as if wondering if he should go even deeper. "I know exactly where all this came from. When I was a high school freshman, my parents died in a freak car accident. My two younger siblings and I moved in with our grandparents, but they didn't know how to help us through that very dark period. In hindsight, I realize I went into a deep depression and spent way too much time playing video games. My high school grades were terrible. When I couldn't get into a good university, it really shook me up. I decided to start working super hard to make up for my lack of a fancy degree with brute force. I launched Fisk to try to give my life meaning by serving others. It really means so much to me."

The circle is silent except for the crackling of the digital bonfire. The others are so struck by Jon's vulnerability that they find it hard to make eye contact with him.

Farah breaks the silence by going next. "I went to Stanford and worked at Google, but I still feel really unsure of myself." The room seems to hold its breath. Jacob senses goose bumps, feeling that this moment might've just unlocked something for Jon. "I realize I use positivity and being extra helpful whenever I feel insecure about a situation. I don't have any kind of trauma that remotely compares to Jon's, but my mom always taught me to hide my emotions, like a duck. You know how ducks seem so calm while floating on water? Well, they're actually paddling like crazy under the surface. That's me."

She goes on to share her deepest fear. "It sounds silly, but I was a straight-A student because my parents held me to impossibly high standards. That made me hyperaware of everyone's expectations, and I still always worry about letting people down." After a pause, she adds, "I studied engineering because I was pushed in that direction, but I actually wanted to do something more focused on people. Maybe psychology or something like that. So I love this job running our operations. It's my attempt to not waste my engineering degree but also work closely with people."

Inspired by Jon and Farah, Miguel and Kelly take their own turns at revealing their hidden insecurities. When they finish, the room is silent once again, except for the fire.

Everyone looks around the room, feeling a mix of emotions. A heaviness hangs in the air, reflecting the deep and serious stories shared, and the responsibility the team members now have with that information. At the same time, there's a lightness because, for the first time, they see each other as more than colleagues, and can appreciate being on this tough, tiring, but rewarding journey together.

It's now 3:00 p.m., and the team is happy to take a fifteen-minute break before the day's final push.

Block 4: Resolve Unspoken Issues

At 3:15, they're ready to go again, surprised at how the day has flown by. Jacob tells them that this block is designed to channel what they've learned into concrete actions to help the team move forward. He introduces the concepts of drag and the trap of speed (see chapter 2) and declares, "It's time to slow down so that you can go faster later. Making the right decisions at this point will lead to less drag in the future. Let's build aerodynamics into how you operate as a team, before you hit the gas again."

He hands out and explains the Team Drag Checklist: twenty potential sources of misalignment, miscommunication, and conflict that startups commonly encounter. They include:

> **Equity splits.** Did we make the easy choice of distributing equity in equal shares, since we started as a tight-knit group of peers? If so, what will we do in the future if contributions to the startup start to vary widely and people perform at different levels of quality? What will happen if a pivot makes some cofounders' skill sets less essential?
> **Time commitment.** What hours will we keep? Are we expecting everyone to work part-time, full-time, or all the time? If we started off working part-time (as many startups do), are we aligned on who will later be willing to go full-time and at what point? How will we handle deviations from this time commitment?
> **Gossip.** What will we do when gossip starts to spread within the team? What is each team member's responsibility when they hear one colleague complain about another? When does gossip cross the line from harmless to damaging?
> **Mental health.** What will we do when someone on the team is struggling with their mental health? To what extent are we ready to support our teammates, especially if they need to take temporary breaks from work?
> **Personal stagnation.** If one or more cofounders aren't building their skills fast enough to keep up with the growing

business, what are fair actions to move forward without them?

> **Failure.** At what point will we decide this startup is a failure? What metric do we use: bankruptcy, or a success hurdle such as "x users in y months" or "x dollars in revenue by year y"? What will we do if some members of the team want to keep fighting while others have already mentally moved on?

"I'm asking you to deal with the elephants in the room," says Jacob. "What are the obvious issues that almost everyone sees or anticipates but avoids talking about? Choose three items on your checklist that seem urgent and likely to cause problems later. If you can't narrow them down, focus on ones we haven't yet talked about today." He stops for ten minutes while the team ponders and marks up their checklists.

Then Jacob continues. "In any important team discussion, there are usually four distinct kinds of conversations. One is the actual conversation that everyone hears in the meeting. But there are also private conversations beforehand, as allies align their thoughts in advance. Likewise after the meeting, allies evaluate what happened. And there are silent conversations going on in the minds of every participant—thoughts they don't feel safe sharing with anyone, even their allies. But now we're going to bring all of those conversations into this room for all to hear."

He asks everyone to share their top three sources of drag and tallies them in his copy of the checklist. The top three vote-getters will be addressed over the next eighty minutes.

The item with the most votes is **Failure.** Miguel jumps in to start the discussion: "I feel strongly about this one, but not because I'm anywhere close to wanting to give up. I just think it will help us a lot to have a finish line to look toward and pour all our energy into. Without one, it feels like we might be hustling forever." He turns to Jon to ask, "When we started Fisk, what did you imagine would be the signal to quit?"

Jon replies, "I remember that we were more focused on when we'd know it was time to quit our jobs and do this full-time. I never even thought about giving up."

Miguel is reassuring, not hostile. "I think that's very common for first-time founders. I've read about startups that end up in 'zombie mode,' neither dead nor really alive because they stop growing. I would hate to keep wasting my time if we ever get to that point, just because we're afraid to admit that we screwed up or ran into bad luck."

Kelly jumps in: "Would you say our board will focus on our active user numbers and revenue? Suppose we have three straight months of declines in both. Won't they just pull the plug on us? Then we wouldn't have to be the ones deciding to quit."

"That's probably true about the board," Miguel responds. "But three months of declining numbers feels like two months too many. I think we should agree that if we ever hit a single month of real stagnation, we should have a serious, honest conversation about pivoting or shutting down." After some more back-and-forth, they agree to this new standard.

Similar productive exchanges happen for the other two sources of drag that they cover. When Jacob calls time at 5:00 p.m. and gives them a final ten-minute break, they've all taken a ton of notes, and they feel more aligned than they have in a very long time.

The End—and the Beginning

After the final break, they reconvene so Jacob can wrap up their Bonfire Moment. He briefly recaps what they covered in each of the four blocks, while sharing suggestions and resources for continuing the positive momentum when they return to work on Monday. "While this may have felt like a retreat from the daily grind, you did a lot of hard work today. I hope this feels like a reset for Fisk."

As his final request of the day, Jacob asks them to spend a few minutes reflecting on two questions: "What new insights do you have of yourself, this team, or your work? And what are you most grateful for today?" They go around and share their reflections, all very positive. Then they pack up, thank Jacob, and head out for a happy hour drink to unwind before going their separate ways.

Over the coming months and years, the Fisk team will incorporate many of the elements of the Bonfire Moment into their daily work. They plan to run the leadership assessment for themselves and the managers on their teams at least once a year. They will keep their User Guides easily accessible in a shared folder, update them as needed, and add new ones for new hires. And when they get together for a quarterly company-wide retreat, they will spend time around a real campfire, while getting real about the challenges and insecurities they bring to their work.

With a tighter, more cohesive team, they are on the road to a growing and profitable business.

Chapter 8

Block 1—Face Hard Truths

This is the first of four chapters where we'll take a closer look at each block of the Bonfire Moment.

In the first, Face Hard Truths, we use a research-backed assessment tool—derived from studying hundreds of startup teams worldwide—to help the team reflect on their individual skills and uncover hidden strengths and gaps. By the end of this block, each participant will have undergone a structured self-assessment, gauged their performance relative to our dataset of leaders, and discussed their challenges in a peer coaching process, tapping into the team's wisdom to tackle the most challenging aspects of their work.

In this chapter, we will explore the usefulness of structured reflection, the research behind our assessment tools, and what facilitators and participants need to do in advance to make Block 1 effective. Finally, we'll explain what we call the rhythm of Block 1—how the session should proceed, step-by-step.

We all operate with assumptions about what leads to success, but it's often impossible for us to see where our theory of success might be flawed. Micromanagers don't realize that they're micromanagers—they think they're thorough, cautious, diligent. Workplace jerks believe fear gets results but don't see its negative impact on the loyalty of their best people. And so on. Structured self-reflection and coaching give us an opportunity to evaluate our theories of success. They can help us see past our own gaps in awareness, to process problems that are glaringly obvious to others. This place of "I don't know, but everyone else knows" is sometimes called the *bad breath zone*.

Consider the history of surgery. In the mid-nineteenth century, operations took place in a surgical theater with the patient, doctors, and operating table center stage, and spectators on bleacher-like benches. The audience was without gloves, masks, or sanitary hospital gowns, which to modern eyes seems insane. Not even the doctors wore gloves or masks. They operated in street clothes, and pinned the needles they used for surgery on their lapels. After each use, they'd wipe off the blood and pin them back on. If a bandage fell to the floor, it usually found its way back to the operating table. Surgeons even took pride in the bloodstains as a display of their experience. It's not surprising then that the postsurgical survival rate was low—so low that hospitals often forced patients to pay up front.[1]

The surgeons of that era had a terribly flawed hypothesis about disease transmission called the miasma theory. They believed that infections were the result of a noxious form of "bad air" that came from rotting body parts and fluids on the surgical floor. They continued to innovate with new tools, such as more sophisticated knives, and by airing out the surgical theater for longer periods between operations. But the mortality rate continued to be dismal.

It took a non-surgeon—French chemist Louis Pasteur—to figure out what the surgeons were missing. His experiments on fermentation led to his groundbreaking germ theory of disease. It then took years for him to convince surgeons that infections came from microscopic organisms entering open wounds. When germ theory was finally adopted into surgical practice, masks, gloves, full-body gowns, and sanitized surgical equipment were added to the protocol. Sure enough, the postsurgical survival rate jumped significantly.

It's obvious to us in the twenty-first century, but at the time, this shift was revolutionary for an entire medical field's theory of success. As this exemplifies, sometimes something you don't see, and perhaps are incapable of seeing on your own, hurts you the most in your pursuit of success.

Block 1's structured reflection process will help you reassess your own theory of success, just as surgeons did in the nineteenth century.

A Research-Backed Assessment Tool for Startup Teams

We created the process for Block 1 based on a study we led as the cocreators of the Effective Founders Project with Google for Startups (see appendix A for details). With nearly a thousand growth-stage startup founders and leaders as our study subjects, we asked their investors, cofounders, and direct reports to assess them across thirty-three leadership capabilities. Sixty percent of the participants were CEOs or CTOs, and all other functions were represented. We collected more than 250,000 data points, creating an exceptionally deep and broad assessment of startup leaders around the globe.

The Effective Founders Project dug into that data and put the most and least effective founders under a microscope. Here are the seven key strategies we derived, which are cornerstones of the Bonfire Moment feedback structure:

1. **Treat people like volunteers.** The best employees are like volunteers—they'll work passionately for a challenging but meaningful mission. They also have options. Talented people work where they choose to work, and as the adage goes, people leave bosses, not companies. Create a talent monopoly by understanding the psychology of your employees.
2. **Protect the team from distractions.** While founders are typically seen as easily distracted by new ideas, the best ones

create focus and clarity. Set clear goals and priorities to build momentum for your team, which in turn fuels better performance and morale.

3. **Minimize unnecessary micromanagement.** While data shows that micromanaging can be helpful in certain situations, the most effective leaders aim to delegate work in order to scale both themselves and their businesses. Micromanaging can be a fatal flaw, especially for CEOs.

4. **Invite disagreement.** You want your team to be able to engage in a conflict of ideas, not personalities. Founders consistently undervalue giving teams an opportunity to voice their opinions, while employees value it highly. Encourage open team dialogues early and often.

5. **Preserve interpersonal equity.** Violated expectations are the main source of conflict in startups. The most effective teams openly discuss and document what they expect from each other and constantly evaluate interpersonal equity—does each of you feel that expectations are fair?

6. **Keep pace with expertise.** Leaders need to know enough about each role to hire the right people and help develop their team. Ninety-three percent of the most effective founders have the expertise (e.g., in coding, sales, finance) to manage the work with competence.

7. **Overcome discouragement.** While most would expect self-confidence to grow with time, the most effective founders are not nearly as confident as the least effective. Build a support system, and know how to ask for help in order to overcome doubt.

Taking a Hard Look at Yourself

We've adapted the results of the Effective Founders Project into a question-based self-reflection tool that everyone can access through our website during their Bonfire Moment. While it can be used at any time in any context, we think individuals will gain the most from it during the focused process of the workshop.

After each participant answers about thirty questions, the tool delivers a summary report that provides an overall rating of their (self-assessed) leadership capability across the seven strategies of effective founders. The tool then gives feedback about each of the questions, categorized under each of the seven strategies.

Participants will end up with three types of data points:

1. **Overall assessment:** They'll see which strategies they consciously invest in and excel at, while also uncovering areas they've overlooked due to lack of awareness, effort, or ability.
2. **Comparisons to our dataset of founders/leaders:** They'll see how their self-assessment compares to those of the thousands of leaders who have used this tool. While we recognize that leaders often find themselves in unique contexts that require tailored strategies, we think this benchmarking is useful. Consider it an indication of the level of difficulty of the seven strategies—you may find some of them personally easier or harder to implement compared to our database of prior participants.
3. **Potential hidden strengths and weaknesses:** We indicate which strategies leaders tend to mistakenly think they perform competently (or incompletely). Based on our original study that invited feedback from cofounders, direct reports, managers and investors, the report identifies those areas statistically prone to gaps in awareness. It serves as a reminder that we may sometimes misjudge our own abilities.

We've found that this self-assessment tool uncovers some important areas that participants can reflect more deeply on and address with the help of their team. An alternative option that some Bonfire Moment teams choose is a 360-degree feedback tool, which solicits feedback in advance from the participants' colleagues, managers, and direct reports. The 360-degree option requires a lot more preparation time but can yield even more insights as leaders face hard truths about how others view their leadership styles. Details about getting access to our 360-degree feedback tool can be found in appendix C.

The Rhythm of Block 1

We call the step-by-step outline of what happens next the *rhythm of the block*. Facilitators will find the full rhythm of the day in appendix B. What follows are guidelines for each step of Block 1.

Block 1: Face Hard Truths

9:00 a.m.	**Start:** The facilitator sets the group's expectations by sharing an overview of the day and some ground rules.
9:15 a.m.	**Self-assessment:** The facilitator prepares the team to assess their individual skills by sharing the underlying structure behind the assessment questions. After filling out their questions on the online tool, participants read the summary of insights and write down some of their early reflections.
9:45 a.m.	**Peer coaching:** Each teammate gets twenty minutes to focus on one area where they'd like input from the group. This is an opportunity to untangle the thoughts and reactions they might have from the self-assessment summary.
11:05 a.m.	**Fifteen-minute break:** Congrats! You're now done with the first block.

Start: Setting Up for the Day

We recommend that everyone move their chairs into a circle with no table or other obstructions. This isn't a hard-and-fast rule, but we've found that this setup—with everyone able to see everyone else—creates the space for open, honest dialogue.

The facilitator, in tandem with the team leader, should briefly explain why they're all gathered for a Bonfire Moment. Reminding everyone of their team's backstory can be helpful, whether they've been a team for only a few months or for several years, and whether they're in trouble at the moment or simply trying to upgrade from good to great.

The facilitator should start by citing some of the research covered in chapter 1, noting that people problems are the number one risk to startup success. Next, they talk a bit about what the team is capable of when operating at its best: making better decisions, moving faster, feeling more motivated and energetic. This helps orient the team around the *why*: Why are we here? Why did we pick this agenda? Why now?

The facilitator should then explain the ground rules to help the team maximize this experience. We require at least four major rules:[2]

1. **No screens:** Laptops, phones, and tablets all need to be stowed away, muted, and kept at arm's length, except during breaks. Everyone should take old-school notes, with pen and paper. At some points during the day, there will be options to view or contribute to a shared document, but those will be exceptions.
2. **No bullshit:** One of the core principles of the Bonfire Moment is radical honesty. This is not the time to be in pitch mode; people need to hit pause on their usual default to optimism. This will be time for real talk.
3. **No bragging:** Job titles and credentials are irrelevant today, as the whole team wrestles with their problems as equals. For today, at least, it doesn't matter who went to a top-ten university, who owns the most equity, who has an MBA, or who launched a given feature.
4. **No spilling:** The Bonfire Moment is a confidential and private space. Everyone should promise to keep these conversations totally confidential. For this reason, we ask investors not to be part of the workshop.

Don't be surprised if some people want to jump ahead to learn what's going to happen during the later blocks of the workshop. A good facilitator will avoid talking about the rest of the day, other than letting people know the general idea behind each block and roughly when the breaks will be. At this point, everyone should be focused entirely on Block 1. After taking any questions about the process or ground rules, the facilitator should dive into the feedback section.

Self-Assessment: Prepare, Complete, and Reflect

Before asking the team to fill out their self-assessments, the facilitator should take five minutes to explain how the assessment is structured (see the discussion on this earlier in the chapter) and offer some advice for responding to areas that need fixing (more on this in a bit). Then everyone gets about twenty-five minutes of silent time to work on their self-assessment, then read, digest, and take notes on the responses provided by the online tool.

The summary at the conclusion of the self-assessment will include an explanation of the seven strategies of effective founders, which align with the questions the participants had just been asked. Then the summary section will give the participants' scores, with benchmarking to the median leaders in our dataset.

One big challenge for the facilitator is helping participants process the summary report, which can reveal important skills they've neglected to develop. It may stir up defensiveness or other negative feelings. No one in the room should ignore these responses, because emotions are data. Emotions help us understand what we care most deeply about, our hopes and fears for the startup, our anxieties about the future, our questions about our self-worth.

Also, everyone should try to avoid the *fundamental attribution error*. Any negative action might be blamed on internal factors (such as a person's character, personality traits, or work ethic) or external factors (such as being dropped into a high-stress situation, lack of sleep, or bad luck). Psychologists have found that people tend to blame external factors for their own shortcomings but internal factors for other people's shortcomings. For instance, if you've ever assumed that someone else failed a test because they were dumb but that *you* failed a test because it was unfairly hard (or the teacher wasn't effective), that's the fundamental attribution error. So be skeptical of any sweeping generalizations about the external factors that contributed to the weaknesses surfaced by this self-assessment.

As participants digest and make notes on their results before returning to the group circle, they can plan to respond to gaps they've discovered in three possible ways:

1. **Ignore.** Sometimes there's a good reason to disregard some strategies in our framework. One founder chose to ignore some aspects of the summary while they were in the middle of a painful cost-cutting period that unforeseen market factors necessitated.
2. **Start.** It's likely the gaps are simply a result of not knowing what great leadership looks like. Before starting, it's important to consider how many of the leadership strategies are relevant in the current situation, and which ones a leader should prioritize given their limited time.
3. **Shift.** Changing habitual behaviors is hard, of course, but the self-assessment can serve as a wake-up call for those who may have previously refused to change their leadership style. This wake-up call can launch a process of seeking help, to learn about new concrete actions to take on the road to personal and professional growth.

Peer Coaching: Get Input on One Area to Fix

After the group processes their self-assessment summary, the facilitator will guide them into the peer coaching phase. The ideal size of a coaching group is four people (though five is better than three), so break up into subgroups if you have more than five. Each team member will get twenty minutes to be coached by the group on a single gap they've surfaced. As we saw in the Fisk example, this person might choose a problem that's especially hard to address. Or they might choose a new gap they had not been aware of previously. Either way, the group will take turns asking questions, listening intently, and brainstorming solutions.

The facilitator should ask the participant who is being coached (the "coachee") four sets of questions, one at a time, in order:

1. **"What challenge do you want to work through in the next twenty minutes and why is it important to you?"** The goal is to gain an appreciation of the problem and not miss any important details. At times, the challenge presented by the coachee needs further clarification if it's overly broad or vague. For instance, one founder wanted to work on motivating her team. As they listened and asked for a few clarifications, it was clear that the founder herself was struggling with motivation after a recent customer pitch that they badly needed to win fell through. She opted to tackle that challenge instead. If anyone attempts to jump into solution mode, it's important to hold them off. Spend three minutes on this question.

2. **"What have you tried so far and what are you thinking of doing?"** This is an opportunity for the participant to speak; the group should respond at this point only with clarifying questions. The goal is to understand the *coachee's* perspective on solutions, such as why certain ideas have worked or failed. The more everyone understands what the coachee has already considered, the more productive the next step will be. Again, you want to hear only questions from the group, not solutions (not even solutions couched in question form). Spend five minutes here.

3. **"Would you like suggestions from the group?"** Once they agree, the coachee is asked to turn their chair around and remain silent while the rest of the group brainstorms possible solutions as if the subject isn't in the room. The participant can take notes but not interrupt. The reason for this is twofold: we want the group to feel unencumbered by the coachee

responding to every idea either verbally or through facial reactions, and we don't want the coachee to feel obliged to accept all suggestions. For the group, the goal is to generate as many suggestions as possible and not spend too much time on any one idea. Suggestions might come in the form of things to do, questions that the coachee might ask, or fresh perspectives on the challenge that might reshape the problem. For instance, someone might say to a founder who struggles with motivation, "I think losing motivation is just a part of the cycle, and once we win the next pitch, things are probably going to feel very different. Maybe the way to address it is not to focus on it." Spend ten minutes brainstorming.

4. **"Which of these ideas interest you enough to act on in the next thirty days?"** When answering this final question, the coachee turns back around to rejoin the group. This might be a good time for the coachee to clarify some points that were unclear. The group should check that the actions chosen are limited to two or three, concrete and doable in the next month. "I'll try harder" is not a clear way forward. "I will block out an hour each week to revisit the vision of our team and how we're tracking" hits the mark. This is a quick two-minute wrap-up, before you move to the next person.

Twenty minutes in the spotlight may feel like a long time, but most participants say it flies by. They often wish the peer coaching session could keep going, because the insights are so helpful.

After each team member gets their turn in the hot seat, Block 1 is completed. Everyone can cool off for fifteen minutes before returning for Block 2.

Chapter 9

Block 2—Notice Hidden Dynamics

The second block of the Bonfire Moment offers your team insight into hidden dynamics—an opportunity to explore the motivations, work preferences, and expectations of team members, who will write User Guides as a tool to address current and anticipated conflicts. At the end of this block, the team is likely to find common ground on their aspirations for the startup and mutual understanding around feedback styles, conflict areas, and potential breakup scenarios.

This chapter offers an overview of the ideas that went into the construction of the User Guide. Then we break down the rhythm of Block 2 and offer guidelines for facilitators as they lead a team through it.

We created the User Guide to give teams access to the same kind of manual they would get with a new smartphone or laptop. Why shouldn't people also come with some basic instructions on how to work with them effectively and troubleshoot when they malfunction? So we brainstormed questions to help teams understand each other, learn how to get the best out of each other, minimize sources of potential conflict, and find healthier ways to resolve the kinds of conflicts that inevitably occur.

The likelihood of smooth sailing through an entire startup journey is virtually zero. Many people assume that as time goes on, a good team will just keep getting better, as this graph illustrates:

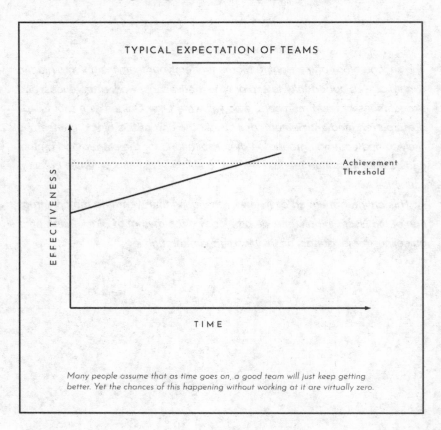

TYPICAL EXPECTATION OF TEAMS

Achievement Threshold

EFFECTIVENESS

TIME

Many people assume that as time goes on, a good team will just keep getting better. Yet the chances of this happening without working at it are virtually zero.

The typical reality for team performance is much less linear, as we learned from the research of Princeton-trained social psychologist Bruce Tuckman. The four stages of team development—*Forming*, *Storming*, *Norming*, and *PERFORMING*—were originally conceptualized in his groundbreaking research, which has maintained its significance through the decades.

Forming is when team members first get to know each other, establish roles and responsibilities, and define team objectives and goals. This period is usually characterized by a positive atmosphere of goodwill, where team members are patient with each other's idiosyncrasies and tolerant of individual approaches to doing the work.

But soon after, team members are likely to experience some conflict and tension as they express their opinions, struggle to find common

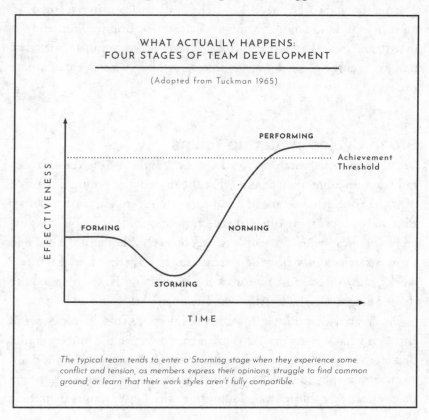

WHAT ACTUALLY HAPPENS:
FOUR STAGES OF TEAM DEVELOPMENT

(Adopted from Tuckman 1965)

PERFORMING

Achievement Threshold

EFFECTIVENESS

FORMING

NORMING

STORMING

TIME

The typical team tends to enter a Storming stage when they experience some conflict and tension, as members express their opinions, struggle to find common ground, or learn that their work styles aren't fully compatible.

ground, or learn that their work styles aren't fully compatible. This is the Storming stage, when many teams begin to doubt whether they'll be successful together. Some even give up at this early point.

If the team progresses, they'll enter the Norming stage, when they start to understand each other's strengths and weaknesses and differences in work style. If they can agree on norms and standards for behavior, communication, and decision-making, they can reach their highest potential in the Performing stage. But the cycle may repeat whenever new members join the team, or when externalities such as new competition or a major strategic pivot push the team back into the Storming stage.[1]

The User Guide is designed to help a team spend as little time as possible Storming and accelerate more quickly to the Norming stage. The reason it's so effective—and the tool that startup teams find most helpful in the months and years after their Bonfire Moment—is that it asks teams to work through the most common factors that lead to recurring, sustained conflicts, which we refer to as storm cycles.

Storm Cycles in Startup Teams

We've found that when personal conflicts and ongoing tensions derail teams, people often assume that the underlying problem is a lack of trust. So they invest money and time on improving trust, whether that means organizing fun events after hours, doing trust-building exercises, or simply urging people to rely on each other more. Although those strategies may provide a temporary boost that lasts for a few weeks, they often fail to address the underlying issues that require deeper diagnosis. The startup is in Tuckman's Storming stage.

We created a diagnostic flowchart of questions to help leaders work through what's going on. As they move down the list, the dynamics become less obvious and it gets harder for leaders to elicit honest answers. But if they succeed in getting answers all the way down, they're more effectively able to design solutions, with better results than these trust-building events. The completed User Guides can be extremely valuable tools in doing this diagnostic:

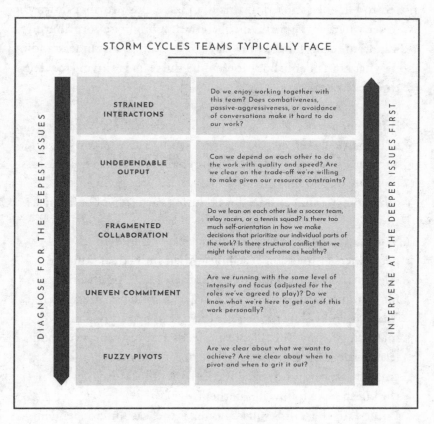

STORM CYCLES TEAMS TYPICALLY FACE

DIAGNOSE FOR THE DEEPEST ISSUES

STRAINED INTERACTIONS	Do we enjoy working together with this team? Does combativeness, passive-aggressiveness, or avoidance of conversations make it hard to do our work?
UNDEPENDABLE OUTPUT	Can we depend on each other to do the work with quality and speed? Are we clear on the trade-off we're willing to make given our resource constraints?
FRAGMENTED COLLABORATION	Do we lean on each other like a soccer team, relay racers, or a tennis squad? Is there too much self-orientation in how we make decisions that prioritize our individual parts of the work? Is there structural conflict that we might tolerate and reframe as healthy?
UNEVEN COMMITMENT	Are we running with the same level of intensity and focus (adjusted for the roles we've agreed to play)? Do we know what we're here to get out of this work personally?
FUZZY PIVOTS	Are we clear about what we want to achieve? Are we clear about when to pivot and when to grit it out?

INTERVENE AT THE DEEPER ISSUES FIRST

Some more detail about these five types of storm cycles, sequenced from easiest to hardest to diagnose:

Strained interactions are at the top because they're likely apparent to every team member and often to outsiders as well. When you spot combative, passive-aggressive, or avoidant behavior, don't rush to fix it immediately. We find that when people gripe about personality conflicts, there's often an underlying issue with dependability. Rarely is the issue simply a "difficult personality."

Undependable output can trigger chronic mistrust, because everyone wants their teammates to deliver work with reliable quality and speed. Everyone gets frustrated when a colleague constantly over-promises and underdelivers, or when deadlines are repeatedly committed to but then missed. If this is an issue, push further down the list to see whether fragmented collaboration might be contributing.

Fragmented collaboration can stem from a misunderstanding about what kind of collaboration model the team is striving for. There are three basic options:

1. **Interdependent,** or the soccer team model, expects teammates to be mutually reliant. One player's work feeds directly into another's, and any weak link in the chain hurts the whole team. Software development teams operate this way, giving each other lots of input and feedback during each step of building a code base.
2. **Sequential,** or the relay race model, expects individual performers to focus on excelling at their individual skill sets. Clean handoffs are important, but there's less opportunity for teammates to cover for each other, as in the soccer model. These assembly-line models are often seen between sales and marketing teams. The sales team needs a steady supply of good leads to do their job. Marketing teams use ads, direct mail, email marketing, and social media to get those leads, and then the salespeople follow up on them.
3. **Pooled,** or the tennis squad model, is the least interdependent. A tennis squad trains together and travels to tournaments together, but all matches are individual contests, and each player is incentivized to focus on their own record. Many business teams unknowingly employ this model, often without realizing that it is not well suited to most situations.

If you haven't already, ask if your startup is trying to act like a soccer team, relay racers, or a tennis squad. You might find that some people need to change the way they collaborate to fit your preferred model. You might also ask if there are any structural conflicts that can be reframed as acceptable or even healthy. (Go back to chapter 4 for a refresher on the differences between personal conflict and structural conflict.) If you determine collaboration is fragmented in an unhealthy way, keep going down the list to uncover what might be causing it.

Uneven commitment can be detected if team members are clearly not operating at the same levels of intensity and focus. This can lead to feelings of unfairness, which if left unaddressed can tear a partnership apart. But it's natural for people in certain roles to have more or less intense workloads at different times. You may have to temper expectations of equal effort by reminding people of those natural ups and downs. If you think the real issue is uneven commitment, dig deeper. The problem could be a confusing change in strategy or a strategy that fails to get people on board.

Fuzzy pivots are shifts in mission or strategy that cause some team members to question whether they want to remain part of the startup. Maybe what you're doing now is not what some members want to sign up for or feel equipped to contribute to effectively. Or maybe the pivot confused the team because it wasn't explained clearly enough or because it wasn't entirely clear in the founders' minds to begin with.

We recommend that leaders tackle this checklist from top to bottom during their initial assessment, but then resolve issues starting from the bottom after evaluating the situation. For instance, after working through the questions, you might find that the deepest source of your storm cycle is a recent pivot that wasn't clearly laid out. It's best to address the fuzzy pivot first, then work back upward to deal with other problems, such as commitment gaps and strained interactions. By addressing a fuzzy pivot, you may find that many of the issues self-resolve. Dig deep to figure out what's really going on, then start at the deepest level to begin an intervention.

The Rhythm of Block 2

Here's an overview of the time you'll spend together in this block, along with guidance for facilitators.

As Block 2 begins, the group has just reflected on their leadership

Block 2: Notice Hidden Dynamics

11:20 a.m.	**User Guide overview:** The facilitator shares the rationale behind the User Guide, its sections, and the right mindset to approach this task.
11:30 a.m.	**Individual authoring:** The team spends an hour filling out their User Guides.
12:30 p.m.	**Team huddle:** The team shares their responses for each section of the User Guide, over a long lunch.
1:50 p.m.	**Ten-minute break:** Well done! Tidy up the space after lunch and take a quick break.

strengths and weaknesses, and each member has gotten the team to help them through an area for improvement. Their current mood might be reflective, affirming, eager for action, or some combination. The facilitator should restart at 11:20 exactly, because there's no time to waste. If the group starts late, it will throw off the rest of the day.

User Guide Overview: Setting Up a Liberating Structure

The group should be back in their circle (chairs only, no table). The facilitator hands out blank copies of the User Guide, downloaded from our website or copied from appendix D. It should be filled out with a pen, not on a laptop or phone. Paper both minimizes distractions and keeps these very private and sensitive thoughts off digital ink, at least until the team is comfortable sharing what's in their User Guides after the session.

The facilitator's first task is to explain that the guide is a *liberating structure* that will help them explore topics that don't naturally come up in casual conversation. While it can be hard for people to disclose personal feelings, this step is key to surfacing points of contention within the team. The idea of a liberating structure in an intentional juxtaposition of seemingly opposing ideas; *liberating* suggests freedom, autonomy, and flexibility, while *structure* implies rules, order, and boundaries.

Imagine being in the middle of a vast empty field with no perimeters —it can be difficult to determine where safety ends and danger begins. But if a perimeter wall is built to enclose the field, you would know exactly where the safety line is, and you might be more inclined to explore all the way up to the wall and even look beyond it. The structure of the User Guide signals that it's a safe space to explore freely.

It's important to stress that the goal is neither fake harmony nor confrontation. Fake harmony won't help the team improve their mutual trust and cohesion. On the other hand, confrontation can trigger damaging reactions such as defensiveness, stonewalling, or aggressive language. Confrontation can also favor some over others; some cultures see it as a useful way to "clear the air," while others may perceive it as a sign of immaturity or a risky lack of self-control, possibly leading someone to say something they will deeply regret.

Even though the three parts of the User Guide are mostly self-explanatory, facilitators should go over them first to build familiarity with the questions and give people a sense of how much time to spend on each. Here are some key points worth making about each section:

Part 1: Personal motivations. Motivations impact the kind of energy each team member brings into the company, how they make decisions, and how they interact with others. Conflicting motivations can easily cause conflict. We ask participants to reflect on a simple heuristic: head, heart, and wallet. Did they mainly join the startup for the intellectual challenge (head), for the chance to make a meaningful impact (heart), or to build their personal capital, either financial or social (wallet)? (You'll find more complete descriptions in the User Guide.)

Part 2: Working style. Each person has a unique way of getting stuff done. The more we understand each other's preferences, and the reasons behind those preferences, the easier it is to collaborate effectively. The questions in this part will clarify the strengths and weaknesses each person brings to their work, how colleagues can bring out the best (and worst) in each other, and the most effective ways to offer feedback and resolve conflict.

Part 3: The partnership. Unclear mutual expectations and feelings of unfairness are two of the biggest sources of conflict in any startup team. This section helps teams clarify what they expect from each other, how fair they feel the partnership has been so far, and how they might plan for worst-case scenarios. This is the hardest section because it asks teams to open up about their deepest frustrations.

At this point, the facilitator can announce the start of a silent hour for reflection and writing. As the team spreads out to private corners of the room, they should be reminded that they will need every minute of the hour to do it properly. In fact, they will probably wish they had even longer.

FAQ for the Reflection and Writing Hour

The facilitator can expect some questions during the writing hour. Here are a few we've been asked repeatedly while people work through their User Guides:

Why is it called a User Guide? We're not products!
Of course you're not products, but the metaphor helps capture the goal: making it easier for colleagues to understand each other's motivations, working styles, expectations, feelings of fairness, and potential challenges. By being explicit about these things, it will be easier to meet each other halfway, build trust, and work more effectively. The goal is not to manipulate or literally use each other, but to promote open communication, empathy, and collaboration.

Will we be forced to share personal details that we're not comfortable disclosing?
No, you won't be forced to disclose anything. We understand that this activity can feel scary, and it only works if people *choose* to take a risk by opening up more than usual. Having said that, we strongly encourage your participation in this exchange of information and feelings. By sharing your motivations, working

style, and expectations, you will create a shared understanding that can help the whole team. If you take a chance by being as candid and vulnerable as possible in your User Guide, the resulting bond with your colleagues can greatly improve your future experience at work.

I don't feel comfortable telling people how to work with me—shouldn't I be able to adapt to other people's styles?

Your discomfort is understandable, but collaboration and communication will suffer if only some members of the team adapt to the needs and preferences of others. The more your colleagues get to know you, the better they can work with you in a way that enables you to be productive and successful. The User Guide is designed to make everyone's experience better, with fewer misunderstandings and fewer avoidable conflicts. But no one will be forced to change the way they relate to each other.

What if my answers evolve over time?

The User Guide is a snapshot of what you're thinking and feeling today. Some of your answers will likely change as your role evolves, as you gain more experience in working and leading, and as the company scales and pivots. Your answers might even change based on feedback you hear from your team during the Bonfire Moment. All of that is fine, and you'll be able to modify your answers in the future.

I'm done, with a lot of time to spare. What should I do?

Please go back through the User Guide again, from the top, and see where you might be able to share more details and insights, with more generosity and team spirit. The more you put into it, the more you will get out of it. Sometimes it helps to put it down for a few minutes and stare out the window while pondering the toughest questions. For people who prefer action, reflection can be hard—but it's worth the effort.

The Team Huddle: Watching Cohesion Take Shape

When the writing hour ends at 12:30 (following ten- and five-minute warnings), the facilitator should announce that it's time for lunch. This will start with a few minutes for people to stretch, use the restroom, and grab whatever food has been ordered. Then the facilitator can explain that the group will discuss their User Guides, one section at a time, while they eat. Everyone will be expected to share their answers and contribute to the discussion prompted by other people's answers.

The facilitator's main role during this huddle is to keep time, take notes, and manage the flow of conversation, making sure everyone gets a chance to share their thoughts. Ideally, the facilitator should speak as little as possible, stepping in only if the conversation stalls or if there are challenges or disagreements that need addressing. On rare occasions (as we saw in the Fisk example), the facilitator might need to join the discussion to help defuse any tense dynamics that emerge. It may be helpful to ask questions that help unpack any disagreements, while trying to keep the exchange respectful and productive.

In most cases, this huddle will bring the team together like nothing else they've experienced in a professional setting. The liberating structure of the User Guide nudges them to talk about sensitive topics they'd probably avoid in any other setting. As people share their different perspectives in turn, listeners may experience flashes of insight. *So that's why she's so obsessed with the user experience! That's why he keeps talking about when we might get acquired or go public! That's why he gets so upset when I check in on how he's progressing toward a deadline!*

In many cases, team members find that they have more in common than they initially thought. They discover shared values, interests, and working styles, which helps to create a stronger sense of unity and alignment.

What's particularly powerful is that—unlike in a typical work meeting—no one can dominate the conversation, and no one can intentionally stay silent, because everyone has to answer every question. The team huddle creates a level playing field, which can be transformative for those who may be more introverted or hesitant to share their thoughts.

As Block 2 ends at 1:50 and everyone helps clean up from lunch, the team might wish this conversation could keep going. The facilitator can reassure them that, in a sense, the huddle will continue long after the Bonfire Moment. Their User Guides will give them the raw material for many future discussions. Some teams have everyone's guides scanned and uploaded to a shared drive, so people can easily consult them in the future. One founder, for instance, became much more comfortable giving feedback once she could revisit her team's User Guides for guidance on how they preferred to receive it. (In chapter 12, we'll share more ways in which startups have extended these tools beyond the workshop.)

After another ten-minute break it's time to begin Block 3, which is often the most transformative part of the Bonfire Moment.

Chapter 10

Block 3—Drop the Masks

You're now entering the most raw and unreserved moment of the day. In Block 3, your team has an opportunity to reflect on their self-doubts, fears, and insecurities.

The main activity for this block is the Bullshit Circle, where we invite teams to reflect on and share the pretenses and self-justifying half-truths they put out into the world, often as a facade to conceal their deeper self-doubts and insecurities. It builds trust and team cohesion better than anything else we've seen.

This chapter shows how we created the Bullshit Circle and why it's effective. You'll also read our own stories of personal vulnerability, which we tell in Bonfire Moments that we facilitate, to show our willingness to make the same kind of disclosures that we ask teams to make. Finally, we'll go through the rhythm of Block 3, along with some essential instructions for facilitators.

The Origins of the Bullshit Circle

We created the Bullshit Circle as an antidote to the brag culture that dominates the startup ecosystem. Many founders feel pressure to project extreme confidence about their big ideas, their credentials, and the early traction of their startups. But privately (as we saw in chapter 5), many are plagued by perfectionist underconfidence, because everyone else seems to know exactly what they're doing.

The Bullshit Circle reassures startup founders that they're not alone, that *everyone* who comes into this work feels some kind of insecurity, anxiety, or self-doubt. It offers teams a psychological ice bath, waking them up to the prevalence of the impostor phenomenon.

We drew inspiration from research on the power of group psychotherapy.[1] Most people don't know that group therapy got its start in the military right after World War II, when there were too few psychologists available in the United States and the UK to do one-on-one counseling with the many veterans who displayed symptoms of post-traumatic stress disorder (PTSD). What began as a necessary compromise was quickly found to be a highly effective new process. By bringing together veterans who'd had similar traumatic experiences, group therapy offered participants a sense of shared understanding and mutual support from peers.[2] Today we know that, at least in some situations, group therapy is more effective than individual therapy.[3]

There are three features from group therapy that we built into the Bullshit Circle.[4]

The first is called *universality*—provoking the realization that the negative feelings participants thought were uniquely theirs are actually being widely experienced by peers. It's hard to wrestle with self-doubt and insecurity, and these challenges are compounded by a sense of isolation. Teammates tend to feel validated and relieved when shown that these difficult emotions are normal for everyone. "I thought it was just me" is a common reaction we hear after a Bullshit Circle.

The second feature is helping participants clarify what therapists call the *index event* behind their fear or insecurity. We ask everyone to reflect on an event or a pattern of experiences, often going back to their childhood or adolescence, that stands out in their memories.

By making connections between past and present, and hearing others make similar connections, team members can begin to explore some unresolved feelings and reduce the distress from those unpleasant memories. This will help them handle future challenges with greater resilience.

Finally, this experience creates a moment of *catharsis*. Sharing guarded personal stories and disclosing insecurities in a safe space can release bottled-up negative feelings. Letting them out can feel so cathartic that people often leave the Bullshit Circle with a surprising sense of lightness or inner calm.

Vulnerability Is a Flex: The Beautiful Mess Effect

It may seem like Block 3 is asking for a surprising level of vulnerability and self-disclosure. It is—but only because the eventual payoff justifies the initial discomfort of opening up to one's peers in this way.

Many people consider self-disclosure to be a sign of weakness or self-indulgence. But what an individual thinks of as a negative disclosure often turns out to be perceived very differently by others. Social psychologists describe a paradox called the *beautiful mess effect*.[5] Through several social experiments, they found that people who display vulnerability worry about appearing weak, inadequate, and flawed—a "mess." Yet others who witness their self-disclosures are more likely to describe those people as admirable, courageous, and strong. Several studies showed that people judged the self-disclosures of their peers about 15 percent more positively than they judged their own.

The researchers explain this incongruence as a matter of psychological distance. We each see our own vulnerability more clearly and intensely, because we have no distance from ourselves. We notice and criticize every flaw and mistake. But when we watch someone else be vulnerable through self-disclosure, we have the distance to be more objective, noticing both good and bad aspects.

In a business context, researchers at Harvard Business School and Wharton found something similar: while people feared seeming incompetent when asking for help, others perceived them as *more* competent. In fact, an advice seeker was judged to be 16 percent more competent than a self-sufficient individual working on the same difficult challenge.[6]

Traditional gender roles can contribute to these dynamics, according to the world's leading expert on vulnerability, Brené Brown. Both traditional masculinity and femininity experience shame in vulnerability, but through different triggers. Those who try to project traditional masculinity tend to avoid looking weak or incapable. And norms of traditional femininity can include perfectionism—the myth that women should "do it all, do it well," and not "let them see you sweat."[7]

By recognizing that vulnerability is a flex rather than a weakness, we can begin to dismantle these shame triggers and cultivate healthier, more authentic relationships with others. Embracing vulnerability allows us to learn from our experiences, grow as individuals, and foster more supportive, inclusive, and resilient teams.

The Bullshit Zone

Think back to what we learned about overconfidence and underconfidence in chapter 5. When you launch a new project or activity, your confidence is usually at its peak. As you learn more and build your skills, your confidence might erode; your growing expertise reveals how far away you currently *are* from true excellence. This awareness can push you to keep trying, working hard, doing your best. But with the pressures of the brag culture common in startups, many instead resort to self-preserving narratives driven by insecurity. At that point, they're entering the bullshit zone, and they begin repeating fundamentally dishonest narratives to their collaborators, investors, clients, friends, and family.

During the Bullshit Circle exercise, we ask participants to reflect on how they operate in their own bullshit zone. Are they subconsciously relying on one of three main types of self-preserving narratives—false optimism, false strength, or false detachment?

(A quick recap from chapter 5: False optimism is positive bravado

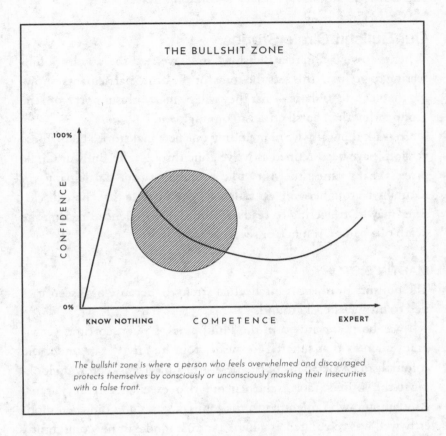

THE BULLSHIT ZONE

The bullshit zone is where a person who feels overwhelmed and discouraged protects themselves by consciously or unconsciously masking their insecurities with a false front.

used to steer the focus to new challenges, leading the team and investors to believe all is well. False strength is highlighting past successes or showing off one's expertise, while perhaps also acting arrogant and hiding any weakness. False detachment is keeping one's head down, trying to appear cool and independent, and using silence to avoid attention.)

When we ask participants to confront their self-preserving narratives, we're helping them articulate emotions that may be hard to describe. As we mentioned in the previous chapter, this establishes a liberating structure: they can better understand and describe behaviors that might have previously gone unnoticed or been misunderstood. Reaching complete self-awareness is a lifelong journey (if not an unattainable one), but participating in a Bullshit Circle can be a key step on that path.

Our Bullshit Circle Stories

Whenever we facilitate a Bullshit Circle, we lead the way by volunteering to go first. This sets the tone for the other participants, showing that it's safe to share—that they will be met with support from the group rather than harsh criticism or judgment.

To walk the walk, we're including our personal stories here. These versions have been refined as we've gone through the Bullshit Circle process many times; the story told by any first-time participant will naturally be rougher and less articulate. Please note that these disclosures may be triggering to readers who have experienced racism, the death of a parent, trauma, or severe anxiety.

MARTIN'S STORY

The bullshit I project is intellectual strength, because of insecurities tied to my racial background.

I was born and raised in the Philippines, a poor, corrupt, yet vibrant country that suffered for nearly four hundred years under the colonialism of the Spanish, Japanese, and Americans. I grew up looking to the United States as the benchmark of excellence in every arena. Any Filipino who migrated to the United States and did even modestly well was celebrated as a hero and role model in my community. So from a young age, I set my sights on doing the same.

But when I moved to the States in 2009 as a graduate student, the intimidation struck me hard. Among all the individuals in my circle, I found myself unconsciously feeling most uneasy around my white male peers. They were articulate and self-confident. I was impressed with their command of English. I grew up multilingual, and between home, school, and work, I had learned to juggle English with a couple of Philippine dialects plus some foreign languages, which made it hard to keep to a single lane in conversation. I often found myself fumbling for the right words and sentence structure in English. I was privately embarrassed by my strong Filipino accent—I thought it made me sound slow, clumsy, and unintelligent when I spoke English. As a result of these insecurities, I found it difficult to build genuine, relaxed friendships with my new peers. And even in my early thirties, when speaking in front of large crowds around the world, my eyes quickly scan for the white male audience members; when I see them, I can viscerally feel my defenses rising.

I believed early in my career that even when striving for the same goals and exerting equal effort as my American counterparts, I would fall short. So instead of feeling sorry for myself, I decided to put my head down and work harder than any of them. Whenever I heard others complain about not having long enough weekends, or dream about a four-day workweek, I told myself that while all that would be nice, it wasn't for me.

Long after grad school, I took great pleasure whenever anyone said they were impressed with my knowledge and research, or that my ideas were sharp and unique. This is a big part of the mask I wear, using a show of intellectual superiority to stand out.

These days, I've learned to embrace my personal history and ethnicity rather than run from them. In 2020, for instance, I was politely called out by a Black colleague for a microaggression against him, of which I was completely unaware. My inner voice wanted to shout back: "But I'm an outsider too! I'm one of you!" Days later, I realized I was no longer that unsure new immigrant in his early twenties. I now had some degree of power and privilege, and with it a moral duty to lift others up. I feel incredibly grateful that my colleague had the courage to speak up and offer me his helpful feedback.

Over the years, I've built strong personal and professional relationships with many kindhearted white colleagues, including Josh. They have helped me realize that the story I tell myself about who I am—and who they are—is distorted. Despite how confident people seem, we all privately carry insecurities. And while social privileges are real and shouldn't be ignored, people have more in common than they can see on the surface.

JOSH'S STORY

The bullshit I project is emotional distance, because what I've been really afraid of is looking incapable if people learn about my hidden past with trauma and anxiety.

When I first started working at Google in 2015, I didn't have much of a technical background. I had majored in biology and psychology as an undergrad and worked in the environmental sector for several years, as an outdoor wilderness guide and in a variety of jobs at environmental nonprofits. I moved to San Francisco on a whim to work for my college roommate's startup, which had just closed a Series A. I've always been up for an adventure, so I figured, why not try and see what happens? I had been at the company for six months when things there began to go south and the founder connected me with an entry-level role at Google.

Once I got there, I was working with colleagues who had been in tech their whole careers, some with more than twenty years of experience in the sector. I was immediately intimidated and made up for it by never asking questions, for fear of sounding dumb. I worked very long hours to catch up as fast as possible. But this attempt at self-reliance kept me from seeking out mentors with technical expertise, which could have accelerated my learning.

Even before joining the high-stress environment at Google, I was already predisposed to panic attacks and anxiety. My father unexpectedly passed away under tragic circumstances when I was in my mid-twenties. I was with him when it happened, and the traumatic experience left me with PTSD, as a therapist later diagnosed.

With that burden on my shoulders, and all the pressure to succeed in this unfamiliar and competitive environment, my only real coping strategy was to work even harder. I became obsessed with being the most prepared person in every meeting. I even shaved my beard for the first time in a decade to look more put together!

Then one day, I had a meeting where I was scheduled to present brand-new material to a group of people I had never worked with. I felt unprepared and stressed out, and suddenly, the walls of the small, windowless conference room started to close in on me. I was heading into a full-blown panic attack. I had to awkwardly excuse myself in the middle of my presentation so that I could head to the bathroom and let the panic run its course. It's hard to describe how awful panic attacks can be to those who've never had one: bizarre thoughts, sweating, heart palpitations, hyperventilation. It's an all-consuming feeling of impending doom. Only because I'd had several prior panic attacks did I know that the most severe of these symptoms would pass in a matter of minutes. Afterward, I messaged the group and apologized, giving a somewhat fake excuse that I was feeling unwell. I was too embarrassed to be fully honest.

Since then, I've made it a point to build more balance into my life and show up with more authenticity. I constantly pursue personal growth opportunities, such as attending meditation and health retreats, reading self-improvement books, and trying to pass along what I can to others, such as by working on this book with Martin. I still carry traces of impostor syndrome, and despite all this self-work, I still often tend to present an armored front instead of showing my most authentic self. Like all of us, I suppose, I'm very much a work in progress.

The Power of the Bullshit Circle

Now that you know our Bullshit Circle stories, have your perceptions of us changed? Do we now seem like real people rather than merely authors? Has your level of trust shifted? If we were teammates, how comfortable would you be to share your own story with us? And do you feel we'd be more likely to support you when our team goes through tough times?

Your answers to those questions will show you the potential power of Block 3. When it works, it can have a dramatic, lasting impact on the dynamics of a team. People often tell us they never saw their colleagues the same way again. Dropping their masks allowed them to see each other more clearly, more honestly.

Over time, we've refined the Bonfire Moment to provoke a range of emotions throughout the day. The responses are somewhat different for each participant, but the most common emotional journey looks almost like a roller coaster:

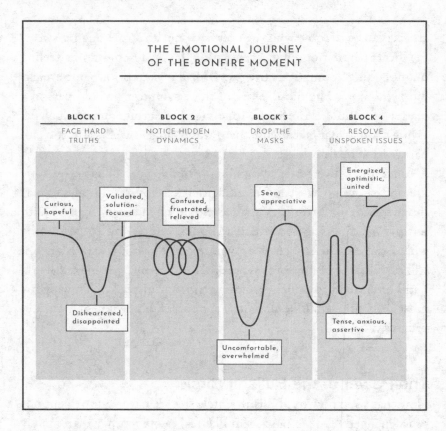

THE EMOTIONAL JOURNEY
OF THE BONFIRE MOMENT

The plunge of Block 3 may look scary, but we assure you, the view looks great from the top. We urge you to find your courage, hold on tight, and try to enjoy the ride!

The Rhythm of Block 3

This block stands out from the others in that it requires significantly more preparation to set up the physical space and frame the tone and guardrails for the activity. It also demands more flexibility, since you can't predict what stories people will share or how the team may react. The facilitator may have to use intuition to pivot in the moment, more like a jazz improviser than a classical pianist playing from sheet music.

Here's the summary, followed by details about each segment.

Block 3: Drop the Masks

Before 2:00 p.m.	**Set up the space:** The facilitator darkens the room and places pillows in a circle on the floor, with four laptops in the center showing the digital bonfire.
2:00 p.m.	**Circle up:** The facilitator explains the goals, structure, and guardrails of the self-disclosure exercise. Then the facilitator offers the first personal story, to set the tone. In silence, everyone else reflects on their fears and insecurities and the self-preserving narratives they may be using to mask them.
2:20 p.m.	**The Bullshit Circle:** Each team member shares their reflections. The others listen without passing judgment or offering advice. It's a time to genuinely connect on a human level.
2:50 p.m.	**Debrief:** After everyone finishes their stories, the team takes ten minutes to decompress, share realizations, and show gratitude for this moment of raw honesty.
3:00 p.m.	**Fifteen-minute break:** Congrats! You just finished the hardest part of the day. Time to stretch and fuel up for the final push.

Set Up the Space: Shift the Environment to Shift the Conversation

We encourage the facilitator to put extra care into preparing the space for Block 3 before the team arrives. Think about how you can use the environment to cue participants that they're about to have a different kind of conversation. While this is ultimately optional, the ideal setup would include:

> A room darkened with the help of heavy curtains.
> Good ventilation and a comfortable temperature.
> Large pillows or beanbags on the floor for sitting in a circle.
> Several laptops in the middle of the circle, playing a video loop of a bonfire with audio on. If you're able to do the Bullshit Circle outdoors and it's feasible to build an actual campfire, that's even better.

The environment really matters, because we're asking the group to do something they're not used to doing. The right setup will help them shift their state of mind. Interior designers call this neuroaesthetics—the use of color, lighting, scents, sounds, and spatial arrangements to induce different emotions. This conscious design of the workshop space will go a long way toward creating a memorable moment of deeper connection for the team.

Circle Up: Preparing for a Moment of Honesty

As we saw in the Fisk example, the facilitator should have the team sit on the floor pillows and prepare them for a moment when they will feel the most raw and vulnerable. The facilitator then walks through these key steps:

› Welcomes the group to the Bullshit Circle and explains what they're here to do. Explains the key ideas of the trap of confidence (see chapter 5) and the bullshit zone (see earlier in this chapter).
› Lays out the reflection task and hands out the fill-in-the-blank statements:

REFLECTION PROMPT FOR THE BULLSHIT CIRCLE

THE BULLSHIT I PROJECT TO OTHERS IS:

_____

BECAUSE WHAT I'M REALLY INSECURE OF IS:

_____

THE EXPERIENCE THAT FIRST CAUSED ME TO FEEL THIS INSECURITY WAS:

_____

› Explains self-preserving narratives (false optimism, false strength, and false detachment) in the context of "the bullshit I project to others." This visual can drive home the types of narratives:

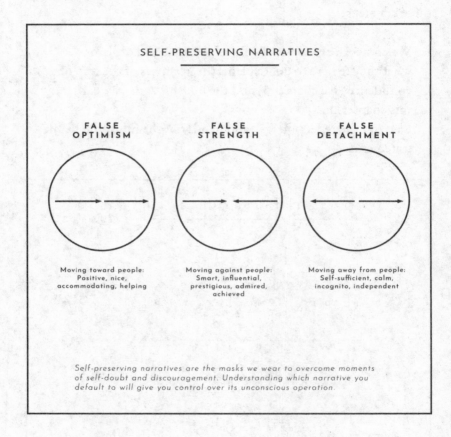

SELF-PRESERVING NARRATIVES

FALSE OPTIMISM

Moving toward people: Positive, nice, accommodating, helping

FALSE STRENGTH

Moving against people: Smart, influential, prestigious, admired, achieved

FALSE DETACHMENT

Moving away from people: Self-sufficient, calm, incognito, independent

Self-preserving narratives are the masks we wear to overcome moments of self-doubt and discouragement. Understanding which narrative you default to will give you control over its unconscious operation.

› Explains the rules of engagement. This will *not* be a discussion, or a time to coach people out of their insecurities. We use the acronym JOIN: don't *judge*, don't *offer* advice, don't *interrupt*, and share *nothing* outside the circle, to protect each other's privacy. Don't even discuss anything said here with each other in the future, unless the speaker is there and explicitly requests a conversation about it. When someone else is sharing, the only acceptable response is appreciation and encouragement.

RULES OF ENGAGEMENT

✕ JUDGE

✕ OFFER ADVICE

✕ INTERRUPT

NOTHING LEAVES THE
BULLSHIT CIRCLE

> Share your own story. This is where the facilitator puts on
  a participant hat. By sharing their own insecurities, the
  facilitator further clarifies the goals of the Bullshit Circle.
  More important, this first story sets the wheels of reciprocal
  self-disclosure in motion. Participants may also see parts of
  themselves in the facilitator's story, drawing them into deeper
  reflection.
> Give people time to reflect on what they want to share. This
  often requires only a few minutes, though some groups might
  need longer.

During all these preliminary steps, the facilitator should try to
maintain a calm, nondramatic tone. Go with what's natural and true
to your communication style. We don't want participants to think

their facilitator has gone into cult leader mode. It's still just a group of colleagues talking, but with more openness and vulnerability than usual. It can help to sprinkle in a bit of humor when it feels appropriate.

A good facilitator will encourage participation without sliding into excessive pressure. Different people will come to this activity with varying degrees of enthusiasm; some might be eager to open up, while others might be deeply inhibited or mistrustful. It's important to acknowledge that most people feel somewhat uncomfortable while sharing their previously private fears and insecurities, but the benefits usually outweigh any discomfort. Nevertheless, a good facilitator won't push any participant so hard as to trigger a fight-or-flight response. No one will be compelled to share.

It can help to line up someone to share first after the facilitator, especially if the group hasn't been very forthcoming during the earlier blocks. Ideally, this first sharer should be respected enough to put the rest of the group at ease. Usually this won't be the most senior person in the room. It's optional to either tell the group that one person was privately invited to go first, or just have the first sharer volunteer to make it seem organic.

The Bullshit Circle: What to Look Out For

If the setup and the circle up have gone smoothly, the facilitator won't need to do much during the actual sharing of personal stories other than keep an eye on the clock and gently rein in any long-winded monologues. At the end of each share, it's important to acknowledge the bravery of the speaker and thank them for participating. But there's usually no need to provide commentary or ask follow-up questions.

Please keep in mind that it's rare for every participant to have a breakthrough during their story. In our experience, about one third of the team will truly go deep with the exercise and reveal something profound. Another third will do the task sincerely but might not have the depth of self-awareness to tell an emotionally resonant story. (Or perhaps they've had the privilege of leading lives with no hidden fears, insecurities, or personal demons.) The final third will struggle with the task and will either begrudgingly put in minimal effort or remain silent. Please don't judge any of these responses. Everyone is at different points in their respective journeys of self-discovery. Even someone who barely participates or who refuses to speak at all may find that this experience triggers private reflections later on, which may benefit both them and the team down the line.

Upon noticing any negative reactions to sharing, the facilitator can help participants self-regulate. For example: "I notice that some of you seem frustrated," or "I'm seeing a lot of discomfort right now." You don't need to ask why or probe further; just acknowledging the vibe out loud can be very helpful.

If a speaker is really struggling at any point, it's okay to call for a break and urge them to stretch, take some deep breaths, or go for a short walk. Reassure them that it's common to experience a range of emotions during the workshop. Others can continue to ponder or journal during an unexpected break.

If there's an awkward moment when you're down to just one or two participants who have declined to share, the facilitator should give them a respectful final nudge, then move on. Say something like, "Let's take a few more seconds to see if anyone else wants to share their story. But remember, no one should feel compelled to do it."

In rarer cases, the facilitator may observe some potentially problematic situations that require special responses:

> **Is the sharer deploying too much humor?** Cracking a joke or two can break the tension when describing a personal problem or a troubling past experience. But if the story begins to sound like a stand-up comedy routine, the speaker may be overly relying on humor as a defense mechanism. You might interrupt at a natural point and try to get back on track with a question like, "How did that experience affect you?"
> **Is the sharer showing physical signs of distress?** A shaking leg, trembling hands, or a facial tic may indicate particularly intense emotions, as can harder-to-spot signs such as sweaty

palms or dilated pupils. If such reactions seem out of character, the sharer may be pushing themselves too hard to express their thoughts clearly. The facilitator might gently interrupt, offer a pause and maybe a glass of water, then let them continue after someone else goes.

> **Is the sharer engaging in excessive post-rationalization?** Some participants will spend 20 percent of their time disclosing the origins of their insecurities but use the other 80 percent to explain lessons learned, insist that everything is great now, or offer advice to others based on their experiences. This could be a sign that they're struggling to dig deeper into their inner life. The facilitator doesn't have to jump in and intervene, but it can be helpful to nudge the story back on track. One might say something like, "Thanks for those great lessons. Can you tell us more about what fears and insecurities you experience when you're working on projects, meeting with investors, or collaborating with your team?"

> **Is the sharer talking about self-harm, suicidal thoughts, depression, or other major problems?** We're not therapists or psychologists, and neither are most facilitators. If someone is showing signs of suicidality or other serious harm to their well-being, it's crucial they receive care. Take them aside (unless doing so would put others in danger), and make sure they receive appropriate professional help.[8] Even if the sharer resists because of the stigma around mental health support, do your best to reassure them that everyone on the team wants them to get help and feel better. Then follow up one-on-one at the end of the day.

Debrief and Move Forward

After everyone who wants to share has had their turn, the final ten minutes of Block 3 are for processing. The facilitator doesn't need to overengineer the debrief by preparing a closing speech. The goal is simply to draw out some organic responses from at least some of the participants. Some potential questions to ask the group:

What stood out for you?

How did it feel to share your fears and insecurities?

How did it feel to listen to others share theirs?

Do you see any of your colleagues differently now than you did yesterday?

Since time is short, the facilitator should encourage people to keep their responses brief. Most people won't fully process this activity until after the day is over. But if a good percentage of the team participated, the whole group will never see each other quite the same way again. They're primed to return to work with more empathy and mutual understanding.

As the group leaves for a fifteen-minute break, the facilitator can reassure them that the final block of the day will be much less introspective, much more action-oriented and practical. Now that the masks are down, it will be much easier for the team to acknowledge, address, and actually *solve* their specific sources of friction and conflict.

Chapter 11

Block 4—Resolve Unspoken Issues

The final block of the Bonfire Moment asks participants to confront the twenty most common friction points that startup teams face, and work together to begin to eliminate them. This list is compiled from our work with founders and their teams around the world, who find that the same sources of conflict tend to crop up over and over. Confronting these thorny problems head-on will strengthen any team. Block 4 builds on the hard work of the earlier blocks, which laid a foundation of awareness and psychological safety to enable the team to acknowledge and address the elephants in the room.

This chapter will help you understand the critical skills that Block 4 cultivates: identifying and addressing serious issues in ways that make everyone on a team feel respected, even amid disagreement.

"People just need to feel like they're part of a winning team, and all the people problems sort themselves out," said a skeptical founder at one of our startup accelerators. In rejecting the need to invest time in building the right foundation for his team, he referred to a Silicon Valley cliché: "Revenue solves all problems." While there's some truth to this aphorism, it can be dangerous if used as an excuse to ignore a dysfunctional culture.

In an article about the halo effect, management professor Phil Rosenzweig described how human psychology leads people to make specific inferences about a company based upon general impressions. He wrote, "When a company is doing well, with rising sales, high profits, and a surging stock price, observers naturally infer that it has a smart strategy, a visionary leader, motivated employees, excellent customer orientation, a vibrant culture, and so on. When that same company suffers a decline—when sales fall and profits shrink—many people are quick to conclude that the company's strategy went wrong, its people became complacent, it neglected its customers, its culture became stodgy, and more."[1]

Suffering from the halo effect at the peak of success is dangerous; it leads to complacency and avoidance of the hard issues. We would revise that old aphorism to: "Revenue *hides* all problems." The halo effect turns deep conflicts into the proverbial elephants in the room—everyone sees them, but no one feels that it's safe to talk about them. During downturns, such conflicts can become fatal to a startup.

This is where the first three blocks of the Bonfire Moment really pay off. So far during this intense day, the team has likely started to see each other and their dynamic in new ways. They've probably shown more vulnerability than ever by making self-disclosures and voicing concerns that are usually left unsaid. Especially after the emotional intensity of Block 3, it's normal for a team to feel a bit drained. But that's by design. The blocks are organized to build the psychological safety needed to get into these specific thorny problems and points of misalignment.

As the Bonfire Moment enters its final stretch, it's time to dig into those challenges so the team can move forward. There will almost certainly be too many issues to resolve today, such as how future decisions will be made, how the startup will raise and spend future capital, and what to do about teammates who don't have the skills or commitment the startup needs. The point of Block 4 isn't to solve every problem immediately but to establish a new problem-solving model that can endure for the long run.

This final sprint will be worth the effort to dig deep and finish strong. Block 4 can lead to breakthrough agreements about important, foundational issues.

Naming the Elephants in the Room

In chapter 2, we explored the trap of speed—the intense pressure on new startups to rush into developing products, selling to early adopters, and fundraising from investors, while putting equally critical but longer-term issues on the back burner. Many startup leaders put blinders on so they can focus relentlessly on urgent challenges, while making snap decisions about process and culture that later create significant drag and limit the startup's potential. The longer all those other issues are left on the back burner, the more likely they will fester and break the team apart.

We designed Block 4 to push a team to notice, name, and talk about such issues without the usual evasion or stalling tactics. The key, according to Harvard professors Ronald Heifetz and Marty Linsky, is to create an environment where courageous conversations require less courage.[2] If a team can make addressing the elephant in the room a normal and common practice, people will feel less anxiety and discomfort when speaking up. The newfound depth of relationships developed during the earlier blocks of the Bonfire Moment should significantly help this shift.

Heifetz and Linsky note that for important team meetings, there are usually four distinct conversations happening. The first is the conversation in the room, the one everyone can hear. The second takes place privately in advance, with each person confiding in one or two teammates they closely align with, to express their true attitudes and decide how transparent they want to be in the room. The third conversation, after the meeting, is where those same small clusters of allies privately discuss what happened. And the fourth conversation happens inside each team member's head—their unfiltered, private thoughts and feelings—concurrent with the other three. The key, Heifetz and Linsky say, is to merge the second, third, and fourth conversations into the first, so everyone can hear and discuss those normally private thoughts.

A good way to foster more honest interaction is to block time for meetings *without* any action-oriented goals. This goes against the conventional wisdom that a good meeting always ends with clear decisions and the assigning of action steps; anything less is supposedly a waste of time. But Liran Belenzon, the cofounder and CEO of BenchSci, whom we met in chapter 2, disproves this conventional wisdom. He sometimes sets up meetings that *don't* attempt to solve any problem, simply to gather honest, uncensored thoughts and perspectives on a particular subject. A few days later, a follow-up meeting can use those diverse perspectives to hammer out a plan of action. "Once the team agrees that we have the problem, the rest is easy," says Belenzon.[3]

Strive for Class 2 Disagreements

In chapter 3, we met Bob Taylor, the leader of Xerox's Palo Alto Research Center in the 1970s, when its many innovations led to blockbuster products for Apple and other companies.[4] Taylor's team thrived in part because he enforced a culture of positive contention, stressing the difference between what he called Class 1 and Class 2 disagreements. Class 1 meant that neither party truly understood each other's point of view, and as a result people often resorted to straw man arguments, exaggerating what the other person was saying until it was easily rebutted. In contrast, Class 2 disagreements required the parties to study the strongest aspects of each other's positions, and not attempt a rebuttal until they could accurately explain the opponent's point of view. This took longer and required "steel man" rather than straw man arguments.

As you work through the potential sources of misalignment and conflict during Block 4, strive for Class 2 disagreements, no matter how tempting it is to fall into the typical Class 1 style of workplace debate. The more psychological safety everyone on the team feels, the more everyone will benefit from hearing opposing views. Here are some useful tactics:

> Focus on the conversation, without screens or other distractions. Don't engage in side conversations. Don't interrupt the speaker or allow interruptions from others.
> Ask as many questions as it takes to fully understand an opposing point of view.
> Respond verbally to show engagement (e.g., "Yes, I understand") and rephrase points to show understanding (e.g., "What I heard you say is ____; is that right?").
> Use nonverbal cues such as nodding to show understanding, and try to avoid negative facial expressions.
> Don't tolerate personal attacks, including those against anyone not in the room at the time.
> Avoid rushing too quickly to propose solutions.
> Avoid assigning blame.
> Invite the team to challenge your perspective and not hold back any opinions.
> Acknowledge any doubts about your current opinion, or when you're open to see evidence that might disprove your position.

The Rhythm of Block 4

Here's the overview of this final leg of today's journey:

Block 4: Resolve Unspoken Issues

3:15 p.m.	**Set up the challenge:** The facilitator explains the goals of Block 4, then invites the team to read and reflect on the tactics that lead to Class 2 productive, respectful disagreements.
3:25 p.m.	**Go over the Team Drag Checklist:** The team reviews the twenty critical sources of misalignment, miscommunication, and conflict that startups commonly encounter. The team votes on three of these "elephants in the room" that seem most worthy of immediate attention.
3:40 p.m.	**Dive in:** The team discusses their three most urgent sources of team drag, or as many as they can get through in eighty minutes, using the Class 2 disagreement guidelines.
5:00 p.m.	**Ten-minute break:** The last break of the day, a quick mental reset before the sprint to the finish line.
5:10 p.m.	**Wrap up:** After a long day of hard work, the team gathers one more time while standing in a circle. They briefly share what insights stood out and summarize the progress they made together.
5:30 p.m.	**End:** That's it; you're all done!

Set Up the Challenge and Discussion Tactics

The facilitator has the team sit in a circle of chairs, with no table. If people seem tired or discouraged, they can be reassured that this block will be more practical and less introspective than Block 3, and encouraged to dig deep to finish the day strongly.

Then the facilitator briefly explains the purpose of Block 4, the importance of addressing the elephants in the room, and why that should be easier for everyone at this point in their Bonfire Moment. Each team member gets a copy of the list of Class 2 discussion tactics (see above), which should keep disagreements from collapsing into personal attacks.

Go Over the Team Drag Checklist

The facilitator then hands out copies of the Team Drag Checklist from chapter 2 (reprinted below, and available for download at www .bonfiremoment.com). The explanation: these are big issues that tend to get downplayed or ignored due to the trap of speed, often with dire consequences later on.

Each teammate can take a few minutes to choose three items from this checklist that seem to be important unresolved or unexplored issues. Anyone can also propose an issue that's not on this checklist, since every team might have its own idiosyncratic challenges. The facilitator tabulates the votes, and the three items that get the most votes become the topics of discussion.

The team should be told that if there's any time left over before 5:00 p.m., they can begin to address a fourth item. But if they run out of time while still on the first or second item (a more likely scenario), they can continue Block 4 during a future meeting on a normal workday.

The Team Drag Checklist

Initiation:

1. **Mission.** Is our work trying to solve an important, meaningful problem, and has that higher mission been clearly articulated for the team?
2. **Skills and networks.** Do the people on our team have mostly overlapping skills or networks? Do we have enough diversity to open a wide range of prospective employees, customers, and funding?
3. **Equity splits.** Did we make the easy choice of distributing equity in equal shares, since we started as a tight-knit group of peers? If so, what will we do in the future if contributions to the startup start to

vary widely and people perform at different levels of quality? What will happen if a pivot makes some cofounders' skill sets less essential?

4. **Colocation.** How do we feel about having everyone based in the same city, working from the same physical space, or taking advantage of options for remote work? How often do we expect people to be physically in the same place? How flexible will we be when making exceptions?

5. **Representing the team.** Who will be the face of the startup when a media outlet or conference allows only one cofounder to represent us? Will it always be the same person? How do we prevent any of us from feeling invisible?

Operation:

6. **Decision-making.** Will we make important decisions based on data, intuition, or a combination of the two? In scenarios when there isn't good data, whose intuition do we lean on?

7. **Raising money.** What kinds of investors are we willing to work with? Are we clear about the pros and cons of receiving money from family or friends? Whom are we going to turn down for financing? Will those guidelines change if we get desperate?

8. **Spending.** How much will we spend on non-revenue-generating expenses, such as a nice office? Are we aligned on whether certain kinds of expenses help attract talent or build confidence with customers, or if they're empty ways to feed our egos?

9. **Running out of money.** If we're ever about to run out of money, what are we prepared to do? Do we ask friends or relatives for help, put in our own money, and/or take no salary? Should we make exceptions to salary cuts based on personal circumstances?

10. **Hiring and firing.** Will culture and values be a key part of our hiring decisions? Are we willing to turn away highly credentialed people who fail those tests? Should we fire people who undermine the culture, in addition to firing for underperformance? How much time should we give people to address constructive feedback?

Interaction:

11. **Time commitment.** What hours will we keep? Are we expecting everyone to work part-time, full-time, or all the time? If we started off working part-time (as many startups do), are we aligned on who will later be willing to go full-time and at what point? How will we handle deviations from this time commitment?

12. **Conflict.** How do we handle conflict in the team? What are the rules of engagement for resolving issues without damaging relationships?

13. **Expressing stress and anger.** What are acceptable expressions of stress and anger? Will we tolerate profanity, yelling, incivility, or property damage? What are we prepared to do to enforce our norms?

14. **Gossip.** What will we do when gossip starts to spread within the team? What is each team member's responsibility when they hear one colleague complain about another? When does gossip cross the line from harmless to damaging?

15. **Mental health.** What will we do when someone on the team is struggling with their mental health? To what extent are we ready to support our teammates, especially if they need to take temporary breaks from work?

16. **Friendship outside of work.** Is spending time in social activities with colleagues outside working hours optional, encouraged, or expected? Are we mindful that certain activities (such as drinking at the pub, playing soccer on Saturdays, or doing recreational drugs) might put some people in an awkward position? Will we allow participation in these social events to define the inner circle of the startup?

Separation:

17. **Personal stagnation.** If one or more cofounders aren't building their skills fast enough to keep up with the growing business, what are fair actions to move forward without them?

18. **Resignations.** What do we consider fair reasons for one of us to resign from the team? Will we support teammates who can't stay due to family responsibilities or financial needs?

19. **Exit plans.** Are we aligned on possible exit plans for the startup? If a large company offers to buy us out before we intend to exit, will we consider selling? Under what conditions would we reject a serious offer?

20. **Failure.** At what point will we decide this startup is a failure? What metric do we use: bankruptcy, or a success hurdle such as "x users in y months" or "x dollars in revenue by year y"? What will we do if some members of the team want to keep fighting while others have already mentally moved on?

Dive In and Look Out for Unproductive Dynamics

Now the team dives in to their three most urgent sources of team drag, or at least as many as they can get through in eighty minutes, using the Class 2 disagreement guidelines. The facilitator should hang back and say as little as possible, while taking notes on any specific plans that are agreed upon. It's important to show the team that they're qualified to self-manage challenging conversations without a facilitator, since they won't have one after today.

Nevertheless, a good facilitator will listen for any dynamics or cues that suggest a need for intervention and adjustments. These may come in three categories:

1. **Verbal signals:** Is one person dominating the conversation? Is anyone slipping into a hostile or disrespectful tone, or cutting other people off instead of listening? Is anyone remaining mostly silent? Are any ideas raised without being acknowledged by the rest of the team?
2. **Nonverbal signals:** Do people seem attentive when their peers are talking? Does anyone seem anxious, withdrawn, or bored, as visible from signs like posture, facial expression, or lack of eye contact? Is anyone doodling, repeatedly checking the clock, fidgeting nonstop, or staring into space?[5]

3. **Action signals:** Is there an imbalance in who brings up a topic, offers commentary, or pushes back on other people's comments? Do some people naturally play the role of peacemaker, by urging the group to slow down, cracking jokes to reduce tension, or emphasizing common ground? Are people advocating for the startup as a whole, or just for their functional roles (sales, engineering, etc.)?

If the facilitator observes any unhealthy dynamics getting in the way of productive decision-making, they can interrupt and share what they're noticing. In these moments, merely stating an observation is often enough to nudge the team in the right direction. Keep it brief, and let the group reassess and adjust.

For instance, if the facilitator notices several people mentally checking out and only a couple truly engaging in discussion, they might say: "I notice that only a few people seem interested in this topic. Do you think we should switch to something else?" Or if the rest of the team repeatedly ignores one person's comments, the facilitator might step in with: "I'm not sure if you noticed that [name] shared an idea and no one responded to it. Why is that?" The goal is to make the team figure out what's going on and what to do about it, rather than give them the answers.

But in most cases, no intervention will be necessary. As we saw in the Fisk example in chapter 7, by this point in the day people tend to be fully engaged and respectful of each other's opinions. If things are going well, the team will come to concrete agreements on at least one or two of their drag topics. The facilitator should write down those agreements and promise to send a follow-up email reminding them of what actions they've committed to.

When time is about to run out, the facilitator can ask the team to end the conversation and take note of where they left off, if they need to continue another day. Ideally, they should immediately choose a date to reconvene and finish discussing these issues. Needing an extension is common, since it's hard to wrestle with three big issues in just eighty minutes.

If all went well, the group will take their final quick break with a sense of significant accomplishment. And they'll realize that Block 4 never really ends—it will become their model for future problem-solving and conflict resolution.

Wrap Up

Everyone returns to the circle one last time, but now standing rather than sitting. This signals that the Bonfire Moment is wrapping up and the last twenty minutes will be brisk. Standing also helps people keep their energy up for the final stretch.

The facilitator should acknowledge the impressive effort, focus, and courage the team has demonstrated by engaging in this important work. After that, we recommend a brief recap of all four blocks, walking through some of the day's key moments. This will help the team process just how far they've come since 9:00 a.m., so the recency of Block 4 won't overshadow the earlier highlights.

Then it's time for each person to respond to two final reflection questions:

1. What was the biggest insight about yourself, your team, or your work that you'll take away from today?
2. What are you most grateful for after today?

Everyone should answer in order around the circle, after taking a minute to think. Once the last person has spoken, the facilitator can congratulate the team on completing the Bonfire Moment. It's been a long day of introspection, challenging conversations, vulnerability around self-disclosures, deepening connections, and roll-up-your-sleeves problem-solving. Some team members might need a few days to fully process everything that happened.

And then comes . . . the rest of their lives, both as individuals and as colleagues. How will today's Bonfire Moment pay off in the weeks, months, and years to come? That's the subject of our next chapter.

Chapter 12

After Your Bonfire Moment

When we designed the earliest versions of the Bonfire Moment, we focused on a simple goal: to build a one-day workshop that would tackle a startup's hardest people problems. We didn't think much about how teams might continue to apply elements of the workshop in the weeks, months, and years to come.

We were humbled when early participants told us that the Bonfire Moment had permanently changed the way they saw themselves as leaders and interacted as teams. And we were surprised to learn that quite a few of those teams were developing their own ways to replicate, adapt, and extend their experience into their daily work habits.

In this final chapter, we share a number of ongoing practices that can help you carry the impact of your Bonfire Moment into the future. We're deeply grateful to the founders, participants, and facilitators from around the world who encouraged us to pass along their stories and suggestions. In the following pages, you'll hear from some of these amazing partners from Amsterdam, Bangalore, Belfast, Bogotá, Cape Town, Delhi, Jakarta, Lagos, London, Philadelphia, San Francisco, São Paulo, Singapore, Stockholm, Tokyo, and Zurich.

Kate Gray, a seasoned Bonfire Moment facilitator who helped us scale the program in Scandinavia, wisely told us, "Avoid, as in all good practices, the one and done approach. This workshop is something you want to return to. If you don't, the unhelpful patterns of behavior will likely reemerge."

In asking participants how they've brought the workshop's ideas and practices into their daily lives, we were impressed by their creativity and commitment. Though their insights could fill a workbook, eight common themes surfaced:

1. Rerun the Bonfire Moment as a team reset.
2. Use the Bonfire Moment's tools to normalize ongoing feedback.
3. Tap into the User Guides for easier onboarding and collaboration.
4. Block undistracted time for candid discussions on hard topics.
5. Work with an executive coach.
6. Think like a leader, not just a doer.
7. Figure out if conflicts are insurmountable, and have the courage to part ways if so.
8. Facilitate the Bonfire Moment for other teams.

As we explore some interesting variations and examples of these best practices, you'll notice that while some stick to practical actions, others delve into more profound shifts in mindsets and personal values.

Rerun the Bonfire Moment as a Team Reset

Bonfire Moment alumni have found that it can be particularly beneficial to rerun the workshop when the team is in need of a reset—that might mean as early as six months later. You'll recognize when your team needs it, but here are some critical moments to look out for:

> **Team members join or depart.** It's important to assume that with new people in key roles, the team dynamic will shift. Effectively integrating them requires breaking up any inner

circles and making sure everyone feels like part of the team. Conversely, when key people leave, it helps to realign the team and fill the gaps in skills or roles that their departure may have caused.

> **Responsibilities of team members shift.** The Bonfire Moment can provide an opportunity to clarify new expectations, ensure that everyone understands their roles, and reestablish working and communication norms.

> **The startup undergoes a pivot.** Be careful that your pivot isn't a fuzzy pivot (see chapter 9). During a Bonfire Moment, teams can discuss these changes, reset expectations of each other, and make sure everyone is on board with the new direction.

> **Significant conflicts arise.** By stepping away from the daily work environment, teams can tackle conflicts with a greater sense of calm and perspective. The Bonfire Moment will create an open space conducive to productive dialogue and problem-solving.

> **A new phase of growth begins.** Following successful funding rounds and subsequent growth of the team, the original team will need to adapt to their expanding leadership roles. They'll need to depend on each other differently, and develop as individuals to keep pace with the scaling business.

When one of these big moments arrives, it's beneficial to gather your team for a Bonfire Moment after you've handled all the immediate tasks introduced by the transition and things have calmed down. This usually means about a month later. You'll want to wait until everyone has had time to understand all the changes that need to be made and isn't overwhelmed by a long to-do list.

Use the Bonfire Moment's Tools to Normalize Ongoing Feedback

Remember the structured approach to self-assessment in Block 1, including the peer coaching sessions? Quite a few teams turned the feedback process into a regular practice for the team. Every six or twelve months, they gather candid inputs for the leaders from colleagues and direct reports. (For details on our advanced feedback tools beyond those in Block 1, see appendix C.)

Kerry O'Shea, a Google leader and Bonfire Moment facilitator based in Singapore, saw how this worked at a Bangalore-based delivery startup. During the workshop, its CEO and his management team received challenging yet incredibly useful feedback. Soon after the workshop, they adopted the same feedback process for every manager in the company. The CEO noted that before their encounter with these tools, "We didn't have a framework to think about leadership in concrete terms. This gave us the structure for it. We now do this periodically and use data to track our improvements."

If you adopt a data-driven approach to feedback, don't forget that creating a team culture where you can coach each other through challenges is equally important.

Kate Gray once facilitated a Bonfire Moment in Stockholm with several startups in the same room. One team showed up in matching tracksuits with a big company logo across their backs, like a high school gang in the movies. The team's CEO did all the talking, while the other cofounders kept their heads down. "He was incredibly and delightfully aggressive, challenging and questioning me," recalls Kate. She dreaded how painful the dialogue-based activities of the Bonfire Moment would probably be. But during the peer coaching activity, when the CEO had to turn his seat around and say nothing while his team discussed his challenges, the dynamic started to shift. By the end of the day, several members of the tracksuit team separately and privately approached Kate, whispering variations of "Thank you; we really needed that."

You can experiment with running peer coaching sessions at various intervals, to see what works best for your specific needs. One team got into a good rhythm of doing them the last Friday of every month, to tackle tough challenges together.

Tap into the User Guides for Easier Onboarding and Collaboration

Numerous startups have found that the User Guides from Block 2 are a useful tool for onboarding new people, keeping conversations transparent, and providing useful reminders during team conflicts.

Bogotá-based facilitator Annamaria Pino, who advises founders and first-time managers in startups across Latin America, swears by this practice. "It's my go-to whenever I start working with new teams. I tell them that I have this little document that's a shortcut for you to understand my brain and how it works and how to make the best of it." People usually respond with a puzzled look, not sure what she means. But once they read Annamaria's User Guide, they nearly always respond positively, noting how similar or different their work styles are. Who could resist a line like this: "I am direct . . . well, by Colombian standards. According to my grandmother, I use German grammar when I speak Spanish." Annamaria doesn't hesitate to share her User Guide with anyone. "It's a beautiful tool to connect people, especially when my work is often done remotely."

Felix Spira, a cofounder of SkillLab, an Amsterdam-based career guidance app that helps marginalized job seekers, embraced User Guides for his whole team. Starting when they had only about a dozen staffers, interns, and volunteers, SkillLab set up a section of their intranet for everyone's User Guides. As the head of operations and people, Felix himself refers to them whenever he's preparing to give someone feedback, or when he tries to anticipate a teammate's reactions.

South African cofounders Benji Meltzer and James Paterson found that working through the User Guide questions left a lasting mark on their partnership. They hadn't known each other long when they launched Aerobotics, a data analytics company that uses aerial imagery and machine learning to optimize crop performance for farmers. Their Bonfire Moment came a few years after they began collaborating, when they were raising money for a Series A round. They needed to come together on some big decisions, and were finding they had some differing opinions about the future of their business.

As two engineers who tended to avoid conflict, they had previously shied away from topics that seemed contentious or personal. But while discussing their User Guides during Block 2, Benji began to understand why they had different opinions about the future of their business. While discussing their sources of motivation, whether "head, heart, or wallet," he had a moment of clarity. "James comes from this domain, having grown up in a family of farmers. So a huge thing for him is making an impact, contributing to this industry, leaving a legacy that improves the way farming works. Since I don't come from this background, while I enjoy the space and find fulfillment in what we do, I'm motivated by building a team, working with great people, building something special with them, and making money along the way."

Benji added that this very personal disclosure, along with their blunt discussions around other questions in the User Guide, "meant that all our subsequent conversations were real and raw. We couldn't have known the power of that conversation back then."

Since their Bonfire Moment, Benji and James have come back to these sensitive topics time and time again. They have invested considerable effort in aligning their growing team (now more than seventy people) around the "why" behind their decisions. They dedicate time to virtual meetings for the entire company and an annual management gathering of their widely dispersed leaders from South Africa, Portugal, Australia, and the United States. They use these opportunities to go beyond strategy and planning discussions, to also engage in honest, transparent dialogues about the company's current state, its future aspirations, and the road map to get there.

The founders themselves spend time onboarding new employees, coming back to some of the clarifying parts of their User Guide around the goals they have for the company.

It all seems to be paying off. As we write this in 2023, Aerobotics has raised more than $30 million and is serving farmers across twenty countries worldwide, including five of the six biggest citrus companies in the United States.

Block Undistracted Time for Candid Discussions on Hard Topics

Many Bonfire Moment alumni have found immense value in blocking time away from the daily grind to discuss difficult aspects of their journey together. Some have gone to great lengths to replicate that feeling of having a protected space and time for deeper discussions, and to reconnect as teammates. For instance, some have gone on hikes in the mountains, where they were forced to unplug from the internet. Others set up off-site retreats and suspended everyone's email and Slack accounts for a day.

Some reproduced the entire Bonfire Moment at their retreats, while others chose just a few select elements to incorporate. Some included recreational activities, while others kept the focus on serious conversations. There's no one-size-fits-all model, and it's worth experimenting with different kinds of off-sites on different timetables. The key is to block time far in advance, so people know that they will have an opportunity to engage in difficult conversations in a supportive setting.

SkillLab found affordable ways to get their whole team together in person twice a year, even while on a tight budget as a seed-stage startup. One off-site location was in the mountains in Austria, another on the Belgian coast. "With remote teams, it was essential to get them together in person for these retreats. We were able to lift the company to new heights," said Felix Spira.

SkillLab used these retreats to focus everyone's attention on a pressing problem, or to brainstorm new offerings. Tactics included using problem trees to work through challenges, building out user personas to better understand potential customers, and having structured discussions around their diverging definitions of success.[1] Early on, they introduced the User Guide to the entire team; everyone filled it out individually, then they all spent a couple of hours talking about them. Before each retreat, a simple survey determined which topics had the most urgent need for attention.

If you're planning a retreat-like experience as a follow-up to your Bonfire Moment, here are three key takeaways from alumni:

1. Invest three times as much time in preparation and planning as in actual participation. For instance, allocate six days of planning and preparation for a two-day retreat. Assign someone on your team as the point person to make sure your plan is meticulous, so participants won't feel like their time was wasted.

2. Prioritize your agenda with a bias toward addressing the elephants in the room (see chapter 11). What issues would most benefit from an extended, deep discussion among the team? Examples include interpersonal tensions, a lack of clarity about a strategic pivot, a lack of alignment on priorities, or a recent setback. Topics less in need of focused time can be covered in weekly stand-ups.

3. Make sure every element of the plan is inclusive. Here are a few examples of things that can unintentionally exclude team members: alcohol or drug use, physically strenuous activities, a lack of food options for participants with special dietary needs, or awkward sleeping arrangements (such as room sharing).

Work with an Executive Coach

Initially, we didn't recommend executive coaches, in part because coaches often aren't focused on quick solutions to pressing issues. But we eventually realized that we were biased by the trap of speed. An urgent intervention like the Bonfire Moment can be very valuable, but so can the long-term mentorship of a skilled executive coach. We both changed our views after working with coaches who helped us expand the limits of our personal growth.

Martin says: "I've relied on an executive coach during several pivotal career transitions, including my 2020 move into a global role at Google and relocation with my family (at the height of the pandemic!) from Taipei to Silicon Valley. During such challenging periods, biweekly coaching sessions were instrumental in helping me get centered and adjust to radical changes."

Josh says: "I benefited from executive coaching when I was considering a career shift in 2019, from leading the Startup Accelerator program to a chief of staff role. I met several times with one of the leading mentors in the accelerator program, who helped me figure out my aspirations and how to achieve them."

Rafael Figueroa, the dynamic CEO of Portal Telemedicina, made huge strides in his leadership approach while working with an executive coach. Portal Telemedicina is a Brazilian healthcare startup that uses artificial intelligence to support doctors in underserved, remote areas by providing fast, low-cost, reliable diagnostics. Founded in 2013 by Rafael and his brother Roberto, the company started in São Paulo with two trucks, three nurses, and a grant to provide rudimentary checkups to patients. We met Rafael and Roberto in 2017, when they participated in one of the earliest runs of what would later become the Bonfire Moment. By 2022, their company was serving hospitals and clinics in three hundred cities across Latin America and Africa, and has become the pacesetter for bringing advanced artificial intelligence into healthcare in the developing world.

As the company grew, Rafael needed to find ways to expend his energy sustainably. An executive coach helped him discover his "Red Bulls and Kryptonites"—the factors that energized and drained him. These insights helped Rafael focus his calendar on challenges where he truly excelled and which he also enjoyed (complex R & D projects, collaborations with major partners, pitching, and fundraising), while building a team that could cover his Kryptonites (accounting, tax, and legal issues). The coach also taught him that one person's Kryptonite is another person's Red Bull, so there's an opportunity to assign every facet of a company's operations to someone with the passion and proficiency to thrive at it.

Ulrich Scharf, founder and managing director of SkillLab, found that creating his User Guide was only the beginning of a journey into understanding his personal values. He and several of his cofounders received the support of executive coaches through their participation in Google's accelerator program.[2] With his coach, Ulrich looked back at some of his key decisions to see how they reflected his core values.

He remembered starting SkillLab with nine cofounders, giving everyone equity based on a complex equation of time and contributions. But when a couple of them started to engage in ego-driven power plays while being very calculated in their commitment, Ulrich knew he had to make the tough decision to let them go. Their ego games clashed with his own values of being mission-focused, humble, and collaborative.

During those tough periods, Ulrich learned he had a powerful personal resolve. "I wasn't sure if I was strong enough to push through on what I knew was the right thing to do. But in retrospect, safeguarding the culture and values of the team was the best thing I did for my startup," he told us.

To find the right executive coach, evaluate your options on three levels of compatibility. First, find someone familiar with the pressures of the startup environment. Big company executive coaches will sometimes struggle to understand the challenges you face. Second, select a coach who understands the cultural nuances of your workspace. You're likely to encounter frustrations unique to the culture of your country or city, so select a coach who has a deep understanding of these challenges, even if they are not based there. Finally, make sure you share good personal chemistry with your coach. This should be an individual who not only understands your professional aspirations but also resonates with your personal values and understands your motivations; who has a communication style (whether straightforward or empathetic, structured or spontaneous) that best supports your growth; and whom you can trust, respect, and enjoy spending time with.

Chances are that founders or investors you know have worked with a coach they're willing to recommend. You might find others through local coaching networks, discoverable through a simple search. However you find them, speak to at least three before deciding to work with one. If finding a suitable coach proves difficult, consider working with an informal mentor who has experience with challenges similar to yours. However, be ready to adapt a mentor's advice—which will be based on their unique experiences—to fit your particular context.

Think like a Leader, Not Just a Doer

One of the most profound shifts we've seen in Bonfire Moment alums is how they think about their role. They begin to see themselves as leaders, a sometimes lofty designation for those who began with the concrete goal of building a product. This tends to play out differently between first-time founders and experienced ones.

First-time leaders who don't yet have the scar tissue of serious misjudgments may start their Bonfire Moment with an attitude of skepticism, if not scorn. *Who has time for all this chatter about people stuff? We have serious work to do!* But by the end of the day, many realize that it's important to see themselves as leaders, not merely doers. It's one thing to lay the bricks, and another to architect a grand structure. Leaders craft the vision and inspire their teams to work tirelessly toward it. This mindset shift can color everything they do.

More seasoned founders and executives tend to see the Bonfire Moment as an opportunity to reflect on past mistakes from a new perspective. They take the time to untangle the roots of past conflicts and think about what they might have done differently. They usually emerge from the day with more clarity about what's squarely on their shoulders to improve in the teams they lead.

Let's come back to brothers Rafael and Roberto Figueroa of Portal Telemedicina, the Brazilian healthcare startup. Roberto, the COO, fondly recounted that "Rafael originally did not want to be the CEO." Rafael was a former banker who wanted to focus on learning about medical and AI research, an interest that influenced the build-out of their diagnostic products. He had a remarkable vision for the technology, yet also meticulously engaged with the details of running the company, a balancing act often required of early-stage startup CEOs. But as the company grew, Rafael felt the strain of centralizing too many decisions and making everyone too dependent on him.

Realizing that his overinvolvement could limit his company's ability to scale, Rafael decided to count how many people asked him to make small decisions in a single day. The total was fifty-eight, including someone asking him if he preferred white or blue folders for an upcoming event. After that moment of clarity, he began to change his leadership style, prioritizing purpose-driven delegation. As Rafael recalled recently, "I changed over the past few years, realizing that if I am too precise about direct orders, my team won't go above and beyond. Today, I tell the team my vision, give them the budget, and have them own it. I tell them to take more risks and make decisions themselves." He now leads by setting OKRs, establishing milestones, and giving autonomy. "We maximize our potential by leading and guiding, versus executing." To do that well, the brothers stay intensely focused on hiring well, living by the principle that "A players hire A players; B players hire C players."

Not all founders are in a place to hire and scale as much as the Figueroa brothers have in recent years, but the lesson holds true at any stage of growth: only once a founder becomes a true leader are their teams able to reach their highest potential.

Figure Out If Conflicts Are Insurmountable, and Have the Courage to Part Ways If So

The Bonfire Moment was never intended to provoke the dissolution of founding teams, but sometimes that has been the result. Usually participants find that some interpersonal conflicts can be solved quickly, others can be solved over time with a lot of effort, and still others can't be solved. In some cases, confronting hard realities during the Bonfire Moment required accepting that some team members would never be able to coexist.

When we hear that the workshop has led to a partnership's ending, we don't see that outcome as a failure of the Bonfire Moment, or of the people involved. Quite the contrary; we're grateful if our workshop helped them gain clarity about a situation that might have otherwise continued to make them miserable for months or years to come.

During a Bonfire Moment in 2023, veteran facilitator Tony McGaharan[3] was leading a group of women founders from the Asia Pacific region through the User Guide process when one pulled Tony aside. "These hypothetical breakup scenarios in our User Guide . . . I wish I had considered them earlier." Akako was one of three former classmates who had launched a Tokyo-based startup offering Japanese women access to fitness services. They had split the equity equally, raised capital, and survived the pandemic in 2020 by pivoting to digital offerings. But even as their product started to gain traction, tensions emerged in the trio's working relationships.

Akako, the COO, was increasingly frustrated by the work style and seeming lack of long-term commitment of their CEO, Aiya. The latter was often quick to harshly criticize everything her teammates did, including very preliminary ideas that emerged during design sprints. This dynamic surfaced while discussing their User Guides, as did other sources of conflict. For the rest of the day, Akako noticed that Aiya was visibly pensive.

A few weeks later, as Aiya left for a summer vacation, she gave her two cofounders a document outlining her plan to leave the startup, making them co-CEOs. Aiya wrote, "I'm the type of person who wants to take on full responsibility. I realize I'm not happy relying on others, and I'm having a hard time meeting VCs when they say repeatedly that having three equal partners is a problem." The note ended with Aiya's request to be bought out in cash, for three times the startup's value as of the last financing round.

Knowing that it would be impossible to cash out at this very early stage, and that taking out a big loan would hurt the company, Akako was determined to work things out with Aiya at first. But as she later told Tony, "I consulted my mentors, and we came back time and time again to our experience in the workshop. We only clearly realized in that workshop that this would not work itself out, even if we tried hard."

After negotiations, Aiya did leave the startup, but on less punishing financial terms. Rather than seeing their separation as a failure, Akako and her other partner set out to heal the toxic team dynamic and refocus on growing the startup. Now the team is on a healthier path, continuing to improve the well-being of women all over Japan.

Facilitate the Bonfire Moment for Other Teams

We first realized the Bonfire Moment had potential when we returned to São Paulo in 2018, a year after first seeding the program there. We were surprised to see quite a few of the founders who had sat diligently in our workshops now sharing our frameworks and tools with people at their companies and at other startups.

Two of our earliest Brazilian alumni, Allan Panossian and Marcelo Furtado, had even taken photos of our materials, reverse engineered our leadership assessment, and created a Portuguese-language version of the workshop. Allan is a serial entrepreneur who built a local version of Yelp and a food delivery platform for restaurants. Marcelo is the cofounder of a Latin American HR tech startup. They discovered so much value from their Bonfire Moment that between the two of them, they spread their unofficial, translated version to an estimated thousand leaders across Brazil from 2016 to 2022.

When they apologetically let us know in 2017 about their boot-leg version of our tools, they were surprised to see us overjoyed, not threatened. They opened our eyes to the possibilities for sharing it with broader audiences in new ways, including through this book.

Speaking with us again in 2023, Allan called the Bonfire Moment a game changer. "I first facilitated the workshop with my leadership team at a time when two of my more seasoned leaders had left the company," he told us. "It was so transformational that I genuinely wanted other founders to have it too. It was my way of giving back, to help build better companies for the future."

Marcelo added, "I had been a founder for many years and had experienced several accelerator programs, startup meetups, and big tech conferences. But they all lacked material to prepare us in dealing with our most important asset, our team. The Bonfire Moment helped me deconstruct the image of a great leader who knows everything, and instead helped me understand that a great leader is someone who can extract maximum brilliance from their team. The Bonfire Moment provides an environment for individuals to reflect, challenge themselves, and leave with practical actions."

Nicole Yap first encountered our program while she was managing director of Digitaraya in Indonesia. Together with its founder, Yansen Kamto, Nicole helped us scale the workshop as a facilitator to many Indonesian startups. "Every time I've led, participated in, or observed, the feedback has been the same: everyone wishes that they had done this earlier, that they had carved out the time to think about their leadership and the importance of being open and honest with their team and cofounders."

After leaving Digitaraya, Nicole continued to facilitate the workshop for founders, later joining Google for Startups as the partnerships manager for Asia Pacific. She puts special emphasis on using the Bonfire Moment to empower female entrepreneurs. She told us: "The women I've seen go through this workshop are used to feeling out of place and challenged on their credibility, purely on the basis of gender. This workshop puts them front and center, often uncomfortably so, and affirms all their strengths and unique perspectives. I've seen women walk away from this workshop with renewed confidence and appreciation for their roles as founders."

Another great role model is Jeremy Neuner, cofounder and former CEO of NextSpace, one of the world's first coworking companies. In 2018, he took a leadership role on Google's Developer Ecosystem team and not long after he had participated in a Bonfire Moment. He became such a strong advocate for it that he volunteered to facilitate the workshop about fifty times over the next few years. He has personally shared these ideas and experiences with about a thousand founders around the world—"From Vietnam to Venezuela and everyplace in between," as Jeremy put it. "The Bonfire Moment is magical because it asks founders to reckon with both the boldness and the humility that is inherent in any entrepreneurial endeavor. Too often, we celebrate only the boldness of entrepreneurs. And we forget about—and fail to celebrate—the humility that comes from trying, failing, learning, trying again, probably failing again, and perhaps eventually succeeding. It crosses the boundaries of countries and cultures. Founders need someone to remind them that founders are human, a reminder too few of them get," he said. "I'm paying forward the advice, the kindness, and the tough love I was lucky enough to receive during my own journey as an entrepreneur."

We're honored that several dozen official facilitators (and counting) have been certified around the world, on top of an uncountable number of alumni who are informally running Bonfire Moments and adapting them for their local contexts. (You can find information on becoming a facilitator at www.bonfiremoment.com.)

Final Thoughts

As we've just seen, people around the world have come up with many ways to integrate the ideas and tools of the Bonfire Moment into the daily flow of their work. We encourage you to play around with them as well. Test out your own innovations, and share them with colleagues and friends. Don't worry about the possibility of a false step during these experiments. As the tennis champion Arthur Ashe put it: "Start where you are, use what you have, and do what you can."

When we got started with our first rudimentary workshops, addressing people problems felt like the frontier in supporting startups. Hardly anyone in the startup ecosystem—including founders, investors, and accelerators—was paying attention to the help founders needed to navigate team conflicts and build healthy cultures. Early in this journey, we kept hearing similar versions of what one Brazil-based founder told us: "Of all the programs I've done, including a few of the most respected ones in the world, it was your workshop that gave me the best tools I have today to build my team."

Our greatest hope is that someday soon, our emphasis on people will stop being a frontier. And that we evolve how all startup teams operate, everywhere. We want to see a future where these topics are part of the curriculum at every startup accelerator and business school entrepreneurship program. We hope that more and more founders will realize that if they want to change their industries, their communities, and the world, they can't merely focus on product development, sales, marketing, and fundraising. They also have to focus on the people, even when, as we said at the start of this book, teams are harder than tech.

In the meantime, we hope that the Bonfire Moment will help you unlock the boundless potential of your team—and that the stories of other companies on that journey will inspire you to keep working and pushing and making things better, even when the people stuff seems impossibly hard.

We are cheering you on.

Appendix A

About the Effective Founders Project

The Effective Founders Project is a global research program we initiated at Google for Startups in 2015, with the goal of putting the world's most effective founders under a microscope. We set out to understand the strategies such founders use to build great tech companies, drawing on similar analytic techniques that Google has used to develop leaders and build its culture.

On June 15, 2022, Google released a fifty-nine-page report on our findings that we authored, titled *The Effective Founders Project: Seven Leadership Strategies to Overcome the Biggest Risk to Startup Success.* As soon as we announced the report on Google's official blog, the Keyword,[1] it started to draw significant interest from the startup community.

This book builds on and further develops the preliminary insights of that report. This appendix will give you a brief background of the Effective Founders research study, and we encourage you to download the full report for more details.

Why Use Data?

We resolved to anchor our research on data, in part because we saw the startup ecosystem being far too beholden to the personality cults of famous tech founders. It seemed like every conference stage hosted a succession of charismatic, successful founders who ascended to iconic status by talking up their achievements. Meanwhile, young, aspiring founders hung on every word from the "gurus" onstage.

Yet we knew that building great companies requires a lot more than blind adherence to the inspirational (often inconsistent) advice of already-successful founders. We also knew that Google's ongoing success has depended in large part not on seeking out best practices developed by others but on the use of research and data in their own unique context—even when that data contradicted the wisdom of iconic founders.

For instance, consider this thought experiment: What if Steve Jobs had been the CEO of Google, or Larry Page the CEO of Apple? Would their successes have been as remarkable? It's arguable that the emphasis on focus and design excellence that defines a hardware company like Apple needed Steve Jobs at its helm. Similarly, the explosion of innovation and engineering prowess at a software company like Google might have necessitated someone like Larry Page. An oft-told anecdote illustrates their contrasting approaches: Jobs once remarked to Page, "The problem with Google is that you're doing too much." To which Page retorted, "Well, the problem with Apple is that you're doing too little."

That's why we felt a strong sense of responsibility to lean on evidence, rather than media hype about famous founders or even the culture we have personally experienced at Google. No single company can be a role model for everyone.

The Dataset

To understand what set the most effective founders apart, our research team analyzed data on more than nine hundred founders and startup leaders across forty countries on nearly every continent. At the time of the study, this was the deepest and broadest dataset on growth-stage founder capabilities in the world. The dataset covered different roles, including CEO, CTO, operations, product, commercial, finance, and HR leaders. The data on each subject of the study was taken from a multi-rater feedback tool, which was used as part of a leadership workshop embedded within the Google for Startups Accelerator called LeadersLab. Subjects had an average of seven evaluators (cofounders, employees, investors, advisors) providing input on each subject's leadership capabilities. The analysis included more than 230,000 impressions on this global set of founders.

How We Measured Founder Effectiveness

The ideal methodology would compare subjective observations by those who work closely with founders with objective metrics such as startup valuations, profit and loss statements, user growth, and employee departures. But that approach had some significant challenges. Disclosure at the pre-IPO stage is very limited, and even when shared, metrics of business growth are subject to a wide range of internal and external factors, making it difficult to draw attributions. For instance, when a well-funded startup shows exceptionally strong user growth, it is dangerous to conclude that the founder was therefore effective. Maybe the founder was just giving away a valuable product or service below costs.

So in an attempt to get as close as possible to accurate observations of how founders operate, we focused on the anonymous evaluations of their teams, cofounders, investors, and mentors. We also excluded from our analysis founders who received ratings only from their own teams; we didn't want the likability of someone in a position of power to overly influence perceptions of effectiveness. So to make sure this wasn't a popularity contest, the study considered a founder highly effective only if employees, cofounders, investors, and mentors shared a unanimous view of their effectiveness. We asked on a five-point scale:

> "[Name] is a leader I would recommend others to work with."
> "[Name] is the kind of leader that others should aspire to become."
> "Overall, [Name] is a very effective leader."

We then looked carefully at how these observers would rate the founder on a host of leadership capabilities:

> How good are they at communicating an inspiring vision?
> How good are they at making decisions quickly and effectively, even with imperfect data?
> How good are they at achieving high-quality results through their team?

Another thirty questions delved more into the details of specific capabilities.

We also asked the founders to rate themselves by answering the same questions. This gave us the ability to compare each founder's self-perception with how their closest collaborators rated them.

By comparing the top quartile of most effective founders with the bottom quartile of those least effective, we were able to see what leadership capabilities differentiated the two groups. This comparative analysis was meant to overcome survivor bias—the tendency to look at successful entrepreneurs and assume that whatever they did made them successful, without checking if those who failed had behaved the same way.

Key Findings

The study uncovered seven strategies that set the most effective founders apart.

1. **Treat people like volunteers.** The best employees are like volunteers—they'll work passionately for a challenging but meaningful mission. They also have options. Talented people work where they choose to work, and as the adage goes, people leave bosses, not companies. Create a talent monopoly by understanding the psychology of your employees.
2. **Protect the team from distractions.** While founders are typically seen as easily distracted by new ideas, the best ones

create focus and clarity. Set clear goals and priorities to build momentum for your team, which in turn fuels better performance and morale.

3. **Minimize unnecessary micromanagement.** While data shows that micromanaging can be helpful in certain situations, the most effective leaders aim to delegate work in order to scale both themselves and their businesses. Micromanaging can be a fatal flaw, especially for CEOs.

4. **Invite disagreement.** You want your team to be able to engage in a conflict of ideas, not personalities. Founders consistently undervalue giving teams an opportunity to voice their opinions, while employees value it highly. Encourage open team dialogues early and often.

5. **Preserve interpersonal equity.** Violated expectations are the main source of conflict in startups. The most effective teams openly discuss and document what they expect from each other and constantly reevaluate interpersonal equity—does each of you feel that expectations are fair?

6. **Keep pace with expertise.** Leaders need to know enough about each role to hire the right people and help develop their team. Ninety-three percent of the most effective founders have the technical expertise (e.g., in coding, sales, finance) to manage the work with competence.

7. **Overcome discouragement.** While most would expect self-confidence to grow with time, the most effective founders are not nearly as confident as the least effective. Build a support system, and know how to ask for help in order to overcome doubt.

Industry and Geographic Differences

We carefully looked at any discernible differences across industries and geographies. For instance, we assumed that software startups might show different results from e-commerce or hardware startups, or that Japanese workplace culture would be different from British culture. Our dataset was not deep enough in any single country to make generalizable claims about the quality of founders by nationality. We were, however, able to see how valued certain capabilities are over others.

One useful difference we found had to do with the leadership strategy that correlated most strongly with effectiveness: *treat people like volunteers*. Leaders who assume that good people want to work on challenging, meaningful goals will inspire their teams with the mission, instead of relying on carrot-and-stick incentives. This finding from our study sounded disappointingly predictable, and very "Silicon Valley." So we disaggregated the data to see if it held true in other countries and industries. Interestingly, the correlations were even

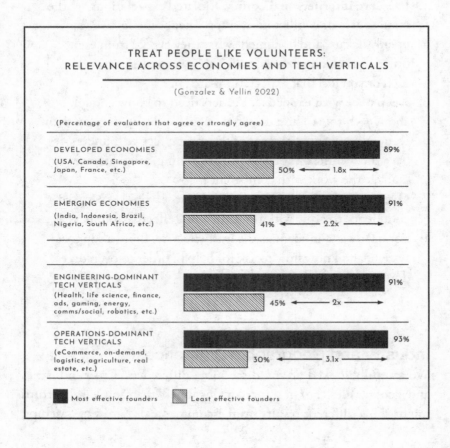

TREAT PEOPLE LIKE VOLUNTEERS:
RELEVANCE ACROSS ECONOMIES AND TECH VERTICALS

(Gonzalez & Yellin 2022)

(Percentage of evaluators that agree or strongly agree)

DEVELOPED ECONOMIES
(USA, Canada, Singapore, Japan, France, etc.)
89%
50% ← 1.8x →

EMERGING ECONOMIES
(India, Indonesia, Brazil, Nigeria, South Africa, etc.)
91%
41% ← 2.2x →

ENGINEERING-DOMINANT TECH VERTICALS
(Health, life science, finance, ads, gaming, energy, comms/social, robotics, etc.)
91%
45% ← 2x →

OPERATIONS-DOMINANT TECH VERTICALS
(eCommerce, on-demand, logistics, agriculture, real estate, etc.)
93%
30% ← 3.1x →

■ Most effective founders   ▨ Least effective founders

more robust for emerging startup ecosystems outside Silicon Valley and for operations-dominant companies.

Data like this comes with a risk of creating a false sense of precision. So it is still important to keep in mind the British statistician George Box's famous warning: "All models are wrong, but some are useful."[2] In writing *The Bonfire Moment*, we've leaned on this research for broad guidelines, not ironclad rules.

The Facilitator's Playbook

This appendix includes:

> An easy guide for current or aspiring facilitators of the Bonfire Moment.
> Preparation checklists, room layout, the flow of the day, and outlines for each module.
> Tweaks to make for larger groups.

We urge facilitators to begin by reviewing the preparation checklists as soon as they commit to running a Bonfire Moment.

Preparation checklists

One month prior to the workshop:
> Select a date and block it from 9:00 a.m. to 5:00 p.m.
> Ideally, choose a Friday (or the day at the end of the workweek), soon after a milestone event or big deadline and never right before.
> Keep all calendars clear of side meetings.
> Decide who should participate.

> **For an early-stage startup:** Everyone working full-time or a large portion of their time (cofounders and early employees).
> **For a larger startup:** The CEO and their leadership team (direct reports to the CEO).
> **For a team within a larger organization:** The team leader and their direct reports, sometimes called "the intact team." Do not include others in different parts of the organization.
> **Don't include:** Investors or board members.
>> Mentors (excluding the facilitator if applicable).
>> Interns.
>> External or internal customers.
> Find a venue that will allow for focused, distraction-free dialogue.
> Consider another office space (not your own), a living room, rented room at a coworking space or business hotel, or the outdoors.
> Avoid your day-to-day work area.
> Decide which feedback tool you will use. The experience will be meaningful and effective regardless of whether you use the self-assessment or the 360-degree assessment, but they require different preparation (see appendix C).

One week prior to the workshop:

> Send a reminder to participants along with some guidelines: that they block off the full day, prepare to part with their devices, and settle any urgent work tasks prior.
> Set aside a notebook for taking notes, and an internet-enabled device (mobile, tablet, laptop) to be left at a device parking lot and used only at designated times.
> Print participant workbooks[1] or have copies of this book available.

› Gather optional additional materials:
  › Whiteboard and marker to write any notes or topics to revisit when time runs out
  › Post-its, pens
  › Single-purpose timer to keep track of time and stay off your phone

One day prior to the workshop:
› Ensure that all materials are complete.
› Set up the space for the day: chairs in a circle with no tables.
› Have a plan to shift the space for Block 3's Bullshit Circle: floor pillows or bean bags, a darkened room, laptops playing a bonfire video.[2]
› Arrange for food delivery so as not to waste time moving to a different location for lunch.

Overview of the Day

One-minute overview: The Bonfire Moment is split into four blocks across one full day.

› **Block 1: Face Hard Truths.** Participants reflect on their leadership skills with the help of a structured self-assessment (or the 360-degree assessment if they chose this option), and receive coaching from their peers.
› **Block 2: Notice Hidden Dynamics.** Participants write up their individual User Guides that contain their personal motivations, work styles and preferences, expectations, and exit scenarios, and share them with the team.
› **Block 3: Drop the Masks.** Team members reflect and share the self-doubts and insecurities they bring to work and the ways they cope.
› **Block 4: Resolve Unspoken Issues.** The team selects from a list of common sources of conflict and aligns on the most burning issues and elephants in the room.

Five-minute rhythm of the day: This is a blow-by-blow overview of the day, as discussed in chapters 8 through 11.

Block 1: Face Hard Truths

Time required:
2 hours and 5 minutes +
15-minute break

Materials needed:
› Participant workbook or copies of this book
› Phones/laptops to access self-assessment
› Chairs in a circle, no table
› Timer

9:00 a.m.	**Start:** The facilitator sets the group's expectations by sharing an overview of the day and some ground rules: no screens, no bullshit, no bragging, no spilling.
9:15 a.m.	**Self-assessment:** The facilitator prepares the team to assess their individual skills by sharing the underlying structure behind the assessment questions. After filling out their questions on the online tool, participants read the summary of insights and write down some of their early reflections. (For an option to conduct a 360-degree feedback assessment, see appendix C.)

To quickly access the self-assessment, have participants scan this QR code:

9:45 a.m.	**Peer coaching:** Each teammate gets 20 minutes to focus on one area where they'd like input from the group. This is an opportunity to untangle the thoughts and reactions they might have from the self-assessment summary (see chapter 8).
11:05 a.m.	**Fifteen-minute break:** Congrats! You're now done with the first block.

Block 2: Notice Hidden Dynamics

Time required:
2 hours and 30 minutes
(including a working lunch) +
10-minute break

Materials needed:
› Participant workbook or copies of this book
› Lunch provisions

11:20 a.m.   **User Guide overview:** The facilitator shares the rationale behind the User Guide, its sections, and the right mindset to approach this task.

11:30 a.m.   **Individual authoring:** The team spends an hour filling out their User Guides. (See appendix D for a User Guide template.)

12:30 p.m.   **Team huddle:** The team shares their responses for each section of the User Guide, over a long lunch.

1:50 p.m.   **Ten-minute break:** Well done! Tidy up the space after lunch and take a quick break.

Block 3: Drop the Masks

Time required:
1 hour + 15-minute break

Materials needed:
> Change of environment
> Four laptops playing a video of digital bonfire
> Timer

Before 2:00 p.m.	**Set up the space:** The facilitator darkens the room and places pillows in a circle on the floor, with four laptops in the center showing a digital bonfire.
2:00 p.m.	**Circle up:** The facilitator explains the goals, structure, and guardrails of the self-disclosure exercise. Then the facilitator offers the first personal story, to set the tone. In silence, everyone else reflects on their fears and insecurities and the self-preserving narratives they may be using to hide them. (See chapter 10 for the key questions.)
2:20 p.m.	**The Bullshit Circle:** Each team member shares their reflections. The others listen without passing judgment or offering advice. It's a time to genuinely connect on a human level.
2:50 p.m.	**Debrief:** After everyone finishes their stories, take 10 minutes to decompress, share realizations, and show gratitude for this moment of raw honesty.
3:00 p.m.	**Fifteen-minute break:** Congrats! You just finished the hardest part of the day. Time to stretch and fuel up for the final push.

Block 4: Resolve Unspoken Issues

Time required:
2 hours and 5 minutes +
10-minute break

Materials needed:
> Participant workbook or copies of this book

3:15 p.m.	**Set up the challenge:** The facilitator explains the goals of Block 4, then invites the team to read and reflect on the tactics that lead to "Class 2," productive, respectful disagreements.
3:25 p.m.	**The Team Drag Checklist:** The team reviews the twenty critical sources of misalignment, miscommunication, and conflict that startups commonly encounter. The team votes on three of these "elephants in the room" that seem most worthy of immediate attention. (See chapter 11 for the checklist.)
3:40 p.m.	**Dive in:** The team discusses their three most urgent sources of team drag, or as many as they can get through in eighty minutes, using the Class 2 disagreement guidelines.
5:00 p.m.	**Ten-minute break:** The last break of the day, a quick mental reset before the sprint to the finish line.
5:10 p.m.	**Wrap up:** After a long day of hard work, the team gathers one more time while standing in a circle. They briefly share what insights stood out and summarize the progress they made together.
5:30 p.m.	**End:** That's it. You're all done!

Supporting the Group Throughout the Day

Be ready to support the group through the emotional journey they will be on. No two Bonfire Moments are going to be alike, so continually read the room and see how you can best guide the team through it. Negative emotions are part of the design of the day, so don't try to smooth them over. However, if the vibe gets too heavy and unproductive, it's part of your job as facilitator to call for a break, to give people a chance to cool down and reset.

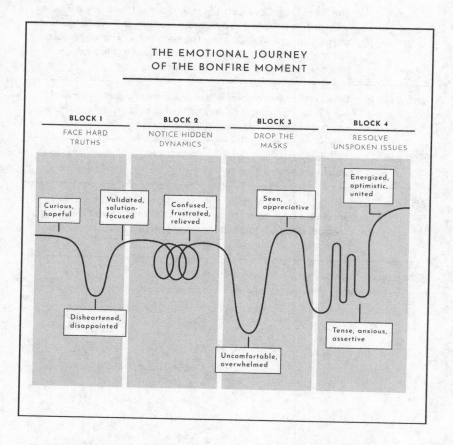

THE EMOTIONAL JOURNEY
OF THE BONFIRE MOMENT

| BLOCK 1 | BLOCK 2 | BLOCK 3 | BLOCK 4 |
| FACE HARD TRUTHS | NOTICE HIDDEN DYNAMICS | DROP THE MASKS | RESOLVE UNSPOKEN ISSUES |

Curious, hopeful

Validated, solution-focused

Confused, frustrated, relieved

Seen, appreciative

Energized, optimistic, united

Disheartened, disappointed

Tense, anxious, assertive

Uncomfortable, overwhelmed

Here are some of the most powerful tactics, explored across chapters 6 through 12, to help you build and safeguard the psychological safety of the group, encourage their best possible responses, and nail your Bonfire Moment:

> Meet with each participant before the workshop to understand their current experience of the team and their expectations of the workshop, and reinforce the seriousness of what's at stake.

> Continually acknowledge that these topics are difficult to work on, but that doing so is essential to helping the team find common ground. Model curiosity by asking a lot of questions.

> Be careful not to use the "parent voice."

> Find an appropriate location that pulls the team away from day-to-day distractions. If you run your Bonfire Moment virtually, be ready to set clear ground rules and follow through on them.

> Start the day with just enough of an overview to manage people's anxieties about blocking off the time, but withhold details so participants can go through the psychological journey without worrying about the difficulty of some activities.

> Watch out for these behaviors in participants: vacationing, absenteeism, hypercriticism. Prepare yourself to manage big egos in the room.

> Keep revisiting the ground rules—no screens, no bullshit, no bragging, no spilling—especially when you observe them being violated.

> Keep an eye on the clock, and don't hesitate to pause conversations that go off topic or over time. There's a lot to cover in just one day, and tangents can easily derail the schedule.

> Help participants understand where they are in the process, especially at the start of each block. Signpost what's coming, and always let the group know how much time is allocated for each segment.

> Invest in your own personal growth as a facilitator. After the day is over, you can ask the team for feedback. You can also ask a seasoned facilitator to shadow you and provide input, or ask permission to observe more experienced facilitators at work.

Tweaks for Larger Groups

When you are facilitating for multiple startup teams at the same time in the same room, or for several teams within a larger company, there are a few important variations to consider:

> **Facilitators:** We recommend having an experienced facilitator run the workshop for any group larger than ten people. For workshops that exceed twenty participants, consider adding an extra facilitator for every twenty additional people. With enough facilitators, we've been able to scale the workshop to as many as eighty people simultaneously.
> **Room setup:** The larger the group gets, the longer it takes to move them from one location to another. So we recommend designing the space so there is minimal travel between the workshop, break, and meal areas.
> **Time:** The time blocks in this playbook work well for smaller groups. With larger groups, assume there will be more interruptions, more participant questions, and more logistical instructions to handle. So be ready to expand the time if necessary, and be more precise with the time limits you give the group.
> Changes by block:

Block 1: During the peer coaching sessions, consider grouping similar functions (e.g., CEOs together, sales managers together). This is optional, but we've found the relatability of having similar role-related challenges adds depth to the conversation.

Block 2: During the User Guide team huddle, keep startup teams intact. If some solo participants have come to attend the workshop without their teams, put them into a group and have them share their personal realizations and how they intend to invite their teams to write up their own User Guides. You can expect them to finish much sooner and enjoy a longer break than the intact teams.

Block 3: For the Bullshit Circle, break up a large group into a maximum of ten per circle, and cap the sharing time for each person to two minutes (this won't feel rushed, and it will allow you to get through as many people without dragging into the night). It's optional to have members of different startups circle up together, or else keep the teams intact.

Block 4: Keep startup teams intact.

Appendix C

Assessment Tools

Block 1 of the Bonfire Moment requires an assessment of each team member participating in the workshop. There are two proprietary assessment options that we have designed and support: a self-assessment and a 360-degree assessment. Both can be accessed at www.bonfiremoment.com. This appendix will give you some additional details about them.

The *self-assessment* is the default option for the Bonfire Moment. We highlighted it in the Fisk story in chapter 7, and we described how it works in chapter 8. This option is free and can be done the day of the Bonfire Moment, with no pre-work required. At the appropriate moment during Block 1, the facilitator will cue the team to go to www.bonfiremoment.com to answer the self-assessment questions and see the results.

The *360-degree assessment* is a more rigorous and time-consuming option that will deepen the Bonfire Moment experience. It involves collecting feedback from a full circle of people with whom the individual interacts—their peers, direct reports, investors, managers, board members, and more—with the aim of providing a comprehensive view of a leader's capabilities from multiple perspectives. This option requires a few weeks of lead time to prepare and requires a payment per user.

Which Assessment Should You Choose?

If you're not sure which assessment to use, consider this comparative table:

	Self-assessment	360-degree assessment
Best for	All, especially at the beginning of the startup journey	Founders and leaders who've worked with four or more close collaborators for at least three months
Preparation	None (it is completed on the day of the Bonfire Moment)	A minimum of four weeks of advance preparation and at least four submitted feedback responses to generate a report[1]
Facilitator's role	Facilitate as outlined in chapter 8	Increased coordination in the weeks ahead and on the day of the Bonfire Moment, and additional expertise to debrief the feedback with participants
Benefit	Valuable self-reflection that will lead to a meaningful peer coaching session	A deeper reflection enhanced by feedback, which often uncovers additional insights that the self-assessment may miss
Cost	Free	See our website for latest pricing
Summary	Effective for a team with a tight budget, an inexperienced facilitator, or a short time frame that won't allow for at least four weeks of advance preparation	More effective for a team that has the budget to use it, a more experienced facilitator, and the advance time to do the required pre-work starting at least four weeks prior to the workshop

Please note that any team that uses the self-assessment still has the option to assign the 360-degree assessment after the workshop, or to make it an option for individual team members who want it.

Gathering Feedback in Advance via the 360-Degree Assessment

If you plan to pursue the 360-degree assessment option, this section will talk you through the process. The first step is that at least four weeks before the scheduled Bonfire Moment, everyone on the team should register for the 360-degree assessment at www.bonfiremoment.com. Starting even earlier is better, to allow adequate time for reviewers to submit their feedback.

Each team member will need to decide who should provide feedback. People will be tempted to invite only those who will have favorable things to say, so the facilitator or team leader should explain why that would undermine the entire process. It would be like lying to your doctor about embarrassing symptoms, or lying to your defense lawyer about a humiliating alibi.

The goal is to obtain around eight completed feedback surveys for each participant, with a 360-degree range of working relationships. As a rule of thumb, assume a two-thirds response rate, given a four-week deadline to complete the survey. So everyone should invite at least twelve people to get eight full responses. More is better, both to build the feedback pool and to protect the anonymity of respondents.

Each participant should take the phrase "360-degree feedback" literally, inviting everyone they work with closely, no matter what the formal reporting relationship on the org chart—up, down, sideways, or diagonal. If we call the leader being assessed X, surveys should go beyond X's manager and direct reports. They should also include X's manager's manager, plus the CEO or other C-level executives, if they've worked together closely. Surveys should also go to close internal collaborators from other departments, and perhaps to people a layer or two below X's direct reports. You can even look diagonally upward to the peers of X's manager, or diagonally downward to the direct reports of X's peers, if applicable.

Some people should be excluded, including anyone who used to work closely with X but who hasn't done so in the past six months; their feedback will be outdated. Likewise, use your judgment about anyone who joined the startup within the last three months, whether as a manager, peer, or direct report. They might not have much insight yet, and might skew the data with overly positive feedback during their honeymoon phase, when underlying problems may not yet be visible.

Once each participant's list has been determined, the online feedback tool will notify the reviewers and provide instructions for taking the survey. It's good practice for the participant to make a personal request of them as well, so they'll know that the person receiving feedback is open to it. This is also an opportunity to reassure the reviewers that the process depends on honesty, not false niceness.

The survey will take only about fifteen minutes. Each participant will be able to monitor how many people have submitted feedback at any point in the three-week window. The online tool will require each Bonfire Moment participant to take the same questionnaire as a self-assessment, which will allow them to compare self-perception with how colleagues see them.

The feedback report will be generated by the online tool after the deadline, assuming that at least four people have completed the assessment. The facilitator will print the reports[2] and keep them hidden until Block 1 starts, so the team can take the journey together.

Backup Plan: If Someone Doesn't or Can't Complete the 360-Degree Assessment

Sometimes one or more members of the team will not be able to complete the 360-degree assessment process in time for the workshop. Some examples of circumstances that may hinder some participants:

> They're new to the team and there hasn't been enough time for any feedback to be offered by the people around them. When possible, we recommend the team delay their Bonfire Moment until all team members have been working together for at least three months. This will allow the initial onboarding dust to settle, and will give people enough interactions to reflect on.

> They did not receive enough feedback to hit our reporting threshold of three assessors. This should be avoidable if the

participant does their own nudging outside of the automated system.

In these cases, we recommend having the affected participants fill out the self-assessment, even if everyone else on the team is using the 360-degree assessment. This will not hinder anyone's ability to participate in the coaching circle, and they can always pursue a full 360-degree assessment sometime after the workshop.

In summary, we encourage people to do the 360-degree assessment for a valuable dose of external feedback. But the self-assessment option will still work to orient participants toward healthy leadership behaviors that make for successful founders.

To quickly jump into the self-assessment, use this QR code:

Appendix D

The User Guide

User Guides offer a quick and easy way to reduce friction and improve trust within a startup team. They work especially well for a leadership team of founders and functional heads.

Humans are complex, and sometimes we all need a little help to understand how to get the best out of our colleagues—and how others can get the best out of us.

We designed this User Guide to prompt short explanations of your personal reasons for being here, how you prefer to work and communicate, your expectations of yourself and others, and how you manage conflict. It includes three sections:

> Section 1: Personal motivations
> Section 2: Working style
> Section 3: Our partnership

Printable versions of the User Guide and a completed sample can be found in the resources section of our website: www.bonfiremoment .com.

Section 1 | Personal Motivations

There are three sources of personal motivation:
> **Head**—the intellectual drive to solve a market challenge or user need with fresh technology, a service, a business model, or a localized value chain. Demotivation arises when the problem becomes unsolvable or no longer challenging.
> **Heart**—a deep passion and commitment for target users, the sector of society, the specific industry, the nation. Demotivation arises when the problem becomes irrelevant or the solution incremental.
> **Wallet**—the personal benefits of the startup, both financial (salary, equity) and nonfinancial (status, title, access to important people). Demotivation arises when a profitable exit seems unlikely or the startup loses prestige.

Use this section to:
> **Reflect on your personal reasons for joining and staying with this startup.** Are you primarily motivated by your head, heart, or wallet? Being clear about this will allow you to more easily make trade-offs along the way.
> **Openly share with your colleagues.** It's important to be explicit about your motivations, which will reduce second-guessing about each other's intentions.
> **Get into alignment.** When a team is in fundamental disagreement about why they're doing what they're doing, it can lead to major conflicts down the road.

What motivates you about your startup?

Head: The intellectual pursuit

Heart: Deep passion for the mission and impact

Wallet: Personal rewards, financial and otherwise

Does your team differ widely on motivations? What conflicts might that cause?

Section 2 | Working Style

Each person has a unique way of getting stuff done. To work more effectively as a team, it helps if you're all explicit about your individual preferences and the reasons behind them.

Highly effective teams understand each other's styles and are flexible in accommodating each other's preferences.

In this section, you'll be clarifying:

> **Your strengths and weaknesses.** You will verify if your colleagues view you the same way you see yourself. When speaking about your weaknesses, you can clarify (1) what help you'll need to improve in those areas and (2) in what areas you need your team to step in and complement you.
> **How others can draw out your best performance and how you can sometimes be misunderstood.** Consider this advice you are giving those on your team on how to best work with you.
> **How you prefer to receive feedback and resolve conflict.** Being able to receive and give feedback, and resolve conflict, will ensure that you're constantly learning and bouncing back from mistakes. Your goal is not to eliminate any need for feedback or conflict. Your goal is to learn how to deal with feedback and conflict in healthy and productive ways.

	What strengths do you bring to the team?	What gaps do you need help with? What kinds of help?
Your list		
Additional input from your team		

People get the best out of me by . . .

People get the worst out of me by . . .

I can sometimes be misunderstood when . . .

The best way to give me feedback is to . . .

When I get into conflict with others, the best way to resolve it with me is to . . .

Section 3 | The Partnership

Unclear expectations of each other and feelings of unfairness are two of the largest sources of conflict within a startup team.

Spend this section clarifying with your team what you expect from yourselves and from each other. Check in about how fair you feel this arrangement has been so far, and do some planning for potential worst-case scenarios.

In this section, you'll be clarifying:

> **Expectations.** Delivering on the expectations that others have of you creates trust, but unmet expectations erode trust and can be a big source of conflict. A startup team can minimize this conflict potential by making sure that expectations are clear, detailed, and aligned.

> **Interpersonal equity.** Just as a business has financial equity, teams have interpersonal equity: fairness in the give-and-take between their members. Interpersonal equity is each person's perception of the balance between what they're putting into and getting out of the business, and what others are giving and taking. "Giving" can include working hours, capital investment, connections, and expertise. "Taking" can include salary, equity ownership, social status, work flexibility, and degree of control. When the balance feels very unfair, it creates tension and may even lead some people to give up on the business.

> **Breakdown scenarios.** These are hypothetical future conflicts that can cause great tension within a startup team. Imagine that your startup has failed a year from now, due to interpersonal conflicts within the team. What relationship reasons (not business reasons) could explain the failure? Responses to this question will help the team preempt some of these future risks.

What contributions are you making or do you plan to make for this startup to succeed?

What expectations do you think others have of you?

What specific expectations do you have of your teammates?

Name

Expectations

Interpersonal Equity Assessment

How satisfied are you with what you contribute as compared to what your teammates contribute?	○	○	○	○	○
	Not satisfied			Very satisfied	

How satisfied are you with what you receive as compared to what your teammates receive?	○	○	○	○	○
	Not satisfied			Very satisfied	

How fair do you feel your arrangement is overall?	○	○	○	○	○
	Not fair			Very fair	

What can you and your cofounders do to make this a 10 rating on all points?

Let's suppose our startup hypothetically fails within the next year because of interpersonal (not business) challenges within our team. What are three of the most likely reasons for this failure?

What can we do now to minimize this future risk?

Acknowledgments

Given the focus of our book, you'd expect us to be serious about assembling an exceptional team. And indeed we were. We embraced our own advice in forming a team that supported us in our debut as authors. We leaned hard on this team to learn the many new skills this journey demanded—finding the time and space for this deep work, conquering the tyranny of the blank page, or moving from bullet-point-style thinking to crafting engaging narratives. And when self-doubt struck hard, they were there to keep us focused and encouraged. It was an exhilarating—and daunting—adventure, bringing this book to life.

Here's the dream team behind *The Bonfire Moment*.

Our literary agent, Sylvie Carr, was an extraordinary partner all along the way, caring for this project as much as we did. Her dedication surpassed that of most agents; she expertly guided us through the intricacies of the publishing industry, worked tirelessly alongside us for nearly a year to transform our messy ideas into a polished book proposal, and meticulously read every word of the early drafts. She was an editor, producer, publicist, coach, mentor, and agent rolled into one.

Hollis Heimbouch, our Harper Business editor, captivated us in our first meeting with her enthusiasm and commitment to our vision, confirming we should not write, in her words, "another boring team book." She was exactly the publisher we needed; her expertise gave us confidence and calm throughout the process. Alongside Hollis, James Neidhardt was an extraordinary collaborator, as was the incredible team backing them up: production editor David Koral, designers Joanne O'Neill and Leah Carlson-Stanisic, Rachel Elinsky and Amanda Pritzker for the marketing and publicity, the skilled copy editors, and the supply-chain team.

Will Weisser, our developmental editor, is as sharp as they get; he offered strategic advice we trusted fully, patiently navigated our tendency to overthink, and moderated our perfectionism. This book would have been unbearable to read without his guidance. Sara Grace brought the needed polish to our prose and helped us eloquently define the metaphor of the Bonfire Moment. Felice Laverne, our sensitivity reader, kept us in check and reassured us our methodology was inclusive. And Jihan Anwar, our superstar researcher, was meticulous in leaving no stone unturned and fact-checking our content. Jared Fenton, visionary founder of the Reflect Organization, offered an editorial eye to our manuscript, ensuring we treated matters of mental health and well-being with utmost sensitivity, and spent the summer of 2023 designing our facilitator certification program.

We built the leadership assessment with the rigorous tools of organizational psychologists. We benefited from the guidance of Lindred Greer (then in the Stanford Graduate School of Business), Michelle Bligh (Claremont Graduate University), Don Ferrin (Singapore Management University), Dana Landis (leadership assessment whisperer, formerly at Google). Meredith Wells Lepley (University of Southern California) worked with us to validate the tool and guided us as we developed the version that's offered through this book. Valentina A. Assenova and Ndubuisi Ugwuanyi (Wharton) collaborated with Martin to validate the assessment tool even further, checking if it linked to important performance outcomes such as revenue, innovation productivity, fundraising, and longevity in a peer-reviewed study titled, "Do Leadership Capabilities Shape the Performance Trajectories of Early-Stage Startups?"

The leadership assessment was brought to life through the wizardry of Roger Planes, the founder of Silicon Rhino and longtime Google Accelerator mentor, and his team, which includes Phil Hardy, Charli Palmer, Andrew Joubert, Jeff Brou, and Ramón Polidura.

Our design team was phenomenal: Matteo Vianello created a cover we feel proud to share with the world, Meagan Geer crafted the aesthetics for graphs and charts, and Justin Ng polished the book art and online assets. Special thanks to Emma Scripps for running the design sprint that got us to our title, and to the many others who helped us search the universe for book title options (Gennifer Birnbach, Kristina Hassaram, and Dave Bowman).

The Google for Startups, Accelerator, and Developer Relations teams were instrumental in helping us scale the workshop and our insights over the years. While it's challenging to name everyone involved, we're fortunate to have directly collaborated with these individuals. The global team included (in alphabetical order): Brett Kamita, Erica Hanson, Garrett Wood, Hannah Curran, Jennifer Harvey, Jeremy Neuner, Kevin O'Toole, Michael Seiler, Rio Otoya, Roy Glasberg, Sami Kizilbash, and Shiri Sivan. The teams across the regions: André Barrence, Anuj Duggal, Ashley Francisco, Fernanda Caloi, Fola Olatunji-David, Francisco Solsona, Gal Agadi, Gibran Khan, Jose Papo, Joséphine Kant, Jowynne Khor, Magdalena Przelaskowska, Marcus Foon, Nicole Yap, Onajite Emerhor, Paul Ravindranath, Rodrigo Carraresi, and Thye Yeow Bok.

Cadres of facilitators around the world joined us on our mission, adapting our workshop's messages to various industries, countries, and languages. As we mentioned in the book's final chapter, tracking every facilitator eventually became impossible, but we relied on and worked with a select few to both share and refine our content: Allan Panossian, Annamaria Pino, Annika Stephan, Greg Albrecht, Hannah Parker, Jan Beránek, Kate Gray, Kerry O'Shea, Lucas Mendes, Lucero Tagle, Marcelo Furtado, Meghan Shakar, Nancy Paez Henriques, Natalie Wei, Rafael Figueroa, Vu Lam, and Zach Ross. Tony McGaharan played a key role in both co-designing the initial workshop and skillfully adapting it for online sessions when Covid-19 hit. He's taken the workshop to founders all across Asia, Latin America, and Europe. He has an uncommon energy and brilliance for leadership development and he's been a valued partner and friend to the Bonfire Moment.

Then there's the long list of book mentors who offered advice on the writing, publishing, or launch process. Our chief mentor, Jake Knapp (author of *Sprint* and *Make Time*), introduced us to Sylvie Carr, answered our calls and texts in moments of frustration, confusion, or desperation, and ran a sprint for our book positioning and title (yes, a sprint from *the* creator of the sprint—how lucky were we?). Through the years, we've leaned on the wisdom and experience of these friends, colleagues, and mentors: Andre Martin, Arnobio Morelix, Elizabeth Churchill, Gorick Ng, Huggy Rao, Jake Breeden, Jenny Blake, Jenny Wood, Jerry Colonna, Jonathan Rosenberg, Kate Esparza, Kim Scott, Liz Wiseman, Liz Fosslien, Neil Hoyne, Noam Wasserman, Phanish Puranam, Rafi Sands, Robert Sutton, Sara Roberts, Scott Hartley, Todd Henshaw, and Yansen Kamto.

Currently, we are in the process of assembling our launch team, which will include specialists in social media, marketing, public relations, and event planning. We're confident this team will be a formidable powerhouse.

Martin's Acknowledgments

Writing this book in the middle of everything in life and work was hard. But it was also an incredible feat for the people that surrounded me.

So my first word of gratitude goes to my unwavering supporter and spouse, Bea. She patiently endured my 4 a.m. alarms so that I could get to writing, gave me time on family vacations to chip away at chapters, and was a clarifying force for the tempest in my mind that troubled over the many aspects of this creative process.

My children—Noelle, Jaime, and Andrea—were my biggest cheerleaders, often waking up to *Papa* hunched over a laptop screen in the dark, sitting on my lap to watch me put one word after another, questioning the use of "bad words" in my writing, and eagerly sharing their excitement about the book with their teachers. Kids: remember that you can do hard things.

My parents, Chito and Nannie, taught me to focus, hustle, persist, and make the most of every opportunity. When I was growing up, my mom sent us off to school every day, saying, "Do a lot of good today." That has stayed with me. My dad, truly as good as they come, showed me through his quiet and humble example how to do the small things well so that the big things are entrusted to you, tirelessly support his kids' dreams, and be generous to a sometimes excessive degree. I'm grateful that he did not flinch when I asked to forgo business school and instead pursue this unconventional path of leadership development. As a finance executive, he likely saw my education choice as risky and silently wrote off the investment. I hope to make good on his blind bet someday!

Finally, thanks to my mentors, friends, managers, and teammates who fueled my love for organization and leadership development. They've been key in shaping my career from the earliest days. Agnes Ycasiano, Anthony Pangilinan, Cooey La'O, Jenny Gonzalez, Jerry Kliatchko, Josiah Go, Joy Ycasiano-Dejos, Luke Yuhico, Maribelle Pelayo, Owi Salazar, Taffy Ledesma, and Tim Liong helped me discern my path, opened doors, and taught me to play the long game. From my time at the Boston Consulting Group: Bernd Walterman, Dean Tong, Peter Cho, and Vikram Bhalla helped me navigate into the firm's people and organization practice. From my nearly ten years at Google, the bosses and colleagues that encouraged me on my journey: Alana Weiss, Alap Bharadwaj, Amelie Villeneuve, Andrew Dahlkemper, Anna Davda, Ben Connell, Brian Glaser, Carmen Law, Claudy Jules, Dana Landis, Eeran Chawla, Geeta Singh, Gina Pelucca, Karen May, Lindsey MacLean, Michelle Cronin, Mike Murphy, Sarah Philippart, Steve Maxwell, Sunil Setlur, Tania Copeland, and Trudi McCanna.

Lastly, I'm grateful to Josh who saw the possibility of this book long before I did, and who had the strategic foresight on important decisions that led us here. This book isn't just a capstone to our decade-long collaboration but a memento of the great friendship that resulted from it.

Josh's Acknowledgments

As Martin pointed out, working on a project as significant as this book while also having other important commitments was challenging—not only for me but for those closest to me as well.

Every day, as I walk my dog, Moses, I use that time to make phone calls to those closest to me, seeking support and guidance on the day's topics. It's during these walks that I've had countless conversations with my mom (Wendy Yellin), sister (Lindsay Yellin), brother (Matt Yellin), brother-in-law (Cary Hayner), and friend (Katherine Shirley), who have all been invaluable in their advice and support. I'd like to thank my late father, Norman Yellin, whom I think about on many of my walks. He led his life with integrity and joy and helped shape me into who I am today. I'd like to also give little Moses a shout-out, as he sparks joy wherever he goes and lightens up my days.

My managers and partners at Google helped champion my growth and ambitions, both personally and professionally. This wouldn't have been possible without the help of Maggie Johnson, David McLaughlin, Roy Glasberg, Sami Kizilbash, Dan Feld, Roni Bonjack, Jake Knapp, Zoubin Gharamani, Jarek Wilkiewicz, Amy McDonald Sandjideh, Geoff Stirling, Bryant Meckley, Kim Roberts, Maya Kulycky, and Simon Bouton.

My sincere thanks also extend to my dear friends, who were helpful in this project for many reasons, some directly in support and some through broader moral support: Charles Otto, Rodrigo Carraresi, Gal Agadi, Fred Alcober, Evan Rappaport, Rich O'Halloran, Jeff Reist, Martin Stroka, Tim Ottowitz, Mitchell Lee, Autl Gera, Samantha Palmer, Brent Hoyer, Kyle Smith, Zach Damato, Nick Wesley, Phil Nicodemus, Victor Anton Valades, Bar Vinograd, Hai Habot, Adam Berk, Jacob Greenshpan, and Barak Hachamov.

Last but not least, I need to give the biggest acknowledgment to Martin. His expertise and motivation on this project have been truly extraordinary. Once we sparked the vision, often my main role was clearing the way for him and finding ways to put wind behind his sails. I couldn't be more proud we got this to the finish line and achieved the vision we set out on so many years ago—we did it, brother!

Notes

Introduction: Teams Are Harder than Tech

1. Michael Gorman and William A. Sahlman, "What Do Venture Capitalists Do?" *Journal of Business Venturing* 4, no. 4 (July 1989): 231–48, https://doi.org/10.1016/0883-9026(89)90014-1.

2. Michael Riordan and Lillian Hoddeson, *Crystal Fire: The Invention of the Transistor and the Birth of the Information Age* (New York: W.W. Norton, 1998).

3. Danielle Newnham, "The Founder Behind Silicon Valley's Most Important Failure, General Magic," *Medium*, July 15, 2021, https://daniellenewnham.medium.com/the-founder-behind-silicon-valleys-most-important-failure-general-magic-5248abf65efd.

4. *General Magic*, 2019, https://www.generalmagicthemovie.com.

5. Newnham, "Founder behind Silicon Valley's Most Important Failure."

6. You might have noticed that the stories so far are disappointingly lacking in gender and racial diversity. There was indeed a time in technology's history when leadership roles went mostly to white men, who had disproportionate access to the resources and inner circles needed to succeed as entrepreneurs. The landscape has, thankfully, started to change, and in this book we capture stories of entrepreneurs from around the world and from all genders.

7. Growth-stage startups are companies that have successfully passed through the early stages of formation, established product-market fit, and started experiencing rapid growth. These startups are generally characterized by a robust, growing user base, consistent revenue streams, and a clear and scalable business model.

8. Google gives its people time to engage in passion projects that help build Google's products and services, and they can spend 20 percent of their time on them. In reality, this often means Googlers work 120 percent of the time, but because these projects are deeply interesting, they feel more like play and less like work.

Chapter 1: Startups Have a People Problem

1. This is a goal-setting system called "objectives and key results." While there are differences with other popular systems like key performance indicators,

key result areas, balanced scorecard, or OGSM (objective, goals, strategies, and measures), the differences aren't relevant for our discussion.

2.   Michael Gorman and William A. Sahlman, "What Do Venture Capitalists Do?," *Journal of Business Venturing* 4, no. 4 (July 1989): 231–48, https://doi.org/10.1016/0883-9026(89)90014-1.

3.   Paul A. Gompers et al., "How Do Venture Capitalists Make Decisions?" *Journal of Financial Economics* 135, no. 1 (January 2020): 169–90, https://doi.org/10.1016/j.jfineco.2019.06.011.

4.   Noam Wasserman, *The Founder's Dilemmas: Anticipating and Avoiding the Pitfalls That Can Sink a Startup* (Princeton, NJ: Princeton University Press, 2013).

5.   Tom Nicholas, *VC: An American History* (Cambridge, MA: Harvard University Press, 2019).

6.   Gompers et al., "How Do Venture Capitalists Make Decisions?"

7.   Charles A. O'Reilly et al., "The Promise and Problems of Organizational Culture," *Group & Organization Management* 39, no. 6 (December 2014): 595–625, https://doi.org/10.1177/1059601114550713.

8.   Hamid Boustanifar and Young Dae Kang, "Employee Satisfaction and Long-Run Stock Returns, 1984–2020," *Financial Analyst Journal* 78, no. 3 (September 30, 2021): 129–51, https://doi.org/10.2139/ssrn.3933687.

9.   Not only is Aldi a capable entrepreneur, but he was also the springboard for Gojek's founder, Nadiem Makarim. Having met Aldi at Harvard, Nadiem was his summer intern in 2010, and the rest, as they say, is history.

10. This business model might seem to uphold traditional gender roles, putting pressure on women to work tirelessly for their families. But this kind of microfinancing achieves exactly the opposite in places like Indonesia: women have shown that they can be just as capable of financially supporting their families. In fact, there's some evidence that when a family's money is earned by the woman, more of it is put toward productive use, such as starting a business or education. Aldi's model empowers women because they will take their families out of poverty, and not reinforce the domestic responsibilities of the gender stereotype.

11. Rosemarie Lloyd, "Discretionary Effort and the Performance Domain," *Australasian Journal of Organisational Psychology* 1, no. 1 (August 2008): 22–34, https://doi.org/10.1375/ajop.1.1.22.

12. Wasserman, *The Founder's Dilemmas.*

Chapter 2: The Trap of Speed

1.   Technical debt happens when a development team takes actions to expedite a product or feature launch that will later need to be fixed or redone. Buggy code, latency, and lack of documentation all contribute to technical debt. It's a common result of prioritizing speed over quality code.

2.   "Smart money" investors also invest their time, expertise, and a network from which startups can source early customers and employees.

3.   In the startup space, when you don't have the resources to pay a market-

competitive salary, the promise of future income (i.e., ownership of a stock that could be worth a lot one day) is the best you can offer.

4. Till Grüne-Yanoff, "Models of Temporal Discounting 1937–2000: An Inter-disciplinary Exchange between Economics and Psychology," *Science in Context* 28, no. 4 (December 2015): 675–713, doi:10.1017/S0269889715000307.

5. *Night Guy, Morning Guy*, Jerry Seinfeld, 2017, https://www.youtube.com/watch?v=UEe2pN8oksc.

6. Alessandro Acquisti and Jens Grossklags, "Privacy Attitudes and Privacy Behavior," in *Economics of Information Security* (New York: Springer, 2004), 165–78, https://doi.org/10.1007/1-4020-8090-5_13.

7. P. D. Sozou, "On Hyperbolic Discounting and Uncertain Hazard Rates," *Proceedings of the Royal Society of London, Series B: Biological Sciences* 265, no. 1409 (October 22, 1998): 2015–20, https://doi.org/10.1098/rspb.1998.0534.

8. Laszlo Bock, *Work Rules! Insights from Inside Google That Will Transform How You Live and Lead* (London: John Murray, 2016).

9. To be clear, we don't think all forms of hierarchy are dangerous. When the goal of a startup is primarily optimizing for commercial success, which requires focus, execution discipline, and rapid tie-breaking, a healthy hierarchy is better than flat org charts. Manager-free implementation teams tend to result in haphazard execution, power struggles between peers, and aimless idea explorations. Good managers play an important role in lowering operational ambiguity. More on this in chapter 4.

10. "Best Workplaces in Canada 2022," Great Place to Work, Accessed August 1, 2022. https://www.greatplacetowork.ca/en/best-workplaces-in-canada-2022-100-999-employees#2022-best-100-999-employees/view-sub-list-details92/5e5d41536b959f00151724fe/.

11. James N. Baron and Michael T. Hannan, "Organizational Blueprints for Success in High-Tech Start-Ups: Lessons from the Stanford Project on Emerging Companies," *California Management Review* 44, no. 3 (April 2002): 8–36, https://doi.org/10.2307/41166130.

12. Keep in mind that as a company gets big, it will probably begin to use more than one of these blueprints for different departments or business units that operate independently.

13. The study defines failure as bankruptcy, a liquidation event, or a merger that was seen as a financial or technological failure, to underscore the fact that not all mergers are failures.

14. Robert I. Sutton, "How Bosses Waste Their Employees' Time," *Wall Street Journal*, December 7, 2018, https://www.wsj.com/articles/how-bosses-waste-their-employees-time-1534126140?mod=searchresults&page=1&pos=1.

15. It is hard to overstate the importance of mental health in startup environments, given that entrepreneurs are estimated to be twice as likely to suffer from depression, three times more likely to suffer from substance abuse, and twice as likely to require psychiatric hospitalization compared to the general population (Michael Freeman et al., "Are Entrepreneurs 'Touched

with Fire'?" (unpublished manuscript, April 17, 2015). Retrieved from https://michaelfreemanmd.com/Research_files/Are%20Entrepreneurs%20 Touched%20with%20Fire%20(pre-pub%20n)%204-17-15.pdf.

Chapter 3: The Trap of the Inner Circle

1. Peter M. Senge, *The Fifth Discipline: The Art & Practice of the Learning Organization* (London: Random House Business, 2006).

2. Cass R. Sunstein and Reid Hastie, *Wiser: Getting beyond Groupthink to Make Groups Smarter* (Boston: Harvard Business School Press, 2014).

3. Details of the rescue are taken from Héctor Tobar, "Sixty-Nine Days," *New Yorker*, June 30, 2014, https://www.newyorker.com/magazine/2014/07/07 /sixty-nine-days, as well as Eliott C. McLaughlin, "Down Below, Chilean Miners Found Hope in Family, the Little Things," CNN, October 9, 2010, https://edition.cnn.com/2010/WORLD/americas/10/09/chile.miners.res cue.nears/index.html; Eliott C. McLaughlin, "Days 1 through 69: How Best of Man, Machine Saved Chile's Miners," CNN, October 16, 2010, https:// edition.cnn.com/2010/WORLD/americas/10/15/chile.mine.rescue.rcap/ index.html; and Rory Carroll, and Jonathan Franklin, "Chilean Miners Emerge to Glare of Sunlight and Publicity as World Rejoices," *Guardian*, October 13, 2010, https://www.theguardian.com/world/2010/oct/13 /chilean-miners-rescue-world-rejoices.

4. Paul Saffo, "Strong Opinions Weakly Held," personal blog, September 26, 2008, https://www.saffo.com/02008/07/26/strong-opinions-weakly-held.

5. Noam Wasserman, *The Founder's Dilemmas: Anticipating and Avoiding the Pitfalls That Can Sink a Startup* (Princeton, NJ: Princeton University Press, 2013).

6. Irving L. Janis, *Victims of Groupthink: A Psychological Study of Foreign-Policy Decisions and Fiascoes* (Boston: Houghton Mifflin, 1972).

7. Dan M. Kahan et al., "Motivated Numeracy and Enlightened Self-Government," *Behavioural Public Policy* 1, no. 1 (May 2017): 54–86, https:// doi.org/10.1017/bpp.2016.2.

8. David Gelles, "If the Pandemic Hit a Year Earlier, 'We Might Not Have Been in the Position to Respond This Fast,' Say BioNTech Co-Founders. Here's Why," Atlantic Council, November 8, 2021, https://www.atlanticcouncil.org/blogs /new-atlanticist/if-the-pandemic-hit-a-year-earlier-we-might-not-have-been-in-the-position-to-respond-this-fast-say-biontech-co-founders-hres-why.

9. Philip Oltermann, "Uğur Şahin and Özlem Türeci: German 'Dream Team' behind Vaccine," *Guardian*, November 10, 2020, https://www.theguardian .com/world/2020/nov/10/ugur-sahin-and-ozlem-tureci-german-dream -team-behind-vaccine.

10. *Uğur Şahin and Özlem Türeci: Meet the Scientist Couple Driving an MRNA Vaccine Revolution*, YouTube, TED, 2021, https://www.youtube.com /watch?v=VdqnAhNrqPU.

11. Bojan Pancevski, "How a Couple's Quest to Cure Cancer Led to the West's First Covid-19 Vaccine," *Wall Street Journal*, December 2, 2020.

12. Steffen Klusmann and Thomas Schulz, "BioNTech Founders Türeci and Şahin on the Battle against Covid-19," *Spiegel* International, January 4, 2021, https://www.spiegel.de/international/world/biontech-founders-tuereci-and-sahin-on-the-battle-against-covid-19-to-see-people-finally-benefitting-from-our-work-is-really-moving-a-41ce9633-5b27-4b9c-b1d7-1bf94c29aa43.

13. Stefan Stern, "BioNTech Founders Özlem Türeci and Uğur Şahin: 'Courage Is Essential for Research,'" *Prospect*, December 22, 2021, https://www.prospectmagazine.co.uk/science-and-technology/biontech-founders-ozlem-tureci-and-ugur-sahin-courage-is-essential-for-research.

14. Martin Gonzalez and Joshua Yellin, *The Effective Founders Project: Seven Leadership Strategies to Overcome the Biggest Risk to Startup Success* (Mountain View, CA: Google for Startups, 2022).

15. Ming-Hong Tsai and Corinne Bendersky, "The Pursuit of Information Sharing: Expressing Task Conflicts as Debates vs. Disagreements Increases Perceived Receptivity to Dissenting Opinions in Groups," *Organization Science* 27, no. 1 (January–February 2016): 141–56, https://doi.org/10.1287/orsc.2015.1025.

16. Gonzalez and Yellin, *The Effective Founders Project*.

17. Leslie Berlin, "You've Never Heard of Bob Taylor, but He Invented 'Almost Everything,'" *Wired*, April 21, 2017, https://www.wired.com/2017/04/youve-never-heard-tech-legend-bob-taylor-invented-almost-everything.

18. Michael A. Hiltzik, *Dealers of Lightning: Xerox PARC and the Dawn of the Computer Age* (New York: HarperBusiness, 2007).

19. The researchers defined social diversity as people who came from different social groupings within their universities, where alliances with people outside one's social group were seen as reputationally risky. See Katherine W. Phillips, Katie A. Liljenquist, and Margaret A Neale, "Is the Pain Worth the Gain? The Advantages and Liabilities of Agreeing with Socially Distinct Newcomers," *Personality and Social Psychology Bulletin* 35, no. 3 (March 2009): 336–50, https://doi.org/https://doi.org/10.1177/0146167208328062.

20. Christopher Bingham, Bradley Hendricks, and Travis Howell, "Do Founder CEOs Tune Out Their Teams?," *MIT Sloan Management Review*, October 26, 2020, https://sloanreview.mit.edu/article/do-founder-ceos-tune-out-their-teams.

Chapter 4: The Trap of the Maverick Mindset

1. Noam Wasserman and Thomas Hellmann, "The Very First Mistake Most Startup Founders Make," *Harvard Business Review*, February 23, 2016, https://hbr.org/2016/02/the-very-first-mistake-most-startup-founders-make.

2. Thomas Hellmann and Noam Wasserman, "The First Deal: The Division of Founder Equity in New Ventures," *Management Science* 63, no. 8 (August 2017): 2647–66, https://doi.org/10.1287/mnsc.2016.2474.

3. Jason Greenberg, "Lifeblood or Liability? The Contingent Value of Co-Founders in Startups" (working paper, New York University, New York, 2015).

4.   Martin Gonzalez and Joshua Yellin, *The Effective Founders Project: Seven Leadership Strategies to Overcome the Biggest Risk to Startup Success* (Mountain View, CA: Google for Startups, 2022).

5.   Ben Horowitz, "Shared Command," Andreessen Horowitz, July 3, 2013, https://a16z.com/2013/07/03/shared-command-2.

6.   Garry Tan, "Co-Founder Conflict," *TechCrunch*, February 18, 2017, https://techcrunch.com/2017/02/18/co-founder-conflict.

7.   Ibid.

8.   Garry Tan, "Should You Be the CEO?" *Medium*, October 29, 2020, https://medium.com/initialized-capital/should-you-be-the-ceo-5a79e34e835.

9.   Phanish Puranam, *The Microstructure of Organizations* (New York: Oxford University Press, 2018).

10.   David A. Garvin, "How Google Sold Its Engineers on Management," *Harvard Business Review*, December 2013, https://hbr.org/2013/12/how-google-sold-its-engineers-on-management.

11.   Aimee Groth, "Is Holacracy the Future of Work or a Management Cult?" *Quartz*, October 9, 2018, https://qz.com/work/1397516/is-holacracy-the-future-of-work-or-a-management-cult.

12.   Aimee Groth, "Zappos Has Quietly Backed Away from Holacracy," *Quartz*, January 29, 2020, https://qz.com/work/1776841/zappos-has-quietly-backed-away-from-holacracy.

13.   Adam Galinsky and Maurice Schweitzer, *Friend and Foe: When to Cooperate, When to Compete, and How to Succeed at Both* (New York: Random House Business, 2016).

14.   Saerom Lee, "The Myth of the Flat Start-up: Reconsidering the Organizational Structure of Start-ups," *Strategic Management Journal* 43, no. 1 (January 2022): 58–92, https://doi.org/10.1002/smj.3333. The true opportunity cost of the modest decline in product quality remains unknown, primarily because this large-scale, quantitative study is merely correlational.

15.   Puranam, *The Microstructure of Organizations*.

16.   Liz Wiseman, *Multipliers: How the Best Leaders Make Everyone Smarter* (New York: HarperBusiness, 2017).

17.   Alex Komoroske, "A Dangerous Addiction," *Medium*, September 25, 2022, https://medium.com/@komorama/a-dangerous-addiction-c71e76105da6.

Chapter 5: The Trap of Confidence

1.   Please see appendix A for details.

2.   Justin Kruger and David Dunning, "Unskilled and Unaware of It: How Difficulties in Recognizing One's Own Incompetence Lead to Inflated Self-Assessments," *Journal of Personality and Social Psychology* 77, no. 6 (December 1999): 1121–34, https://doi.org/10.1037/0022-3514.77.6.1121.

3.   There have been challenges posed to the Dunning-Kruger effect, suggesting that Dunning and Kruger's conclusions were mostly a statistical illusion. But

Dunning, Kruger, and other researchers have continued to conduct experiments that overcome some of those challenges, with evidence that the effect really exists. For more details: David Dunning, "The Dunning-Kruger Effect and Its Discontents," *Psychologist*, March 7, 2022, https://www.bps.org.uk/psychologist/dunning-kruger-effect-and-its-discontents.

4. Robert Hughes, "Modernism's Patriarch," *Time*, June 10, 1996.

5. *Daniel Ek: A Playlist for Entrepreneurs. Stanford ECorner*, 2012, https://www.youtube.com/watch?v=Nps7hHoWVn8.

6. Rupert Neate, "Daniel Ek Profile: 'Spotify Will Be Worth Tens of Billions,'" *Telegraph*, February 17, 2010, https://www.telegraph.co.uk/finance/newsbysector/mediatechnologyandtelecoms/media/7259509/Daniel-Ek-profile-Spotify-will-be-worth-tens-of-billions.html.

7. Ibid.

8. Tom Christiansen, brian d foy, Larry Wall, and Jon Orwant, *Programming Perl* (New York: O'Reilly & Associates, 1991).

9. Albert O. Hirschman, *The Principle of the Hiding Hand* (Washington, DC: Brookings Institution, 1967).

10. Don A. Moore and Derek Schatz, "The Three Faces of Overconfidence," *Social & Personality Psychology Compass* 11, no. 8 (August 2017), https://doi.org/10.1111/spc3.12331.

11. Jeffrey B. Vancouver, Kristen M. More, and Ryan J. Yoder, "Self-Efficacy and Resource Allocation: Support for a Nonmonotonic, Discontinuous Model," *Journal of Applied Psychology* 93, no. 1 (January 2008): 35–47, https://doi.org/10.1037/0021-9010.93.1.35.

12. Ulrike Malmendier and Geoffrey Tate, "CEO Overconfidence and Corporate Investment" (working paper 10807, National Bureau of Economic Research, Cambridge, MA, October 2004), https://doi.org/10.3386/w10807.

13. Eric Schmidt, Jonathan Rosenberg, and Alan Eagle, *Trillion Dollar Coach: The Leadership Playbook of Silicon Valley's Bill Campbell* (New York: HarperBusiness, 2019).

14. *Jonathan Rosenberg—Trillion Dollar Coach: Leadership Playbook of Silicon Valley*, Claremont McKenna College, 2020, https://www.youtube.com/watch?v=FIThn4do1P4.

15. This rebuke wasn't meant as an endorsement of Jobs's infamous temper. Campbell, then an Apple executive, allegedly supported his firing as CEO in 1985. See https://allaboutstevejobs.com/bio/key_people/bill_campbell.

16. Jonathan Rosenberg, interview by Martin Gonzalez, August 23, 2022.

17. Hubert J. O'Gorman, "The Discovery of Pluralistic Ignorance: An Ironic Lesson," *Journal of the History of the Behavioral Sciences* 22, no. 4 (October 1986): 333–47, https://doi.org/10.1002/1520-6696(198610)22:4<333::aid-jhbs2300220405>3.0.co;2-x.

18. Pauline Rose Clance and Suzanne Ament Imes, "The Imposter Phenomenon in High Achieving Women: Dynamics and Therapeutic Intervention,"

Psychotherapy: Theory, Research & Practice 15, no. 3 (Fall 1978): 241–47, https://doi.org/10.1037/h0086006.

19. Studies on the impostor phenomenon have largely homed in on heteronormative genders. We hope to see more studies on gender-fluid individuals.

20. Kay Brauer and René T. Proyer, "The Impostor Phenomenon and Causal Attributions of Positive Feedback on Intelligence Tests," *Personality and Individual Differences* 194 (August 2022): 111663, https://doi.org/10.1016/j.paid.2022.111663.

21. Jen Brown, "Re:Work—Worried You're an Impostor? You're Not Alone!" Google Re:Work, November 15, 2016, https://rework.withgoogle.com/blog/worried-youre-an-impostor-youre-not-alone.

22. *Impostor Syndrome | Mike Cannon-Brookes*, TEDxSydney, 2017, https://www.youtube.com/watch?v=zNBmHXS3A6I.

23. Sana Zafar, "Entrepreneurial Impostor Phenomenon" (PhD diss., Auburn University, 2022).

24. Jared Fenton, in conversation with Martin Gonzalez, January 31, 2023.

25. Michael A. Freeman et al., "Are Entrepreneurs 'Touched with Fire'?" (unpublished manuscript, April 17, 2015). Retrieved from https://michaelafreemanmd.com/Research_files/Are%20Entrepreneurs%20Touched%20with%20Fire%20(pre-pub%20n)%204-17-15.pdf.

26. Basima Tewfik, "The Unexpected Benefits of Doubting Your Own Competence," Wharton IDEAS Lab, https://ideas.wharton.upenn.edu/research/imposter-syndrome-unexpected-benefits.

27. Bradley P. Owens, Angela S. Wallace, and David A. Waldman, "Leader Narcissism and Follower Outcomes: The Counterbalancing Effect of Leader Humility," *Journal of Applied Psychology* 100, no. 4 (July 2015): 1203–13, https://doi.org/10.1037/a0038698.

28. Hongyu Zhang et al., "CEO Humility, Narcissism and Firm Innovation: A Paradox Perspective on CEO Traits," *Leadership Quarterly* 28, no. 5 (October 2017): 585–604, https://doi.org/10.1016/j.leaqua.2017.01.003.

29. Owens, Wallace, and Waldman, "Leader Narcissism and Follower Outcomes."

30. Danielle Newnham, "The Founder behind Silicon Valley's Most Important Failure, General Magic," *Medium*, July 15, 2021, https://daniellenewnham.medium.com/the-founder-behind-silicon-valleys-most-important-failure-general-magic-5248abf65efd#:~:text=And%2C%20oddly%2C%20there's%20a%20paradox,very%20well%20to%20those%20things.

31. Owens, Wallace, and Waldman, "Leader Narcissism and Follower Outcomes."

32. Robert Safian, "Spotify CEO Daniel Ek on Apple, Facebook, Netflix—and the Future," *Fast Company*, August 7, 2018, https://www.fastcompany.com/90213545/exclusive-spotify-ceo-daniel-ek-on-apple-facebook-netflix-and-the-future-of-music.

33. "Daniel Ek, CEO of Spotify," *The Tim Ferriss Show*, December 6, 2020.

34. Ibid.

Chapter 6: The Bonfire Moment

1. Not his real name.

2. Jake Knapp, *Sprint: How to Solve Big Problems and Test New Ideas in Just Five Days* (New York: Simon & Schuster, 2016).

3. For a team of four to five going through the process. It may take longer for larger groups. See appendix B for guidance on how to tweak the workshop.

4. Expert judgment, as it turns out, is merely domain-specific recognition. Chess experts have studied the many possible moves in the game and can access them using rapid recall. They don't have better general memory than the average person. They've honed their specific memory for plays in chess. The study by Chase and Simon (1973) is often cited here; it shows that when you have randomly laid out chess pieces, a chess master isn't able to recall the play more than an amateur player. But when the chess pieces are placed in a configuration that represents an authentic game, chess masters perform significantly better. The researchers conclude that experts have a catalog of common configurations stored in long-term memory, and when they have a rapid response that is usually correct, they impress the rest of us who are just figuring out what the heck is going on. Source: William G. Chase and Herbert A. Simon, "Perception in Chess," *Cognitive Psychology* 4, no. 1 (January 1973), 55–81, https://doi.org/10.1016/0010-0285(73)90004-2.

5. D. Kahneman and G. Klein, "Conditions for Intuitive Expertise: A Failure to Disagree," *American Psychologist* 64, no. 6 (September 2009): 515–26, https://doi.org/10.1037/a0016755.

6. Richard Stanley Melton, "A Comparison of Clinical and Actuarial Methods of Prediction: With an Assessment of the Relative Accuracy of Different Clinicians" (PhD diss., University of Minnesota, 1952).

7. Daniel Kahneman, *Thinking, Fast and Slow* (New York: Farrar, Straus and Giroux, 2011).

8. Ben Horowitz, *The Hard Thing About Hard Things: Building a Business When There Are No Easy Answers* (New York: HarperBusiness, 2014).

9. Emre Soyer and Robin M. Hogarth, *The Myth of Experience: Why We Learn the Wrong Lessons and Ways to Correct Them* (New York: PublicAffairs, 2020).

10. Tom Peters, foreword in *An Invented Life: Reflections on Leadership and Change* (Reading, MA: Addison-Wesley, 1993).

11. Julia Kirby, "Warren Bennis, Leadership Pioneer," *Harvard Business Review*, August 4, 2014. Retrieved August 11, 2022, from https://hbr.org/2014/08/warren-bennis-leadership-pioneer.

12. Warren Bennis and Robert J. Thomas, "Crucibles of Leadership," *Harvard Business Review*, September/October 2002. Retrieved August 11, 2022, from https://hbr.org/2002/09/crucibles-of-leadership.

13. Alison King, "From Sage on the Stage to Guide on the Side," *College Teaching* 41, no. 1 (Winter 1993), 30–35, https://doi.org/10.1080/87567555.1993.9926781.

Chapter 7: Inside a Startup's Bonfire Moment

1. The origin of this adage is hard to trace, but it was recently repopularized by Brené Brown in her book *Daring Greatly: How the Courage to Be Vulnerable Transforms the Way We Live, Love, Parent, and Lead* (New York: Avery, 2015).

Chapter 8: Block 1—Face Hard Truths

1. William Wan, "Screams, Torture and So Much Blood: The Gruesome World of 19th-Century Surgery," *Washington Post*, October 26, 2021, https://www.washingtonpost.com/news/to-your-health/wp/2017/10/31/screams-torture-and-so-much-blood-the-gruesome-world-of-19th-century-surgery/.
2. Some groups add their own specific rules on top of these basics.

Chapter 9: Block 2—Notice Hidden Dynamics

1. Bruce W. Tuckman, "Developmental Sequence in Small Groups," *Psychological Bulletin* 63, no. 6 (June 1965): 384–99, https://doi.org/10.1037/h0022100.

Chapter 10: Block 3—Drop the Masks

1. To be clear, it's important not to confuse this with formal therapy, and it should not be used as an alternative to professional help from a licensed psychologist.
2. Les R. Greene et al., "Psychological Work with Groups in the Veterans Administration," in *Handbook of Group Counseling and Psychotherapy* (Thousand Oaks, CA: Sage, 2004), 322–37, https://doi.org/10.4135/9781452229683.n23.
3. Saul Scheidlinger, "Group Psychotherapy and Related Helping Groups Today: An Overview," *American Journal of Psychotherapy* 58, no. 3 (July 2004): 265–80, https://doi.org/10.1176/appi.psychotherapy.2004.58.3.265.
4. Irvin D. Yalom and Molyn Leszcz, *The Theory and Practice of Group Psychotherapy*, 6th ed. (New York: Basic Books, 2020).
5. Anna Bruk, Sabine G. Scholl, and Herbert Bless, "Beautiful Mess Effect: Self–Other Differences in Evaluation of Showing Vulnerability," *Journal of Personality and Social Psychology* 115, no. 2 (August 2018): 192–205, https://doi.org/10.1037/pspa0000120.
6. Alison Wood Brooks, Francesca Gino, and Maurice E. Schweitzer, "Smart People Ask for (My) Advice: Seeking Advice Boosts Perceptions of Competence," *Management Science* 61, no. 6 (June 2015): 1421–35, https://doi.org/10.1287/mnsc.2014.2054.
7. "Brené Brown on What Vulnerability Isn't," *Re:Thinking with Adam Grant*, 2023, https://www.youtube.com/watch?v=uXVhDSBiZCI.
8. Ensure that you have a trusted professional on call to whom you can refer a participant if they need assistance. If you believe the participant is at immedi-

ate risk of self-harm or suicide, promptly contact the appropriate emergency services. Be vigilant about the laws or professional guidelines in your geographical location or profession around mandatory reporting of self-harm.

Chapter 11: Block 4—Resolve Unspoken Issues

1. Phil Rosenzweig, "Misunderstanding the Nature of Company Performance: The Halo Effect and Other Business Delusions," *California Management Review* 49, no. 4 (July 2007): 6–20, https://doi.org/10.2307/41166403.
2. Ronald Abadian Heifetz, Martin Linsky, and Alexander Grashow, *The Practice of Adaptive Leadership: Tools and Tactics for Changing Your Organization and the World* (Boston: Harvard Business Press, 2009).
3. Liran Belenzon, "Why You Need More Meetings with No Action Items," *Medium*, June 8, 2021, https://liranbelenzon.medium.com/why-you-need-more-meetings-with-no-action-items-5540e2a64343.
4. Xerox PARC is a good example of not falling for the halo effect. By most accounts, it failed to capitalize on its incredible breakthroughs, most of which leaked to companies that eclipsed Xerox's business, including Apple, Adobe, Pixar, and 3Com. Yet leaders like Taylor set up a culture of positive contention worth learning from, even if those failures have denied him and his colleagues the credit they deserve.
5. These behaviors can indicate a lack of engagement. However, for some individuals, especially those with attention-deficit/hyperactivity disorder (ADHD), these same activities actually enhance attention.

Chapter 12: After Your Bonfire Moment

1. A problem tree is a visual tool used to structure and analyze complex issues, identifying root causes and effects in a hierarchical treelike diagram. User personas are fictional representations of potential customers, crafted based on research to aid in understanding their needs, behaviors, and goals.
2. Ali Niederkorn, Lucero Tagle, and Marjes Żammit Blatter, while serving in Google's leadership development function, also act as executive coaches to founders in SkillLab and other startups in Google's network.
3. Tony, an instrumental player in the creation of the Bonfire Moment, now supports founders across Europe, Asia, and the United States from his home in Belfast.

Appendix A: About the Effective Founders Project

1. Martin Gonzalez and Josh Yellin, "What We Learned in Studying the Most Effective Founders," *The Keyword*, June 15, 2022, https://blog.google/outreach-initiatives/entrepreneurs/effective-founders-project/.
2. George E. P. Box, "Science and Statistics," *Journal of the American Statistical Association* 71, no. 356 (May 1976): 791–99, https://doi.org/10.1080/01621459.1976.10480949.

Appendix B: The Facilitator's Playbook

1.   All documents can be found in the resources section of www.bonfiremoment .com. We encourage you to use printouts to minimize distractions or technical difficulties with laptops or smartphones.
2.   Find one on your favorite video platform, like YouTube or Vimeo.

Appendix C: Assessment Tools

1.   This minimum feedback requirement is meant to preserve the anonymity of the people offering feedback.
2.   If your team really hates wasting paper, you have the option of delivering the reports electronically to their devices at the appropriate time.

Index

Index

About the Authors

Martin Gonzalez

Martin is the creator of Google's Effective Founders Project, a global research program that uses people analytics to uncover what makes the best startup founders succeed. He has designed and run leadership courses for thousands of tech startup founders across more than seventy countries in the Americas, Asia, Africa, and Europe. He is a frequent lecturer on entrepreneurship, organization design, and people analytics at Stanford, Wharton, and INSEAD.

Martin is a principal of organization and talent development at Google. He works with Google's senior leaders to shape team culture, develop their people, and expand their leadership, so they can build cool things that matter. In his ten years there, he's worked with leaders across Google Research, DeepMind, Technology & Society, Responsible AI, Pixel, YouTube, Search, and Android, to name a few.

In 2023, the Aspen Institute recognized him as a First Movers Fellow, honoring his pioneering work at Google. The following year, he received the Thinkers50 Radar Award, a prestigious recognition that identifies up-and-coming thinkers whose ideas are predicted to make an important impact on management thinking in the future.

Prior to Google, he was a management consultant with the Boston Consulting Group and a product manager at Johnson & Johnson.

Martin has studied organizational psychology and behavioral science at Columbia University and the London School of Economics. He's a serial immigrant, having lived and worked in New York, Jakarta, Singapore, Taipei, and Manila, where he is originally from. Today he lives in the San Francisco Bay Area with his wife, Bea, and three kids: Noelle, Jaime, and Andrea.

Josh Yellin

Josh is a cofounder of the Google for Startups Accelerator. During his time with Google's Accelerator team, Josh led the growth into eight global locations, partnering closely with more than three hundred of the foremost growth-stage startups from around the world.

Additionally, upon seeing the broad-sweeping global appetite for stronger leadership among the world's top startups, Josh cofounded Google's Effective Founders Project with Martin in 2015. Since its inception, Josh has facilitated workshops with hundreds of founders in several cities around the world and has mentored many startups on various people and operations topics.

In 2019, Josh became a chief of staff in Google Research, supporting organizational strategy and operations for one of Google's foremost Artificial Intelligence research teams. Today Josh is an operational leader in Google DeepMind, which is on a mission to build AI responsibly to benefit humanity.

Josh grew up in Chicago, spent a few years as an outdoor guide in Montana and Alaska, led operations for the largest startup community in Silicon Valley, and cofounded Urban Rivers and Wildlife.ai—two environment-focused nonprofits.

Josh studied biology at the University of Illinois and business at the Wharton School. At the moment, Josh lives in the San Francisco Bay Area, where he can usually be found walking his dog, Moses, on a trail or on the beach.